THROUGHOUT YOUR GENERATIONS FOREVER

THROUGHOUT YOUR GENERATIONS FOREVER

Sacrifice, Religion, and Paternity

NANCY JAY

Foreword by Karen E. Fields

THE UNIVERSITY OF CHICAGO PRESS
Chicago and London

The University of Chicago Press, Chicago 60637
The University of Chicago Press, Ltd., London
© 1992 by The University of Chicago
All rights reserved. Published 1992
Paperback edition 1993
Printed in the United States of America
00 99 98 97 96   5 4 3 2
ISBN 0-226-39572-3 (cloth)
ISBN 0-226-39573-1 (paperback)

Library of Congress Cataloging-in-Publication Data

Jay, Nancy B.
    Throughout your generations forever : sacrifice, religion, and
paternity / Nancy Jay ; foreword by Karen E. Fields.
        p.   cm.
    Includes bibliographical references and index.
    1. Sacrifice.   2. Blood—Religious aspects.   3. Paternity.
I. Title.
GN473.5.J38   1992
306.6'9134—dc20   91-33085
                                                              CIP

Dedicated with Love to My Grandchildren: Zöe, Anna, Maria, Eleni, Luke, Maggie, and Those Who Are Still to Come.

CONTENTS

CONTENTS

PREPARE TO MEET A WRITER of playful yet profound intuition, whose curiosity made her formidably learned, whose company in conversations was an adventure, and whose light touch makes her delightful to read. Those of us who knew her knew to expect the extraordinary, and also extraordinary mixtures: the high-flown with the mundane, the theoretical with the personal, the sublime with the hilarious. Nancy Jay's students at Harvard used at first to be stunned by her invitation to write subjectively about tomes in the sociology of religion—Emile Durkheim's *The Elementary Forms of the Religious Life*, for example—but then to be liberated when they saw how the personal encounter could lead them into the guts of great books. Her fellow lay therapists, conferring over cases at the Cambridgeport Problem Center, must also have been stunned, by her look at least, the day it suddenly came to her that the "psyche" they were talking about was as though materialized as a thing on the table, real as a centerpiece of gladioli. As she recounted that moment of insight to me: Out of a conversation that began about just people, just families, just problems, *paff!* the "psyche," an amazing concept, had bloomed as life. Dinner conversation with Nancy Jay could go from this wonderment at the commonplace abstractions of day-to-day talk to anything at all. She was capable of moving with apparently seamless transition to saying, "You know what? I think I understand Genesis 49:26a." A *Eureka!* moment was at hand. You waited. "You know the one, the verse that comes after 'the blessings of the *breasts* and the *womb*,' the one that says, 'The blessings of thy father have prevailed over the blessings of my progenitors unto the utmost bound of the everlasting hills.'" After a moment of laughter at the ring and the mystique of the language, you waited again. This was going to be interesting.

Utterly in character, therefore, was the turn in conversation one day that began with an unusual revelation: "I've been thinking about blood," she said, and paused. Yes, *blood*. It was odd, wasn't it, that in so

ix

many societies blood both purified and polluted. And wasn't it remarkable that the blood of childbirth and menstruation commonly polluted, while the blood of sacrifice, even of sacrificed animals, could purify? The experience of childbirth could not have produced such an idea, she was sure, using her own bearing of four children as a momentary reference. Nor could its result, new human life, for that was valued everywhere. Characteristically, she talked awhile about childbirth itself, and then told a funny story: about walking one day in Rome, very pregnant, leading eight young children, her own first two children plus six others, to all appearance eight stairsteps of brilliantly fruitful motherhood; about the long glances of awe and the whispered exclamations of "Bellissima!" Then back to the question: If neither the experience of childbirth nor its result accounted for the oddly opposite properties of blood, what might?

It was not long before Nancy Jay was talking about the opposition between sacrifice and childbirth as an opposition between the voluntary and involuntary shedding of blood, then as one between religious conceptions of man and woman, and then as one between society and nature. Her curiosity about facts that most of us know but do not query evolved into the project whose result is this book: a new general theory of blood sacrifice. Although Nancy Jay died February 12, 1991, her curiosity and her company survive in this book. Its erudition has the interdisciplinary scope of nineteenth-century scholarship. Its rigor sparkles in a bright sky of engrossing conversation.

Sacrifice is a territory of ritual that has long fascinated and confounded scholars of religion. In the grand style of their time, nineteenth-century scholars surveyed it panoramically: in the societies of ancient Greece, Israel, and Rome, which had abiding traditional interest; in the ancient Indian society that was coming into view through study of the Vedas; and in a host of societies contemporary with their own, made known to Europeans through colonization. They surveyed this vast and alien territory telescopically as well, for in the mode of their time, one aim of general theory was to bring an alien territory of meanings and motives close enough to reveal how the institution of sacrifice had come to be. But whether set in terms of origins or not, the question of why men sacrifice has been irresistible, and variously answered. Jay's own exploration revisits territory that has been crossed and recrossed by grand theorists the like of Frazer, Wellhausen, Robertson Smith, Hubert and Mauss, Durkheim, Freud, and Lévi-Strauss, to name only a few contributors to an immense literature. Going back more than a hundred years, she re-explores their dead ends, blank spaces, ingenious ideas, and breathtaking inventions.

Part of her exploration was to revisit great error by scholars great enough for their error to instruct. A century ago Robertson Smith noticed the aspect of sacrifice around which this book revolves, the affinity between sacrificing and reckoning lines of descent from father to son. But he did not understand the nature of that affinity. He erred in taking it for granted as natural fact rather than examining it as social artifact. Early in our own century, Freud advanced his famous theory of an aboriginal horde of brothers whose social contract was grounded in an original parricide symbolically remembered in sacrifice and taboo. From her analysis of Freud, Dr. Jay went back in time to an analysis of Hobbes, and then brought the theories of both into focus in a joint photograph, alongside the currently influential theories of Walter Burkert and René Girard. From the joint photograph striking family resemblances emerge, joining the four theories not only to one another but also to sacrificial ideologies. Lévi-Strauss transcended the terms of the old debate about totemism and sacrifice, but threw out sacrifice, because he did not consider it a worthwhile subject for theorizing. By setting forth totemic classification as a recognizably rational enterprise, he abolished its strangeness; but he dismissed sacrifice as rational activity, calling it "a private discourse wanting in good sense" (p. 138). In the deft way she has of acknowledging her debts to great scholars while calling them to account, Jay says her understanding of sacrifice was greatly enriched by what she "fished out of Lévi-Strauss's trash barrel" (p. 138). For her, Lévi-Strauss's timeless discontinuous oppositions were to be set beside the "oriented continuity" of sacrifice, the very medium of which is time.

Nancy Jay crossed the old territory with a feminist commitment to understanding the gender dichotomy that is marked in sacrificial institutions the world over, but widely unremarked in theorizing about those institutions. She did not discover new terrain, but revisited known but unnoticed features of the old. The recurrent father-son themes and the exclusion of childbearing women from sacrificing have been on the well-traveled paths for all to see. So have formulations such as these: sacrifice called "men's childbearing" in Hawaii; sacrificial priests in the African city-state of Benin disguising themselves as pregnant women, having chased away the real women; the Aztec sun rising each day as a result of sacrifice and carrying down with it at sunset the souls of women and children dead in childbirth; the association of femaleness, in many traditions, with that which must be expiated through sacrifice. As she says, like much feminist scholarship, what her theory illuminates "has not been hidden but only ignored, has not been invisible but only irrelevant" (p. 147). But the path toward a feminist theory of sacrifice turned out to be a path toward general theory. To "illuminate aspects of sacrifice that have been regularly left in darkness" (p. 147), she had to try to understand the institution considered as a whole.

Conceiving of the institution as a whole led to scholarly exploration with the scope of her nineteenth-century mentors. It also led back to enduring old problems of social scientific interpretation, for to generalize broadly about rites found the world over was also to interpret them. But sacrifice, especially its inner horizon of meaning, has not only fascinated but confounded, and the theoretical problem of interpreting ritual is a thorny perennial. Like the skillful gardener she was, Jay set the problem out, in the first paragraph of chapter 1, in a display that brings it out vividly against its intellectual landscape: "Without the cutting of wood there is no building of wooden houses" is transparent enough, she says, but not so the meaning of statements such as Heb. 9:22, "Without the shedding of blood there is no remission of sin."

If the fact that men shed blood ritually is a fact readily noticed in countless unrelated traditions, the purpose of that bloodshed has been peculiarly unavailable to learned understanding. Its interpretation has had the "Tower of Babel" quality of disparate proposed meanings. On the one hand, there is the singular opaqueness of statements like the verse from Hebrews. On the other, there is the apparently limitless permeability of ritual as a kind of "sacred Rorschach test" (p. 1), unable to resist any and all interpretations. The thorniness remains, she argues, so long as the meaning of the action is thought of as being "in" the action, "like the gin is in the bottle" (p. 8); for, unlike gin, it cannot be extracted without being adulterated thereby. But if, instead, action and meaning are left together, and ritual is thought of as causing "what it signifies"—a patrilineal clan, for example, or femaleness as that which must be expiated—a more tractable question emerges. What specifically is it, Jay therefore asks, that sacrifice achieves, and how can we understand sacrifice from our own perspective? Sacrificial rituals in this way remain connected to particular contexts of concrete doing. They are what they are and do what they do in context. She compares them to Wittgenstein's brake lever that, separated from the rest of the mechanism, may be anything or nothing. Setting the problem this way renders speculation about inaccessible meanings and motives avoidable. It permits identification of valid limits of interpretation, yet makes no claim of having exhausted all interpretive possibilities. Understanding ritual is not an act of acquisition, Dr. Jay says, but, instead, an act of turning toward the ritual world of the actors from a particular starting point: "Like women's work, [interpretation] is never done but not consequently invalid" (p. 13).

She refers to her own general concepts as constituting "a lens to look through" (p. 23), magnifying, bringing into focus, but leaving to diverse traditions their diverse individuality. She rejects those universalizing modes of theory that arrive at general statements by reducing different sacrificial traditions to "a single strand of meaning or purpose" (p. 147). The metaphor of a lens has another meaning. A lens can focus and amplify for us analogous aspects of sacrifice in different traditions, but it is utterly dependent upon the direction in which the viewer turns it and therefore dependent upon the identity and interests of the viewer. Interpretation is always "situated," as Jay says over and over. There is no Archimedean point from which social phenomena can be observed from nowhere in particular, or from everywhere at once. What is taken as problematic, and therefore what is concluded, follows from the original questions. The result of looking through the lens Jay devises is not a universal theory in the nineteenth-century mode, but it is a comparative and general theory. The value of the lens is to be judged by what it helps clarify and illuminate.

Turning the lens toward ancient Greek, Israelite, and Roman sacrifice, toward Tallensi, Nuer, Hawaiian, Lugbara, and Ashanti sacrifice, and toward the evolution of the Christian Eucharist as sacrifice, Nancy Jay shows how, in unrelated settings, sacrificial ritual enacts patrilineal descent. The important idea is not simply that patrilineal descent is widely associated with sacrifice, the affinity that Robertson Smith noticed, but that patrilineal descent is socially organized and publicly achieved. Thus: Roman descent was established not by birth but by participation in the sacrificial cult. The Tallensi told their ethnographer that clan ties were a consequence of sacrificing together. The Nuer defined patrilineal kin as those who shared the meat of sacrifice. Demosthenes won a probate suit for a man whose patrilineal right to inherit was contested by demonstrating that, years before, no one had contested the man's placing of a sacrifice upon the clan altar. And so on and on. Kinship through the male line is not a biological relation which people merely acknowledge or of which they only need remind themselves in ritual. It is a social relation. Patrilineal kin know they are kin *because* they sacrifice together; they become patrilineal kin by so doing. To so create social and religious paternity is precisely to transcend a natural relation. In this way, sacrifice becomes what Jay calls a "remedy for having been born of woman" or, in her still more expressive phrase, "birth done better." Sacrifice points to distinct "social relations of *re*production" (p. 37).

Nancy Jay compares ancient rituals knowable only through what remains in ancient texts with modern eyewitness accounts by ethnographers. These she compares in turn with documents about the elaboration of the Eucharist in the Roman Catholic Church as a sacrificial cult. She also examines the Church structure, which evolved a single line of descent, as she puts it, "from father to father": the Apostolic Succession of the sacrificing priesthood. This structure made the ordination of women impossible; for as she showed, throughout the world, women cannot sacrifice. Thus old territories that Church historians have mapped separately are remapped together as features of one another. From the standpoint of a hierarchical structure that depends on sacrifice, "to question the eucharistic sacrifice has been to question the social structure, and to reject the social organization has been to question or reject the sacrificial practice" (p. 113). Representing territory that is present to us, and nearby, this new map offers a new view of an active controversy, the key to which is nonetheless deeply grounded in centuries of scholarship.

Despite her movement across great distances of time and space, Jay's exploration never seems acrobatic. It maintains the unbreathless credibility of a conversation that begins in and sustains curiosity about the oddly opposite properties of blood. And the *Eureka!* feeling of marvel in discovery that she shared with friends and colleagues returns on page after page. It returns there along with disciplined recognition that the lens has limits, for it brings into focus only those forms of patriarchy that are constituted in sacrifice. Not all are.

Dr. Jay's lens works panoramically and telescopically. Its formula, so to speak, is elegant and parsimonious, and has three parts: the characteristic contexts of sacrificing, a characteristic social achievement of the ritual, and a characteristic logic of sacrificial ritual. Sacrifice is, as she puts it, "at home" in extended kin groups that require intergenerational continuity to facilitate inheritance, and that establish selective continuity between males. Ancestral cults are typically sacrificial. Sacrifice is alien to hunter-gatherer societies, which lack significant property to transmit, and it withers in the world of exchange and money. But in the contexts where it is "at home," sacrificial ritual solves a problem that is inherent in patriliny: Descent reckoned solely through men is not naturally given but must be socially and religiously created. Ritual provides an event that is as available to the senses as childbirth, but more flexible. There is a characteristic logic of sacrifice that emerges in contexts that otherwise have nothing in common. Sacrificial rituals the world over can be understood to combine in distinctive ways two elements, communion and expiation, or joining and separating, which work as reciprocals of one another in a single unified process. Communion sacrifice joins those worshipers who share in the eating, by that very act separating them from the rest of the world. Expiatory sacrifice separates worshipers from a host of organic and moral conditions, by that very act joining them. By means of this logic, Dr. Jay restores to an English word the forgotten beauty of its origin: "atonement is also always at-one-ment" (p. 19).

The social achievements of sacrifice may be illuminated not only by examples that exhibit "smooth affinities" between sacrifice and patri-liny, but also by seeming counterexamples. Dr. Jay moves from the Greeks and the Romans, and from African peoples like the Tallensi and the Lugbara, societies where the relationships seem relatively straight-forward, to more challenging cases, those of Ashanti, Hawaii, and an-cient Israel, where sacrifice coexists with recognized or latent descent through women. Taking into account features of their landscapes that have "not been hidden but only ignored," chapters on Ashanti and Ha-waii show how building centralized kingship and state power led to specific developments in patriliny and in sacrifice. In Hawaii these de-velopments produced a hierarchy that used a gender vocabulary to dis-tinguish not only between men and women but also between ranks of men. Like the unambiguously patrilineal Romans, Greeks, and Aztecs, the Ashanti and the Hawaiians produced state sacrificial cults and thus a mechanism that efficiently centralized the legitimation of power and succession to power. The mechanism has worked, according to Jay, not because it is the outcome of a biological relationship between the sexes that transcends specific histories, but because gender relations link his-torical social relations to a biological base, making them appear natural and inevitable. Gender is therefore "unequaled as a cornerstone of dom-ination" (p. 148). By bringing into sharp focus analogous features in the Old Testament stories of the patriarchs, the author shows how cer-tain longstanding obscurities in the Blessing of Jacob disappear, and how mysteries of the wife/sister stories, once cumbersomely solved, may be elegantly solved.

In setting forth her solution to the mystery of Gen. 49:26a, she says of other attempts, "Having taken patrilineal descent for granted, schol-ars cannot see its establishment as an achievement, and consequently they cannot ask how it is achieved" (p. 110). Dr. Jay noticed that in ancient Israel the tension of patriliny with latent recognition of descent through women is reflected in differences between the Genesis sources. The J, P, and E sources differ consistently with their different interests in descent and sacrificing, J being the least sacrificial, P most, and E providing the accounts that tell over and over about the remedying of ambiguous patrilineal descent through sacrifice. P, the source of the ev-erlasting "begats," is the source of the book's title, "throughout your generations forever." Applying the logic of sacrifice to these differences, Jay proposes an alternative to the standard explanation for the salience of expiatory sacrifice in post-exilic times, a psychological explanation that Wellhausen devised a hundred years ago. She accounts for the in-creased importance of expiatory sacrifice sociologically, as having to do with the evolution of a theocratic priesthood organized patrilineally and increasingly differentiated from the Israelites as a whole. Finally, observations she made through the telescopic lens led her to infer the existence of a planet, long lost, where sacrificing was once unshrouded by mystery. She shows how passages in Gen. 49 that had already become unintelligible by the time the King James Bible was being created, and that for hundreds of years have been dismissed as textual corruption, become intelligible. In terms of sacrifice as remedy for being born of woman, they can be understood as making perfect sense and as meaning exactly what they say.

In its depth and scope, and in the clarifying power of the general theory it proposes, *Throughout Your Generations Forever* represents a fulfillment of the challenge that feminist scholars embraced when launching a new enterprise two decades ago. Their challenge was to seek truth emancipated from etiquettes of gender dichotomy, from chauvinistic seeing without noticing, and from power prerogatives of veiling, silencing, and outright exclusion. New research was called for, across old territory: To know there, as a character of Zora Neale Hurston's says, you had to go there. The first phase was to fill in the gaps. Women had to be brought back in, silenced voices recovered, and the salience of gender dynamics first demonstrated, then added to the general map of human history. But to imagine this additive phase was immediately to imagine its transcendence, for the challenge had bolder import than the gain of a woman's page, to be inserted or not, read or not, according to preference or commitment. It embodied the faith that restoring half of humanity to truth as knowable through scholarship would necessarily transform not only what our thinking takes into account but also its conceptual topography. If, as suspected, the gaps to be filled were like those large expanses of territory drawn on the map of the world before it was circumnavigated, marked arbitrarily to suit fancy and catechism, inclusion would not long remain a mere matter of taste. For all but the resolutely superstitious, the very outlines of many maps would be transformed. If debate upholds Nancy Jay's theory, the conceptual topography of several fields in religious scholarship will not remain the same.

But two decades ago feminist scholars not only insisted that different voyages were necessary, from different points of embarcation, but also debated the controversial claim that it mattered who the traveler was. To go there, in some sense and in some part, you had to know there, said some. Valid knowledge is independent of identities, said others. And so the question: How does a scholar's identity qualify the questions asked, and how can it serve as a qualification? In the guts of *Throughout Your Generations Forever*, I think, are deeply planted, in dynamic inward relationship, Nancy Jay's singular personal qualifications to create it—not only qualifications like her detailed knowledge of Greek mythology, her profound study in the interpretive theoretical traditions of philosophy, sociology, and anthropology, her reading of the Bible and Bible scholarship, her wide reading of ethnography, including *all* the literature on pre-1820 Hawaii, and much else that went to make up an intense scholarly life; but also qualifications in the flesh-and-blood experience of families, from the different standpoints of mother, daughter, sister, and wife, and the special experience of childbirth. In the conversation we had years ago, she laid out the reality of childbirth as an elemental ground for curiosity about the opposite properties of blood. And in the book, her conversation with Hobbes across the centuries fires back truth so elemental as to be rarely remembered in dissections of social contract theory. To his famous portrayal of men in the original state of nature, where life was "solitary, poor, nasty, brutish and short," she replies, "Probably men's original solitude was not so total that they had never enjoyed the company of their mothers" (p. 129). With such moments in mind, I have tried to imagine discussions of *Throughout Your Generations Forever,* and to imagine how Nancy Jay in action would have chosen to draw upon those layers of intellectual life to which flesh-and-blood experience lends rigor. But now the book has only an objective and final existence. Discussion for or against her conclusions will proceed on the merits, according to the principle that valid knowledge is independent of persons and can be pursued regardless of identity. Nancy Jay's lens passes into other hands. With it we shall see what we shall see.

Karen E. Fields
The University of Rochester
July 1991

ACKNOWLEDGMENTS

THIS WORK HAS BEEN LONG IN THE MAKING, and many people over the years have helped the author with guidance, critical clarity, and enthusiasm. Nancy Jay would have acknowledged all of them, more adequately and generously than I, her husband, am able to. There will be some among them whom I am sure I shall fail to acknowledge; I ask their forgiveness beforehand.

The work was completed in final draft in June 1990. Dr. Jay died in February 1991, shortly after learning that the University of Chicago Press had accepted it for publication as it stood, without need for further revision. I want first to thank those at the Press for their generous support, especially Alan Thomas, the religion editor, who has kept up a strong, committed belief in the work's importance that has powerfully sustained my wife's effort. And I thank the Press's faculty board for their understanding support at a hard time. I want also to thank Jo Ann Kiser, who gave much more than mere duty through her very careful, patient, and clarifying editorial work on the manuscript. Very special thanks are due too to William Scott Green, University of Rochester, who first put Nancy in touch with the Press and other important figures, and took a strong interest in helping see to the publication of her work on Israelite sacrifice (chapter 7) in *Vetus Testamentum*. I wish also to express warm gratitude to Jonathan Z. Smith, University of Chicago, who gave enthusiastic support at a critical time in affirming the work's importance and literary quality. In addition, Valerio Valeri, University of Chicago, kindly read the chapter on Hawaiian religion and sacrifice and provided helpful and encouraging commentary.

In an earlier version, the work was accepted as my wife's doctoral dissertation in the Sociology of Religion at Brandeis University in 1981. Certain faculty and graduate students in the Department of Sociology there were especially important to her during the years of completing the dissertation. Egon Bittner was her adviser and mentor, and guided, nurtured, criticized, and cheered on the work with warm faith and impeccable scholarship. Kurt Wolff, a member of her dissertation committee as well as a good friend, provided sustained critical interest and scholarly support throughout. Among her fellow graduate students, Nancy Chodorow shared with her the strong personal and scholarly interest in mothers and mothering that is so central to the work. Fatima Mernissi gave her continual spirited encouragement, along with her own personal and scholarly knowledge of how women experience themselves in an Islamic society where sacrifice is of major religious importance. James Ault also gave steady intellectual and personal fellowship, and attentive concern to the dissertation in process. Karen Fields, most powerful of all, has been faithful friend, intellectual coconspirator, energizer, and, eventually moving ahead to a position on the Brandeis faculty, member of her dissertation committee. Her work on religious movements in Africa provided Nancy very valuable knowledge and intellectual stimulation. With great generosity of spirit, she has written in the Foreword an intellectual tribute and personal appreciation of Nancy that expresses clearly and poignantly the character of their relationship.

In 1980, my wife began teaching the sociology of religion and related courses at the Harvard Divinity School. During the following years, she made major revisions and additions to the work, readying it for publication. She received much help and encouragement from many of her colleagues and students over that time. Perhaps most deserving of thanks is Kay Shanahan, good friend, who worked with Nancy the whole time, introducing her to the computer and teaching her the value of word processing, while also composing endless copies of revision after revision. Among the many students who supported her work with critical interest and shared excitement, Susan Bruno has been particularly steadfast as critic and friend. Among the faculty, Clarissa Atkinson in particular has been both a warm friend and a source of valuable knowledge and criticism drawn from her work on women and family in religious life during the Middle Ages. Jo Ann Hackett was especially helpful with critical advice on Israelite religion and sacrifice, as well as with sources and translation work from Hebraic and related languages, without which my wife could not have completed the intricate scholarship required. Rosemary Hale gave critical help in handling the difficult German scholarship involved. Bernadette Brooten provided superb scholarly support for sources on ancient Greek society, and her assistant, Denise Buell, gave generous help on transcriptions. Michael Fishbein, while visiting at the Divinity School, took a strong and encouraging interest in the work, while William Franklin, another visitor, shared ideas, sources, and enthusiasm with Nancy on the subject of the Eucharist and the ordination of women in modern Christianity.

Finally, and in more ways than it is possible to tell, her children, and grandchildren, to whom Nancy has affectionately dedicated this book, stimulated and supported her throughout the long years of the work's gestation and birth.

The book must now go on its own journey without the concerned support of its author. As a book's creation is only completed in its reading, thereby undergoing continual re-creation through its readers, thanks are due in advance to all those who will read this work with attention and interest.

Robert Jay

IN NO OTHER MAJOR RELIGIOUS INSTITUTION is gender dichotomy more consistently important, across unrelated traditions, than it is in sacrifice. This is true not only of ancient and so-called primitive religions. Even among contemporary Christians, the more vividly the Eucharist is understood to be itself a real sacrifice, the greater the opposition to ordaining women. Why? Most of the immense literature on sacrifice ignores or takes for granted these gender-related features, even though they appear repeatedly in different traditions. Neither the exclusion of women nor the repeated father-son themes have been seen as needing explanation. Consequently, a study of sacrifice focusing on gender leads to a new understanding: sacrifice as remedy for having been born of woman.

Opposition between sacrifice and childbirth, or between sacrifice and childbearing women, that is, mothers or potential mothers, is present in countless different sacrificial traditions. This opposition is manifested in a number of different ways; for example, the gender roles of sacrificial practice. It is a common feature of unrelated traditions that only adult males—fathers, real and metaphorical—may perform sacrifice.[1] Where women are reported as performing sacrifice it is never as mothers, but almost always in some specifically non-childbearing role: as virgins (or dressed as if they were virgins), as consecrated unmarried women, or as post-menopausal women.[2]

Far more diverse than the gender roles of sacrificers are the symbolic oppositions between sacrifice and childbirth manifested in different traditions. Sometimes these are phrased as logical oppositions between the purifying power of sacrifice and the pollution of childbirth and menstruation. In Greek, Roman, Israelite, and other traditions, sacrifice is necessary to remove the pollution of childbirth or to signify that the period of pollution has ended. But oppositions between sacrifice and childbirth take many forms. The Aztec sun rose accompanied by spirits of male human sacrifice victims whose excised, still beating hearts had been rendered to divinities in fire. Only repeated sacrificing gave the sun life each morning and enabled it to climb actively upward, but it sank passively to its death each evening accompanied by the spirits of women dead in childbirth.

This Aztec sacrifice calls to mind the many vivid metaphors in which sacrifice is opposed to childbirth as birth done better, under deliberate purposeful control, and on a more exalted level than ordinary mothers do it. In Hawaii, sacrifice was "man's childbearing" from which women were rigidly excluded, and sacrificing reproduced not ordinary mortals, but the gods (Valeri 1985:114). The man for whose benefit certain Vedic sacrifices were performed reenacted being born, but he was reborn as a god, not as a helpless infant (Hubert and Mauss 1964: 20–21). In the West African city of Benin, before the many occasions of human sacrifice, all women were driven out of the city by the priests, who masqueraded as pregnant women themselves during the sacrifice (Bradbury 1957: 59). One can go on indefinitely listing similar illustrations, but the problems for interpretation and comparison only become greater and greater. Listing these oppositions as illustrations of some supposed general principle uproots them from their own social and symbolic contexts, and only within these contexts do they become intelligible. If anything can be redeemed from such a list, it is only more questions. What is it about childbirth that needs to be remedied in sacrifice?

The approach taken here will not focus primarily on symbolic representations of childbirth or childbearing women but on the social contexts of sacrificial ritual, especially on the ways the practice of sacrifice affects family structures, the organized social relations of reproduction within which women bear their children. This choice of focus is not simply to avoid the methodological problems of trying to compare different symbol systems. It is because sacrificial religions are very much features of their own social contexts, and they thrive in societies with certain kinds of family structure. When family organization changes, sacrificial practice may be sharply reduced. (Northern Europe at the time of the Protestant Reformation is an example.[3])

Sacrifice is at home in societies where families are integrated into extended kin groups of various kinds: lineages, clans, sibs, and so on. Like sacrificial religions, these extended family structures are concentrated among agrarian and pastoral societies (Paige and Paige 1981: 56–57, 65; Nimkoff and Middleton 1960; J. Z. Smith 1987). Hunter-gatherers and industrial societies resemble each other both in not developing sacrificial traditions and in not organizing families into elaborate kin groups. Unlike these societies, families in agrarian and pastoral societies are organized around important productive property such as farmland and herds, organized in structures of enduring intergenerational continuity that facilitate inheritance. Intergenerational continuity between males is a central concern in such societies, and sacrificial ritual is important in identifying, maintaining, and sometimes in undermining, these enduring social structures. It is no accident that ancestral cults are typically sacrificial cults. As Meyer Fortes said, sacrifice is "the crucial ritual institution of ancestor worship" (1965:140).

Relations between sacrifice and family organization are immensely varied. Every tradition is different, but in general, where intergenerational continuity is figured through fathers and sons, sacrificing directly supports descent structures. Where intergenerational continuity is figured through women, in bilateral or matrilineal systems, sacrificing may work separately from, or even in opposition to genealogical structures.

I have been using the word "sacrifice" as if it were without problems. This word is a gloss covering countless different actions and kinds of actions. Our word lumps together (blended, as it were, in the perspective of great distance) actions that sacrificers themselves do not call by one name. The ancient Israelites had names for many different kinds of sacrifice, but no one word that referred to all of them. In glossing them all under one name we are abandoning their categories. We cannot do otherwise if we want to talk about "sacrifice" from our own perspective, but we need to prevent our category from obliterating sacrificers' own distinctions. This will involve a continual negotiation between our perspective and that of sacrificers themselves, a negotiation that will succeed only if we never uproot sacrificers from their own contexts, and if we do not let what we bring to the study blot out what they say about their own sacrificing. The moment we say, "The celebrants do not and must not comprehend the true role of the sacrificial act" (Girard 1977: 7), we have lost all possibility of gaining any understanding beyond the one we already had and brought along with us. *reduction-istic*

To avoid obliteration by interpretation we must recognize that we cannot even identify an action as sacrifice except within its own tradition. (The most convincing proof of this can be had from post-Vatican II Christian struggles over the obstacle to ecumenical unity posed by disagreement on whether the Eucharist is or is not a sacrifice [see below, Chapter 8].) Not all ritual killings are sacrifices,[4] nor do all sacrifices involve slaughter. In some traditions, a plant may be substituted for an animal victim, and represent that victim. But in other traditions, a vegetable offering may indicate that this is a specifically non-sacrificial offering, or even a subversive refusal to sacrifice. All these can only be distinguished contextually.

Constructing an objective criterion to identify "sacrifice" invariantly across different traditions would be more distorting than it would be clarifying. To bring "sacrifice" under our control as a perfectly defined object of analysis, to cut out and classify its constituent elements, is more like doing sacrifice than understanding it. (The blood you pour out at the base of the altar, the fat you burn, the entrails you wash first and burn later, the skin you . . .) The victim has indeed been brought under a kind of analytic control, but in the process it has been killed.

Because we cannot identify sacrifice objectively, that is, independently of the different meanings sacrificers give to their own rituals, this book is necessarily interpretive sociology (Winch 1971). Consequently, its product will not be "scientific findings" or "laws" regulating all forms of sacrifice, but instead, a way of understanding, a particular perspective that will bring into focus aspects of sacrifice that have been ignored or so taken for granted as to be invisible.[5]

Given the enormous diversity of sacrificial traditions and of their social settings, it is obviously impossible to compare them all. The field of possible candidates for comparison narrows when historical or ethnographic description must be adequate for both ritual practice and social organization. From this narrowed field, I have selected for comparison eight sacrificial traditions, chosen for their religious and social structural diversity. Five traditions are taken from ethnographic accounts: Hawaiian, Ashanti, Tallensi, Lugbara, and Nuer. Israelite sacrifice is included because it is the blood sacrificial tradition most familiar to us, and Greek sacrifice (classical Athenian) because available scholarship has made it far easier to describe than the other major Indo-European traditions such as Roman or Vedic sacrifice. Finally, I include a discussion of post-Vatican II Christian sacrifice, in spite of the obvious complexities involved, because it brings sacrificial ritual to our own time and shows something of the incompatibility between sacrificially maintained social organization and the contemporary world.

This is also an interdisciplinary work, and, as Max Weber said about his own interdisciplinary work, runs the risk of satisfying no one. I am either a debtor or a trespasser, depending on one's point of view, in realms of scholarship such as classics, biblical scholarship, church history, and, especially, ethnography. For sociological theory, I draw on the heritage of Marx, Weber, and Durkheim. From Marx comes the recognition that the mode of production is fundamental for social organization and religion and that all social and religious institutions are historically contingent human products. Interpretive sociology originated with Weber, and I have also adapted his use of ideal types for comparative studies. From Durkheim comes the notion that in ritual action people create and recreate aspects of their own society. Unlike Durkheim, I understand this as being always political action involving

→ *not a consensus decision*

struggles for power, including power over women's reproductive capacities.

Chapter 1 is a discussion of some hazards and strengths of interpretive social science for studies of ritual. Chapter 2 sets forth a model for distinguishing between integrative, communal aspects of sacrifice and differentiating, expiatory aspects. This model is an abstraction with which any real tradition may be compared, and is intended to facilitate understanding of the work of sacrifice in integrating and distinguishing between social groups. Chapter 3 is an introduction to how sacrificing identifies, legitimates, and maintains enduring structures of intergenerational continuity between males that transcend their absolute dependence on women's reproductive powers. Chapter 4 describes this process in four patrilineal societies. In societies that recognize descent through women in important ways, relations between family organization and sacrifice are more diverse and more complicated. Chapter 5 is a study of an intensely sacrificial religion in a primarily matrilineal setting, Ashanti. Chapter 6 is an analogous study of sacrifice in Hawaii, where genealogy was figured through both women and men. Chapters 7 and 8 focus on Israelite and Christian sacrifice. Chapter 9 is a critique of some major theories of sacrifice with reference to their treatment—or lack of treatment—of questions of gender. It is conventional to begin with a review of the literature, but I have left it till last because I am writing not only for those who are already students of sacrifice, but for any reader interested in gender and religion.

ONE

Social-Scientific Interpretation of Ritual

W E ORDINARILY INTERPRET ACTION with reference to the relation between means and ends so that if we know that a man is cutting
wood to build a house, we believe we understand his action. We all
agree that without the cutting of wood there is no building of wooden
houses. But suppose we are told that "without the shedding of blood
there is no remission of sin" (Heb. 9:22)?[1] How do we know whether
the shedding of blood is or is not an indispensable means for remission
of sin? And how do we recognize remission of sin when we see it?

In the interpretation of ritual action even the identification of means
and ends is a stumbling block. Some people have been satisfied with
explaining that ritual is action with non-empirical ends, but that is of
limited help since other people's non-empirical ends are notoriously unintelligible; and also, quite frequently ritual actors claim to pursue what
we understand as empirical ends (curing smallpox, making the sun rise,
ending famines, and so on), and then their means are unintelligible.
Sometimes there appears to be no distinguishing between means and
ends in ritual: the means *are* the ends. The ritual is done because it is
important to do it. Much ritual has to be done exactly right, as if the
way it is done is what is done. It is not enough to do the ritual just well
enough to produce some separate effect. There is no separate effect, it is
all in the doing.

A survey of social-scientific interpretations of other people's ritual
action (especially rituals of so-called primitive religions) looks like a
free-for-all of apparently unlimited combinations of speculation, wild
projective fantasy, and careful scholarship. Interpretations that have
been denounced as nonsense by some—mistaken in content, specious
in reasoning—have been greeted with acclaim by others. It seems at
times as if rituals, like sacred Rorschach tests, are incapable of resisting
any interpretation whatsoever that scholars and even believers wish to
make of them.

The story of social-scientific interpretations of ritual begins in

1

nineteenth-century Britain when a few scholars, certain that positive science would rid the world of all obscurities, focused its light on the dark corners of savage religion. A positivist wanting to interpret a ritual like sacrifice starts off with a very great obstacle built into his or her theory: the complete separation of meaning and matter. For the classical positivist, there existed on the one hand a wholly objective material world, moved only by physical causation, and explainable by the scientists, and on the other hand the one true and pure subjectivity: the scientific mind, unsituated, not located in extended matter, and entirely lucid to itself. This world was, in principle, *perfectly* intelligible, although it was limited to its two modes: objects understood by scientists, and scientists understanding objects.

Those positivists who concentrate on the subjective aspect of the world, those who understand scientists understanding objects, are sometimes called "intellectualists."[2] Nineteenth-century intellectualists, like Tylor, had some relatively enduring success when their topic was religious ideas. These could be interpreted as attempts at making scientific theory, perhaps wrong in content, but rational in form. Scientists and savages were using the same logical processes.[3] But in the interpretation of ritual action (the savage as applied scientist), they ran into difficulties since for them the relation of means to ends of action was only intelligible as it conformed to scientific ideas of causality. For example: the Aztecs sacrificed to make the sun rise (*the* sun, a wholly objective piece of non-representational matter); therefore Aztec astronomy was both wrong and irrational, a "bastard science." Wrote Frazer, "Their cruel system of human sacrifices, the most monstrous on record, sprang in great measure from a mistaken theory of the solar system. No more striking illustration could be given of the disastrous consequences that may flow in practice from a purely speculative error" (1951: 91).[4]

Those positivists who understand material objects have been called "anti-intellectualists," because they focus directly on the wholly objective aspect of the world. Anti-intellectualists are spared many problems since they are not obliged to take into account the ideas of those they study. Insofar as an interpreter is an anti-intellectual positivist, he or she no longer studies fellow human subjects engaged in intellectually meaningful actions, but instead wholly objective biological organisms striving to meet their needs under certain conditions of heredity and environment. In the study of ritual, consequently, anti-intellectualists sometimes disregard very large amounts of information about what people say they are doing and why they do it. A recent interpretation of this kind tells us that Aztec human sacrifice had in fact nothing to do with astronomy, or even with religion: the sacrificers were meat-cutters, not priests, and their ritual was actually a method for the production and distribution of animal protein in an environment in which it was in very short supply.[5]

Robertson Smith's *The Religion of the Semites* (1889) was the first English attempt to escape the positivists' double-ended impasse by focusing on the *symbolic* meaning of ritual and its purely social, or moral, consequences. Smith's ritual actors were neither scientists nor biological organisms, but members of society, and what they expressed in their ritual was not erroneous scientific cosmology, but social forms and values.[6]

Smith, as a social anthropologist, was unique among his nineteenth-century contemporaries in actually doing fieldwork (in Arabia). But most important, he was the foremost Hebrew Bible scholar of the English-speaking world, and a Christian minister and theologian. As a scholar he was deeply familiar with German historical biblical criticism (a non-positivist tradition of interpretation in which hermeneutic philosophies of understanding originated); and as a Christian, believing that the remote origins of his own religion were to be found in Semitic sacrificial rituals, he could not scornfully deny them religious meaning.

Like the positivists who surrounded him, Smith assumed a linear social evolution. But most positivists focused their interest on the bizarre and irrational, and therefore by definition primitive, along the evolutionary path. If there is only one path, these "survivals" are like blazes guiding us back to the remote past, and the journey consists precisely of increasing evidences of ignorance and error. For Robertson Smith the evolutionary path was the development of a common truth in which savages already shared, although in simpler, even cruder, form. What was important was not archaic survivals, but the enduring and common among us; not the deadwood, but the living root.

Understanding ritual as symbolic action opened it to enormously richer interpretation than was possible for the strict positivists. (The great milestone in this shift was, of course, Durkheim's *The Elementary Forms of the Religious Life.*) But once the doors are opened to more than rigid positivistic ideas of intelligible meaning, it is almost impossible to control the flood of potential interpretations and it is very hard indeed to be really convincing about having identified the "true reasons" for ritual. Unless you have some ironbound rule for identifying *the* meaning of ritual, some orthodox doctrine, either religious or positivist, it is exceedingly difficult to determine whose meaning is the valid one and to justify rejecting the "erroneous" or unintelligible meanings offered by the faithful themselves. We will return to this considerable difficulty later.

To think of ritual as symbolic action is to make an analogy with language. There are a variety of ways in which this has been done. The

[handwritten margin note: used to look at purposes of behavior]

3

earliest of these to be developed, and until recently by far the most prominent, interprets ritual by analogy with language as a system of symbols possessing, or referring to, identifiable meanings. According to this approach, as a word is the expression of a meaning so a ritual act, equally arbitrary, that is, wholly conventional, is the expression of a meaning.

Those who interpret ritual in this way ordinarily distinguish between two aspects of action: "instrumental action," which *does* things, which causally affects the material world; and "expressive action," which *says* things or communicates meanings. The instrumental/expressive split is recognized to be an analytic one (any real action will have both instrumental and expressive aspects), but nevertheless interpreters write of expressive action and instrumental action as if they were two different kinds of action. Ritual action in particular tends to be treated in this way, as purely expressive action: it is symbolically meaningful, but it doesn't really *do* anything. In fact, the instrumental/expressive split preserves intact the positivists' separation of meaning and matter. Although what can be accepted as meaningful is greatly expanded, the material world, still subject only to physical causation, remains meaningless, stripped of subjectivity, the realm only of instrumental action. This is an obstacle for understanding sacrifice, which does *not* so divide meaning and matter. Sacrificers act through and upon meaningful matter: the living body. Even transubstantiation claims to affect an aspect of the material world through ritual action.[7]

If an interpreter cuts meaning and matter completely apart, there is no way to make sense of the instrumental claims which sacrificers make for their ritual. These claims become unintelligible and must be got rid of one way or another; consequently, in order to gain intellectual control of ritual action, an operation not unlike sacrifice itself is performed. An action (I am tempted to say a "living" action) is cut in half. Then, rather like some sacrificers themselves (who may, like the Nuer, cut an animal in half from nose to tail, keeping and sharing the right, good, male half and throwing away the left, evil, female half), the analyst decides which half is the good, intelligible, expressive half and which the bad erroneous half, with its unintelligible instrumental claims. The one is kept and shared communally in the social-science literature, and the other is thrown away.

The means-end relation in instrumental action is still, as in positivist interpretations, that of cause and effect; but the means-end relation in ritual (expressive) action has become that between symbol and meaning. That is, the symbol itself is only a means; it is the referent, the thing symbolized, which has value, which "is" the meaning.[8] But this does not fit very well with some of what goes on in ritual. Think of the prophet Hosea saying: "Bring with you words and return to the Lord . . . so we will render the fruit of the lips" (14:2). These symbols seem to be precisely values in themselves. It is certainly not information about something else that is being rendered unto the Lord. Chanting and speaking in tongues are also ritual uses of language whose value or meaning is not reducible to the referents of symbols.

A greater difficulty follows from the arbitrary and conventional nature of relations between symbols and their referents. This means that unless these conventional and arbitrary meanings of ritual are already known, there is no way to understand them. Just as a word is only intelligible when its language is already known, so ritual symbols are only intelligible within their own unique symbol systems. For example, in some Chinese rituals, water is a feminine symbol: like dutiful women in patriarchal society, it always seeks the lowest level, adapts itself instantly and without resistance to whatever container it is put in, and is also essential for the maintenance of life. In some African rituals, however, water is a masculine symbol, analogous to semen and opposed to a feminine symbol, blood.

Just as a Hebrew dictionary will not help you understand Latin words, so Greek, Israelite, Nuer, Aztec, Ashanti, etc., sacrifice each requires its own wholly separate translation. This Tower-of-Babel quality of symbol-referent relations is probably the most important single reason why social scientists have not attempted to make any general theory of sacrifice since the nineteenth century. It simply cannot be done, according to this theory, and there is no way to account for the remarkable worldwide similarities in sacrificial rituals, except as coincidence or diffusion or in terms of "natural symbols" (Douglas 1973).

In order to make a comparative theory of sacrifice, then, we have to think about meanings in some other way than as the already constituted referents of conventional and arbitrary symbolic expressions. One possibility is a structuralist approach in which interest is not in individual signs and their meanings, but in the underlying system of relations *between* signs which makes it possible for them to be meaningful. Although each language is unique, they are ordered by logical structures that may be universal.

There are still other analogies with language that can be made for interpreting ritual. Real acts of speech are not reducible to conventional symbol-referent relations. Instead, they regularly transcend them. Theories of language that find its meaning in its actual use reveal neatly identifiable referents to be rather elusive. Such theories show linguistic expressions to be features of the social situations in which they are used. As Wittgenstein said, "To imagine a language means to imagine a form of life" (1968: 8). In this sense, if there is a recognizable "language" or "language game" which we can call sacrifice, it is rooted in a particular "form of life," and one way to understand sacrifice would be to identify that "form of life."

There are also acts of speech which change the world in the saying of them, which do not merely indicate pre-existing referents, but which constitute a reality which does not exist without the creative act of speech. These are what Austin (1962) called "performatives." Saying "I do" at one's wedding does not merely express a pre-existing social structural reality in words, it calls it into being in deed. Like symbol-referent interpreters, we generally think of the forms of the world as already there and words as labels attached to them. It is only religion, we think, that says "The world was created by the word of God so that what is seen was made out of things which do not appear" (Heb. 11:3). But if symbols create meanings, rather than merely designate already constituted referents, the symbol-meaning relation becomes less neatly distinguishable from the cause-effect relation than instrumental/expressive split advocates have conceived it as being. If our symbolizing creates for us the intended world, the meant and understood world, the social world in which we live, we can perhaps understand why those whose symbolizing has not constituted for them a world divided into mind and matter have also not split apart symbol-meaning and cause-effect.

Finally, all signs are not symbols. Charles Peirce identified three kinds of sign: a *symbol* is related to its object by convention; an *icon*, such as a diagram or map, actually exhibits its object; an *index*, such as an act of pointing, is in existential relation to its object, "connected with it as a matter of fact," said Peirce (1960, vol. 4: 447). Because the relation of sign to signified is not conventional, indices can be understood across cultural and linguistic boundaries. They *indicate* their object rather than represent it. Anyone who has asked for directions in a language she understands poorly knows the advantage of being able to say, "Please point."

Peirce used examples such as a thermometer as an index of temperature, a weathervane as an index of wind direction; and he has been criticized for confusing the cause-effect with the semiotic relation (Burks 1949). But where the relation between sign and signified is existential, the distinction is not so easily made, and for practical action it is irrelevant. For someone sailing in a fog, a compass needle is a sign pointing to magnetic north; that from a theoretical point of view it is instead an effect of causes is not immediately interesting.

Sacrificial victims are given different symbolic meanings in different traditions, but sharing a victim's flesh puts participants in *existential* relation with the victim ("connected with it as a matter of fact"), and with one another. In unrelated traditions, participation in alimentary sacrifice both signifies and *causes* membership in the group with rights to participate. By indexing a social group, by indicating, *"this* group," alimentary sacrifice both identifies and constitutes it. (As practical actors, sacrificers tend to be unconcerned with theoretical distinctions between semiotic and causal relations. If they are drawn to theoretical reflection, like Thomas Aquinas, they may tell you their sacrifice is an "effective sign," one that causes what it signifies [*Summa Theologica,* III. Q62:1].) This way of interpreting sacrifice will be important in following chapters, comparing different traditions with reference to the social organizational powers of sacrificial ritual.[9]

Social scientists have commonly assumed that conventionally established meaning precedes its expression in action: one has first the belief, which leads to the practice. Less commonly, this order has been reversed,[10] beginning with Robertson Smith, who wrote:

> So far as myths consist in explanations of ritual, their value is altogether secondary, and it may be affirmed with confidence that in almost every case the myth was derived from the ritual and not the ritual from the myth; for the ritual was fixed and the myth was variable, the ritual was obligatory and faith in the myth was at the discretion of the worshipper. (1972: 18)

This tells us that action precedes its interpretation, in other words, that action precedes meaning. An action must have already happened for us to be able to examine it reflectively, to interpret it. Many anthropological and sociological interpretations of ritual, although they are themselves *always* produced in reflection upon past ritual action, have ignored this. While producing meanings following action, interpreters theorize about meanings preceding action. And of course this is not without validity. Language as a completed "symbol system" already existing somewhere can be thought of as preceding any particular linguistic expression. But it is nevertheless true that no act of speech can be understood before it is spoken, no text interpreted before it is written.

There is another reason why social-scientific interpreters of ritual have been resistant to thinking of action as preceding meaning. This notion leads to alarming consequences. Robertson Smith told us that "myth is merely the explanation of a religious usage" (1972:18). *The Religion of the Semites* is certainly also the explanation of a religious usage, yet the author does not seem to have thought of himself as merely making another "variable" myth. Perhaps it is the wish to believe in the rightness of their own interpretations that prevents interpreters from seeing that all interpretations (including mine) are such that "their value is altogether secondary." It is this "secondariness" that is behind the wild diversity of interpretations of ritual.

7

Now, from the point of view of action preceding meaning, ritual preceding its interpretations, I want to begin again and look at a variety of actual interpretations to see what they show us about what people do when they interpret ritual action. Begin with interpretations of the simplest possible ritual-like action (a repeated action with non-empirical ends): a baby or very young child pulling in an object on a string and letting it fall away again, apparently for the satisfaction of doing it. Freud watched his grandson do this, and Piaget watched his daughter playing the same game (Anthony 1957). Each produced interpretations important in the development of his own work, but the meanings each found in the action were entirely different. Freud's baby was doing symbolic action; the object represented his absent mother, and his "ritual" enabled him to manage otherwise intolerable emotional stress. Piaget's baby's action was entirely conflict-free, a purely intellectual process of exploring the properties of a non-representational object and its position in space and time, of discovering causal relations and the permanence of material objects.

These two interpretations can be compared to intellectualist (Piaget, scientists understanding objects) and anti-intellectualist (Freud, biologically essential control of stress) interpretations. (Of course Freud, typically, was unable to limit his interpretation to a mere biological one; he let a social relationship get in there changing everything.) The general murkiness of many theories of ritual obscures in them what is immediately evident in this illustration: The nature of an interpretation of action depends as much or more on the interests, purposes, and situation of the interpreter as it does on those of the actor, and this is *not* a consequence of the interpretation being a poor one, inattentive, shallow, or "merely projective."

That interpretation of action depends on the situation of the interpreter is not a failing. It is a consequence of the (obvious but often unrecognized) fact that an action is not the same as an interpretation of it. The meaning of any action not only varies with the way in which it is interpreted, it *is* the way in which it is interpreted. The meaning is not already there in the action, like the gin is in the bottle, in such a way that you can get it out, unadulterated, by performing certain operations on the action. For meaning is not a simple and direct product of action itself, but of reflection upon it. And the act of reflection is always *another* act, socially situated in its own way.[11]

Now consider an account (all accounts are interpretations) of a religious ritual, a circumcision. The fifth chapter of the Book of Joshua tells us how Joshua circumcised the Israelites at a place called the hill of the foreskins. Verse 4 begins: "And this is the reason why Joshua circumcised them: . . . ," and you think, reading it, that you are about

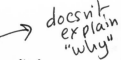

to be given a *real* understanding. But the "reason why" is peculiarly disappointing: "for they were uncircumcised." (You see? The means *are* the ends.) Considerable attention is given to explaining how this state of affairs came about—what with wandering in the wilderness for forty years, not hearkening to the voice of the Lord, and so on. Of course, what is explained is not why Joshua circumcised them in the sense we had hoped for, but why he did it then and there and not at some other time and place. Why he should circumcise them in the first place is not considered to need explanation. What was problematical to the author of Joshua was not circumcision itself, but rather why all those grown-up Israelites were uncircumcised. The interpretation in Joshua 5 is disappointing because it is an explanation for someone else, in some other situation, not one for us. Robertson Smith observed that "everyone who reads the Old Testament with attention is struck with the fact that the origin and rationale of sacrifice are nowhere fully explained" (1972: 3). It would be more accurate to say they are nowhere fully explained for *us;* no interpretation shaped to *our* Here and Now is offered. We are given instead much practical (and therefore for us not immediately useful) information about when it is appropriate to sacrifice, how to do it correctly, how some people do it wrong, and so on.

Now compare the interpretation of Joshua's action with that of David's action (II Sam. 21: 1–14) by the twentieth-century biblical scholar A. S. Kapelrud. Like Joshua 5, this interpretation does not explain a ritual itself; rather, it explains why and when and where it was done. Unlike Joshua 5, it is an interpretation for us, and it is only after thinking about it a while that it begins to seem disappointing.

At the beginning of David's reign there were three straight years of famine. The ritual in question is the killing of the seven sons of Saul, a sacrifice to end the famine. What happened, according to Kapelrud, was this: David, whose new and still precarious position on the throne was threatened by Saul's sons, "needed a pretext and he found it" (1955: 116). He knew that in severe famine a sacrifice of royal children might be required. The Gibeonites were supposed to have an ancient hatred of, and desire for revenge against, Saul. So David asked the Gibeonite oracle what to do and was told (did not offer) to hand over all of Saul's male descendants for sacrifice. Thus David did his royal duty to end the famine, got rid of all competitors for the throne, and kept free of personal responsibility for their deaths, all at once.

In order to understand David's action we ourselves do not need to understand or endorse fertility sacrifices. Kapelrud's interpretation does not even require that David believed in the fertility cult. It was only a feature of the immediate social and political scene that he needed to take into account, and to make use of if possible, for wholly empirical

9

political ends. David appears very like politicians of our own (and Kapelrud's) time. This interpretation makes sense to us even though (perhaps *because*) it has not illuminated fertility sacrifice.

In none of these four examples was it possible for the interpreter to ask the actors themselves the meaning of their action. An obvious objection is that the inaccessibility of the actors as informants is the source of diversity in interpretation. Perhaps where we can question the actors themselves, we can get *the* meaning of ritual. As a final example, consider the account by an American anthropologist of an African (Fang) cult whose members regularly perform a ritual involving dancing all night. Unlike most anthropologists, who usually ask only religious specialists for the interpretation of a ritual, James W. Fernandez interviewed each member of the cult separately about the purpose of the ritual and the meaning of various elements in it. His paper (1965) records a wonderful struggle by a follower of the instrumental/expressive split to make sense of diversity of meanings.

All Fernandez's informants "emphatically subscribed to the efficacy of the ritual" (ibid.:904), but their explanation of its purpose varied widely, and there was similar disagreement on the interpretation of all symbolic elements. For Fernandez, this constitutes a problem:

> What remains of interest is that such highly regularized activity
> betrays such variable perspectives on the meanings involved. This
> is a paradox which challenges explanation.[12]

Of course this is only a paradox for ways of thinking which make meaning directly a feature of action.

Unwilling to abandon the instrumental/expressive split, Fernandez does some fancy theoretical footwork to keep up with his own careful fieldwork. He distinguishes between "logico-meaningful symbols," which express meanings, and "causal-functional signals," which merely tell you what to do (instrumentally) next; and shows that ritual action which has not been reflected upon (causal-functional signals) does not yet have specific interpretations, while ritual that has been interpreted (logico-meaningful symbols) necessarily refers beyond itself to other social situations.

Fernandez shows us still more: The senior members of the cult sit in the back of the chapel to discipline and interpret the ritual while the active dancing members perform it. Interpretation by these junior members is "entirely inappropriate" and taken as "divisive in intent" (ibid.: 915). Of course; interpretation from those without proper authority is not going to be from the right social situation, offering the right perspective.

Fernandez describes this politics of interpretation of ritual as a purely local feature, a consequence of a syncretist religion in a "context of turmoil and anxiety of a society in transition" (ibid.: 916). But, although its intensity varies, wherever there is ritual there is always a politics of its interpretation, because ritual action can always transcend any final perfect interpretation of it, as also interpretations always transcend the action itself, for they necessarily relate it to some particular social situation from which the interpretation is made. The question inevitably arises as to who is socially entitled to a position (perhaps *the* position) from which it is legitimate to interpret ritual. What is being defended in accusations of heresy is not just specific interpretations of texts or actions, but the possession of the only true point of perspective and also the principle that there is such a point.

If ritual action is so unresisting, so vulnerable, to diversity of interpretation, and if that diversity is a feature of the necessary situatedness of the interpreter, how can there be any basis at all for recognizing validity in interpretation? We can sometimes recognize the absurdity of other people's interpretations, but perhaps that is only because we do not share their perspective. For example, consider the savage as idiot in the interpretations of nineteenth-century British scholars of "primitive" religion; as Evans-Pritchard says, "The natives were made to look childish and in obvious need of fatherly administration and missionary zeal" (1965: 8). Now we can see the dark shadow of the British Empire obscuring scholars' vision, but would we have seen it then? Can it be that the more alien an interpreter's social situation, the more distorted we find his or her interpretation? Mid-nineteenth-century West African slave traders explained local human sacrifice as a consequence of the British blockade: a solution to the problem of what to do with an unsalable commodity that was both dangerous and expensive to store. How can we tell whether we are not making similar mistakes?

It is possible to make an analogy between the limitations of social situatedness as an inescapable ground for understanding ritual and some of the ways people have thought about our bodies as unreliable, treacherous sources of partial knowledge about the world. Only as we can transcend sense perception can we trust our knowledge. It is this sort of thinking that led Plato to say, "If we are to have clear knowledge of anything, we must get rid of the body" (*Phaedo*, 66 D11; Tr. Hackforth 1952: 48). But our bodies are not really the main obstacle to knowledge of the world; they are instead our access to the world, the fallible and mortal ways we have of being in the world. So also, it is membership in a social world (that is, our ability to understand meanings) that makes ritual potentially intelligible for us to begin with. What enables us to interpret ritual *at all* is also what prevents us from interpreting it perfectly. In communication with others we can transcend the limits of bodily situatedness and form concepts of objects known not from one, or even from a series of perspectives, but from everywhere. We escape the limits of sense perception by entering the social world. But there is no extra-social unsituated view, no Archimedean point outside or above all social situatedness from which we can interpret ritual as if from everywhere.

We can, however, recognize that sacrificers act within their own social world, which is other than ours, and within which their ritual makes sense in a way it does not in ours. The idiot savage of nineteenth-century scholars is certainly defective, but what he has lost is not his intelligence, but his social context, within which his ritual might be intelligible. There is also no mystery about the interpretations of the West African slave traders. The victim-as-dangerous-inventory interpretations were made to visiting Englishmen and their object was not to understand sacrifice but to discredit the blockade. The social context and intended meanings of sacrificers were wholly irrelevant. No one genuinely trying to understand sacrifice as the action of fellow human beings in their own social context is likely to make that particular kind of mistake.

Of the five illustrations of interpretation of ritual given above, only Piaget's wholly ignores the social setting of the actor. Scientific meanings differ from the meanings of social action in that scientific truths are intelligible without reference to particular social settings. Or course Piaget's baby was doing natural science, so Piaget could get away with it, but those who interpret ordinary ritual will get in trouble if they do likewise.

The social context of ritual action is not a mere background which can be stripped away, as a play is still possible on a stage bare of scenery; it is the element within which ritual has its life. Consider some out-of-context cultural objects, which, unlike actions, can be physically removed from their settings. Years ago, I used to contemplate a small flat piece of carved stone on display in a remote corner of Harvard's Peabody Museum of Archaeology and Ethnology. The faded card beside it read: "A Churinga, the most sacred object of an Australian tribe. The worst disaster that could befall the tribe was to lose its churinga. It must never, under any circumstances, be seen by a woman." The incongruity of the sunny, slightly dusty, matter-of-fact room in the museum and the tragedy and blasphemy of a lost churinga, exposed to the gaze of passing women like myself, was such that I realized that this had once been, but no longer was, a churinga. It was like Confederate money; it is not clear just what that object is now, but certainly it is no longer money. Or even like Wittgenstein's brake lever: "'I set the brake up by connecting rod and lever'—Yes, given the whole rest of the mechanism. Only in conjunction with that is it a brake lever, and separated from its support it is not even a lever; it may be anything, or nothing" (1968: #6). Stripped of its social context, an act of sacrifice may be anything, or nothing.

Attention to the social context of the actors themselves offers real resistance to total freedom of interpretation. But by itself, it does not solve the problem of validity of interpretation. It merely sets limits on the scope of the situatedness of the interpreter, which still remains. The only basis for judging validity of interpretation of ritual action must be either the degree of conformity with established doctrine, or the quality of understanding which the interpretation offers.

The Puritans used to speak of the Spirit "opening" a passage of scripture to them. An interpretation of ritual is valid if it opens what was otherwise closed, if it enables us to understand what had been unintelligible. It can be thought of as more or less valid according to the breadth of understanding it provides, but that will *always* be partial. *[margin: is never all-encompassing]* Action must always be potentially richer than any specific interpretation of it; otherwise it would be eternally tied to the situation of the "perfect" interpreter. If it were not always susceptible to re-interpretation, the past would be split off and frozen; it would be inaccessible to understanding for those in other times and situations, with other perspectives and other interests.

The notion that because we cannot possess *the* meaning we fail is based on a mistaken idea of understanding. Trying to understand the meaning of ritual is not an act of acquisition but a work of relating; the understanding is not an end point that can be reached so much as it is a movement of turning toward the social world of the ritual actors. Like *[margin: Religious study will never be done]* women's work, it is never done but not consequently invalid.

But what is this work of understanding? It cannot be to reach a meaning identical to that of the ritual actors themselves, because their meaning is an organization of their experience which is inaccessible to us. There are two kinds of situatedness, that of the sacrificers and that of the interpreter. The one is unattainable and the other is inescapable. The task is to build some kind of bridge between the two to hold the worlds together, not accurately to decode *their* meaning, but to make what they do and say intelligible for us. This is a kind of negotiating process, a reaching of some agreement, in which we recognize sacrificers as both different from and the same as ourselves. We recognize their differences from us by recognizing their social context, other than our own; by identifying the kind of social world (the form of life) within which sacrifice is meaningfully performed. But we will still not find their symbolic action intelligible unless we can also recognize in it logical structures like our own. I can demonstrate this best by giving the reader an actual experience of recognizing logical structures like our own. I hope to show by this illustration both that when we encounter an "unintelligible" action or expression, if we wish to understand, we must change our way of thinking, play another language game (a kind of stretching process), and also that when we do understand we always grasp the unknown in terms of the known (a kind of scrunching process).

As an exercise, consider Alasdair MacIntyre's criticism of Evans-Pritchard's *Nuer Religion*. Evans-Pritchard's explication of Nuer religion is inadequate, says MacIntyre, for although he shows how it makes sense to the Nuer, he has not done the same for us. There remains an unbridged and, MacIntyre implies, unbridgeable gulf between Nuer logical order and our own. MacIntyre claims (and I think he is right) that "to make a belief and the concepts which it embodies intelligible I cannot avoid invoking my own criteria, or rather the established criteria of my own society" (1971: 71). (This is the inescapable situatedness of the interpreter.) Some Nuer notions of fundamental logical principles do indeed seem to differ radically from our own, and as MacIntyre says, the "Nuer appear to fly in the face of ordinary rules of consistency and contradiction" (ibid.: 65). One gets the impression, reading *Nuer Religion*, that Evens-Pritchard himself was sometimes on the verge of protesting, "But in Nuer it makes perfect sense."

A central obstacle for MacIntyre is the Nuer notion of the divine, *kwoth*, generally translated as "spirit" by Evans-Pritchard. Of *kwoth* itself, in a pure state, Nuer say they have neither experience nor knowledge; it is known only through its manifestations. These many manifestations differ widely from one another, but nevertheless, *kwoth* is believed to be one. Although *kwoth* is fully present in all of its manifestations, none of them can be said to be *kwoth*. For MacIntyre,

> The difficulties in the notion of *kwoth* spring from the fact that *kwoth* is asserted both to be sharply contrasted with the material creation and to be widely present in it. It is both one and many; and the many, as aspects of *kwoth*, are one with each other. (Ibid.: 65)

Nuer logic is revealed by ours to be contradictory, and Nuer religious concepts are unintelligible for us.

Now, stop thinking in terms of identity and contradiction (the "ordinary rules of consistency and contradiction"), and think instead of the relation between *kwoth* and its manifestations, between spirit and material creation, between the one and the many, as being like that between consciousness and the objects or contents of consciousness (what consciousness is conscious *of*). All of these many and widely differing phenomena are manifestations of consciousness (which like *kwoth* is fully present in all of them), although they are not consciousness itself. Of that in a pure state (like the Nuer of *kwoth*) we have neither experience nor knowledge, for all consciousness is consciousness of something. And yet, nevertheless, we are inclined to speak of consciousness as one. Consciousness (like *kwoth*) is both sharply contrasted with the material creation and widely present in it.

MacIntyre tried to understand *kwoth* "objectively," but *kwoth* is more like subjectivity itself. This impossible and contradictory statement reveals the problem, for subjectivity can never be "it," but rather must always be "I." Compare *kwoth* as subject with Yahweh as he revealed himself to Moses:

> Then Moses said to God, "If I come to the people of Israel and say to them, 'The God of your fathers has sent me to you,' and they ask me, 'What is his name?' what shall I say to them?" God said to Moses, "I AM WHO I AM" and he said, "Say this to the people of Israel, "'I AM has sent me to you.'" (Exod. 3:13–14)

It is not Nuer irrationality but our own objectification of spirit that creates the obstacle for understanding. This is, of course, merely an analogy. It is not how the Nuer themselves think of *kwoth*, we have not got *their* meaning; but *kwoth* has become intelligible for us, and what we have recognized is our own mind: consciousness and what it is conscious of.

Harold Garfinkel has shown that even among persons sharing the same social setting "common understandings cannot possibly consist of a measured amount of shared agreement among persons on certain topics" (1967: 39). Instead of possessing precisely overlapping sets of knowledge of what people are talking *about*, we recognize *how* they are talking. This is like Wittgenstein's claim that we understand someone when we know what "language game" she or he is playing (not when we know the exact referents of the words), and that misunderstandings occur when language games are confused. This is the mistake MacIntyre made. He thought the Nuer were playing "rules of consistency and contradiction," and found them playing it very badly; but if we think of them as playing "relation between consciousness and what it is conscious of," we discover them to be skilled players. If it is asked, how can we be certain this is the Nuer's language game? I think we must answer that we cannot. We have not got *their* meaning, we have only found a way of understanding which consists in recognizing them as knowing as we do.

The next steps, in making a comparative sociology of sacrifice, are: first, to find logical structures we can recognize as our own in the varied symbolic actions of sacrificers; second, to identify socially organized contexts (the "forms of life") within which sacrificers act meaningfully and which we recognize as not our own; and finally, to show how these logical structures are grounded in their own social contexts. The following chapter identifies a structure that can help make aspects of sacrificial practice in various traditions intelligible for us. This structure is necessarily abstract, only ideal, so that we may compare widely different real traditions with minimal violence. It is only a lens to look through, not a concrete description of any sacrificial practice.

TWO

The Logic of Sacrifice

S ACRIFICE JOINS PEOPLE TOGETHER IN COMMUNITY, and, conversely, it separates them from defilement, disease, and other dangers. This opposition of joining and separating is so widespread that one of the clearest indications that a ritual killing is properly sacrifice is that it is part of a religious system of this kind. Joining and separating aspects of sacrifice have received different names, for example, "conjunctive" and "disjunctive" (Luc de Heusch 1985), or "collective" and "piacular" (Evans-Pritchard 1956). The traditional terms "communion" and "expiation" recognize a similar distinction. The logic of sacrifice I want to describe is grounded in this opposition.

I shall use the traditional terms, partly for aesthetic reasons, but primarily because they are sacrificial terms themselves. "Joining" and "separating" have a reverse advantage in not originating in a particular tradition, but they are problematic because sacrifice is never so neatly one-sided. For example, Greek alimentary sacrifice was primarily communion sacrifice, but in uniting participants in community it also separated them from foreigners, the defiled, and all those not entitled by descent or invitation to participate.

As "expiation" is traditionally used, it conveys only some of the wide range of meanings of separating sacrifices: appeasement, wiping out (of guilt), turning away (of anger). It is not so appropriate for purification, propitiation, exorcism, scapegoating, and so on. I arbitrarily extend it to cover the whole range of the "separating" aspects of sacrifice.

Communion and expiation are opposed not only as positive and negative but also as the one and the many. Since people are troubled by ills without number, so sacrifices to get rid of them are of many kinds. Some sacrificing societies, including the Israelites, had one form of communion sacrifice but many kinds of expiatory sacrifice. The Greeks had a particularly vivid sense of the multiplicity of real and potential evils. (The contents of Pandora's box were beyond all counting.)[1] In the Greek tradition, one can speak of *the* alimentary sacrifice, uniting participants in community, but there were many different non-alimentary, expiatory sacrifices (Vernant 1980: 112).

Scholars have discussed communion and expiation as if they were wholly separate kinds of action, but their interdependence, both logical and ritual, is a regular feature of unrelated sacrificial traditions. This is so even though one mode may be far more heavily emphasized in any given society at any given historical period. Ethnographic literature may accentuate this imbalance as, according to the interests of the ethnographer, the focus is on one mode to the near exclusion of the other. Ethnographic examples are Meyer Fortes's focus on Tallensi communion sacrifice (1945) and Evans-Pritchards's focus on Nuer expiatory sacrifice (1956). Some scholars ignore expiatory aspects of sacrifice for no apparent reason; for example, van der Leeuw in his phenomenological discussion of sacrifice (1967).

The general tendency, especially among Protestant scholars, has been to shove expiatory sacrifice aside or to treat it as less intelligible than communion sacrifice. Modern scholarly sacrificial literature did this from the beginning. Robertson Smith, following historical biblical scholarship of his time, believed that Israelite worship originally consisted only of communion sacrifice. Expiatory sacrifice was a late introduction, not even a natural development, but a consequence of guilt and despair over the Babylonian exile. More recent biblical scholarship refutes this on several grounds.[2] Jane Harrison reversed this chronology, understanding Greek expiatory sacrifice as a survival from an earlier, primitive (irrational and matriarchal) pre-Greek society. The arrival of the rational Greeks brought only communion sacrifice. She explained the intermingling of the two forms in Greek religion by a supposed chronological superposition of cults, a "theological stratification" (1922: 11). She too has been shown to be mistaken.[3]

Hubert and Mauss, alone among scholars of their time, recognized that expiation "is a primordial component of sacrifice, as primordial and irreducible as communion." Throughout their book they recognized the intermingling of the two modes; but still considering them to be two distinct and logically separate processes, they concluded that the "unity" of sacrifice "must be sought elsewhere" (1964: 6, 17).[4] They did not see that communion and expiation are two aspects of one process, no matter how heavily one or the other may be accented in particular sacrificial acts.

In a formal sense, communion is a kind of integration, and expiation a kind of differentiation, and these are always two aspects of one process. Integration, constituting the oneness of anything, is not possible without differentiating it from other things. Conversely, we cannot differentiate something from the rest of the world without at the same time identifying it as a recognizable whole, without integrating it. So in sacrifice, as that wonderful English word reveals, atonement is also always at-one-ment.[5]

Communion sacrifice unites worshipers in one moral community and at the same time differentiates that community from the rest of the world. Expiatory sacrifice integrates by getting rid of countless different moral and organic undesirable conditions: sin, disease, drought, divine wrath, famine, barrenness, spirit possession, armed invaders, blood guilt, incest, impurity of descent, pollution of childbirth or of corpses, and so on and on, all having in common only that they must be expiated. What is integrated is one. What is differentiated is logically without limit and can be expressed in a single term only negatively, as not the integrated whole, as opposed to it as disorder is to order, as unclean is to clean, or in formal logical terms, as Not-A is to A.

Recognizing this unity of communion and expiation as a formal logical structure makes it possible to understand sacrifice as symbolic action without being stopped short at the boundary of every unique tradition. We can describe a logical structure maintained by sacrificial integration-and-differentiation as a purely formal structure, A vs. Not-A, leaving aside its contents—which do indeed vary from culture to culture. The distinction "Israel/Nations," in which the Nations, unclean in relation to Israel, have in common only that they are not Israel, is unique to Israelite religion, but as a formal structure, "Israel/Nations" is the A/Not-A distinction found everywhere.

The rules describing A/Not-A were first formulated by Aristotle. The most basic of these are: the Principle of Identity (if anything is A it is A); the Principle of Contradiction (nothing can be both A and Not-A); and the Principle of the Excluded Middle (anything and everything must be either A or Not-A). The excluded middle is the crucial "difference" which must be kept between the clean and the unclean (Lev. 10:10, 11:47, 20:25; Ezek. 22:26, 44:23).

In contradictory dichotomy, only one term, A, has positive reality. Not-A is only a privation, a negation or absence of A. This property of contradictories is wonderfully clear in abstract formal logic, but when it is applied directly to the empirical world, strange things happen. For example, when the sexes are conceived as contradictories, only one sex can have positive reality. (Guess which.) This kind of thinking is behind Aristotle's notion of women as misbegotten males. A woman, having no positive sexuality of her own, is only a failure to become a man.

Aristotle mistakenly thought all contrary terms had this contradictory structure (Lloyd 1966: 65), but contraries can be phrased as A/B, both terms having positive reality. Unlike A and Not-A, continuity may be recognized between A and B without shattering the distinction; they do not need an excluded middle. This difference does not lie in things themselves, but in how they are classified, as in the difference between conceiving of men and women as men and not-men, between which there can logically be no continuity, and conceiving of them as two forms of the class "human," which may be supposed to have a good deal in common.[6]

There are further differences between A/Not-A and A/B. Contrast Israel/Nations with Israel/Egypt. Israel/Nations orders all the societies in the world, known and unknown, as either Israel or Nations. When the Assyrians appear on the scene the structure is unchanged. Israel/Nations creates an unchanging order, but Israel/Egypt must change to become Israel/Egypt/Assyria: A/B/C. In A/Not-A distinctions there is no third possibility.

Not-A has a peculiar quality in which B cannot share at all: the "infinitation of the negative." As John Dewey said, "If, say, 'virtue' be assigned to A as its meaning, then Not-A includes not only vice, but triangles, horse-races, symphonies, and the precession of the equinoxes" (1938:192). Not-A is without internal boundaries or order of any kind. The famous contagion of pollution is often considered to be irrational. (An Israelite example (Lev.15:19–24) is that a man who touches a menstruating woman, or anything in contact with her, becomes unclean himself.) But "contagion" is a logically necessary consequence of this structure of formal logic when it is applied directly to the empirical world. Only the excluded middle, the essential empty space between A and Not-A, the "difference" that must be kept between the clean and the unclean, holds the chaos of Not-A at bay. Whatever is contiguous with Not-A is necessarily Not-A itself.

According to John Dewey, direct application of the excluded middle is "the source of more fallacious reasoning in philosophical discourse and in moral and social inquiry than any other sort of fallacy" (1938: 346). Ways of knowing based on contradictories make the understanding of change difficult or impossible, for all change falls into Not-A, which is without discernible order. But suppose it is not merely in our thought, but directly in the social world that we want the unyielding boundaries of the excluded middle. Suppose, like sacrificers, we want not social theory, but social order. Direct application of A/Not-A distinctions, such as pure/impure, is an effective means of achieving just that. The rigidity and resistance to change so troublesome for scientific inquiry is what makes A/Not-A distinctions so useful socially.[7] The only alternative to the one existing order is disorder.

A/Not-A dichotomies, allowing no continuity between terms, and no alternatives to them, are found nowhere in nature. Leviticus (11:47;

20:25) is quite right that such distinctions are made, as is Ezekiel (22:26; 44:23) that they must be taught and learned. They are social creations, not supported by any natural order, and as such, continual work is required to maintain them. Sacrifice is one way of doing this work, creating not just logical structures, but social order.

Integration-and-differentiation is not the only logical structure discoverable in sacrifice. Each tradition has its own unique symbolic structures. Taking classical Greek sacrifice as an example, consider first a symbolic structure unique to that tradition, and secondly the way in which communion and expiation are represented there.

In the Golden Age, says Hesiod,[8] people were all male. They were not born of woman but sprang from the earth. In those days earth produced all its fruits spontaneously: men dined with the gods and did no work. Then Prometheus invented sacrifice and brought about the separation of men and gods. He divided the body of an ox in two: on one side he put the bones, covered with a layer of beautiful white fat; on the other side he put the flesh, covered by the unappetizing stomach and hide. Invited to choose the gods' share, Zeus was deceived by appearances and chose the bones. Ever after, the Greeks feasted on meat at sacrifices while the bones and fat ascended in smoke to the heavenly gods.

Zeus's revenge was to offer his own deceptive gift, and Epimetheus, the stupid twin of wily Prometheus, was dumb enough to accept it. This gift, the first woman, was also beautiful on the outside but worse than bones on the inside. Pandora's first act was to release all the evils males had not known before: hunger, hard labor, disease, old age, and death.

Basing their work on this and other myths, the French classicists Vernant, Detienne, and Vidal-Naquet have described a logical structure of Greek alimentary sacrifice that sets human society midway between the beasts and the gods. Eating cooked meat, which for the Greeks meant sacrifice, is distinguished equally from the beasts' diet of raw flesh and from the gods' diet of fragrant smoke. Like the human condition, the sacrificial meal is "in an intermediary position half-way between the raw and the burned, the rotten and the incorruptible, the bestial and the divine" (Vernant 1980: 137). The same structure encodes sexuality: marriage in the patrilineal family is midway between the sexual promiscuity of beasts and the male purity of the Golden Age.[9] This sacrificial logic is readily intelligible, but it is not found in Israelite, Nuer, Ashanti, etc., sacrificial systems. To identify a logical structure of Greek sacrifice that orders other traditions as well, we need a more elementary structure.

These French classicists are concerned only with alimentary sacrifice. The logical structures they disclose are all grounded in a dietary code. They refer only rarely to a non-alimentary category of Greek sacrifice as "the opposite" of alimentary sacrifice.[10] The two modes of sacrifice were opposed and interdependent as are day and night, heaven and earth, positive and negative, the one and the many. There were different vocabularies as well as different rituals for alimentary sacrifice (*thysia*) and non-alimentary sacrifice (*enagismos*).[11] Victims of non-alimentary sacrifice were destroyed in a variety of ways (including holocaust, meaning "burnt whole"). Sometimes such sacrifices were eaten, but those who partook became polluted and could have no part in alimentary sacrifices.[12]

Thysia was typically a festive daytime celebration with music and procession (*pompe*) to the temple. The victim, ideally white, often a bull decorated with gilded horns and garlands of flowers, was killed with its throat pointing skyward, its head pulled back. The fat and bones were burnt on a raised altar, and the flesh was shared among the participants.

Non-alimentary *enagismos* was commonly a nighttime ritual. Processions were called *apopompe*, a leading *away* from the temple or city. The victims, often rams or pigs, were ideally black and were killed with the throat pointing downward toward the earth. Instead of the raised altar, offerings were made on a ground-level hearth or in a pit in the ground.

Usually the two kinds of sacrifice were offered to two different kinds (or aspects) of divinities. The fragrant smoke of *thysia* ascended to the heavenly gods, the Olympians. Recipients of *enagismos* were the dead and the gods of the earth and of the underworld: chthonic gods. Opposition was sharp between the immortal Olympians and the dead, including those mythical mortals who once had dealings with the gods, the heroes. Defiled persons could sacrifice at the grave of a hero where sacrificial blood could purify blood pollution, but one must be already pure to approach a temple of the Olympians to participate in *thysia*.

The two kinds of sacrifice are commonly called "Olympic" and "chthonic" ritual. But there are troublesome exceptions to this neat categorization.[13] There are records of "Olympic" sacrifice to chthonic divinities. The *orgeones*, localized patrilineal groups of "sacrificing associates," worshiped a hero and heroines, yet their records reveal a "complete absence of chthonic ritual" (Ferguson 1944: 62, 127). The Olympians, especially Hermes and Zeus, had their chthonic aspects and were not consistently heavenly. Consider what Pausanias (8.34.3) said of the Furies, ordinarily chthonic gods:

> When the goddesses were going to drive Orestes mad they are said to have appeared to him all black, and when he bit off his finger they suddenly seemed to turn white, and the sight of them

sobered him and he consumed offerings in fire [holocaust] to turn away their wrath, and performed divine sacrifice [*ethyse*] to the white goddesses.

Notice that the holocaust was to avert their wrath. Alimentary sacrifice was characterized by *therapeia*, service; non-alimentary sacrifice by *apotrope*, aversion or riddance.

Taking our eyes off the gods and looking at the people, it becomes apparent that the consistent difference between alimentary and non-alimentary sacrifice was not who the recipient divinities were, but whether the sacrifice joined people together in alimentary community or, conversely, separated them from defilement and other dangers. All the symbolic elaboration of the opposition, such as the ritual use of day vs. night, black vs. white, oxen vs. pigs, music vs. silence, and especially the Olympic/chthonic opposition, are specifically Greek. But *logically* analogous oppositions of joining and separating are present in very different sacrificial traditions.

In the enormous variety of actual sacrificial rituals of different societies, a claim that people are doing "the same thing" (sacrificial integration-and-differentiation) is only possible in abstraction. It is important to remember that I am using "communion" and "expiation" as ideal types, not real ones. They are not descriptive; they are abstractions which will not adequately describe any actual sacrificial practice. They are lenses that will bring into focus analogous aspects of differing traditions.

The Greek system, in which communion and expiation are relatively separated into two distinct categories of sacrifices, is not representative of all sacrificial traditions. In many other traditions, expiation and communion are thoroughly combined in the same sacrifice; a good example is the Israelite Passover sacrifice in which the blood turns away the destructive power of Yahweh and the flesh provides a communion meal.

Another example is the prescribed series of funeral sacrifices among the East African Gusii. These sacrifices separated the living from the deceased, who by dying had become a source of danger both in spirit and flesh; but these same sacrifices also reintegrated the community that death had damaged. The first sacrifice, a goat, "was explicitly interpreted by informants as intended to placate the deceased," but it was roasted intact, "with the skin on, and the whole thing eaten on the spot; unlike other sacrifices, the meat was not allowed to be taken home" (LeVine 1982: 36).[14] The obligation to consume the victim in this way both identified the mourning group ("the nuclear patrilineal group") and vividly asserted the oneness of this alimentary community (ibid.:

27). In the second sacrifice, communion aspects were more widely extended. "The meat of this goat was distributed to all the houses in the homestead. . . . Each house was likened to a part taken from a whole, emphasizing the unity of the whole without denying its segmentation; the message was similar to *e pluribus unum*" (ibid.: 39). The series concluded with sacrifices at the houses of all the sons and grandsons (sons' sons) of the deceased. Once again, these sacrifices turned away the ill will of the deceased, but at the same time, they identified and affirmed in alimentary community the patrilineal ties uniting the participants.

No sacrificial system can be taken as representative of others. They all combine expiatory and communion aspects in different ways. But we can choose to look at all of them through the lenses of these logical abstractions. In illustrating this logic of sacrifice, my intention is not to cover all the possible variations nor to present any of them as typical or privileged, but only to indicate the variety that exists, and to give readers some experience in recognizing this logical opposition as it appears in different traditions. I have chosen to describe the Greek sacrificial system, and to add to it the following descriptions of Israelite and Nuer systems, simply because they are all different and all relatively easy to describe in this way. But any well-described sacrificial system could serve as an illustration in its own distinctive way.

Sacrificial systems are never fixed, eternal structures. Historical change can dramatically transform them. The best-known example is surely Israelite sacrifice. Expiatory elements strongly predominated in late Israelite sacrifice, but several centuries earlier, communion sacrifice had been of fundamental importance. At no time was sacrifice entirely reduced to one of these modes. Both communion and expiation are *logically* necessary in sacrificial systems, but they need not be equal in any quantified way. They are logical, not statistical, categories.

Biblical accounts of Israelite sacrifice are from different strands of tradition and different historical periods.[15] In the Book of Leviticus, the later priestly authors described their sacrificial system as they claimed it had been inaugurated by Moses (perhaps eight hundred years earlier). Their account may not be historically accurate, but it is unlikely that they would have misrepresented the structure of their own sacrificial system. In this account, they made communion sacrifice (peace offerings) primary even though they themselves rarely, or perhaps never, performed them. Following their example, I will describe Israelite sacrifice as a single system. (See chapter 7 for historical discussion.)

The most important of Israelite sacrifices, the burnt offering, cannot be categorized as either expiatory or communion sacrifice. It appears as a midpoint, flanked on one side by joyful communion "peace offering," and on the other by gloomy expiatory "sin offering." Accounts of communion sacrifice are unelaborated: peace offerings are all pretty much the same.[16] But on the expiatory side of the spectrum the priests distinguished many kinds of sin and guilt offerings, and beyond these, some still more intensely expiatory sacrifices. If you take into account this proliferation of sin offerings, the spectrum of sacrifices (peace-BURNT-sin) is overweighted at the expiatory end. But if you consider only the commonest form of sin offering, the structure is perfectly balanced, for except that only priests could eat it, there was almost no difference in performance between it and peace offering. To make the structure "peace-BURNT-sin" historical, it needs an orienting arrow:

$$\longrightarrow$$
peace-BURNT-sin.

Most early accounts describe burnt and peace offerings performed together; later accounts pair burnt and sin offerings.[17]

Leviticus 1–7 sets out rules for doing sacrifices. They all begin in the same way: The offerer lays his hands upon the victim's head and kills it before the altar; then the priest pours out the blood at the base of the altar. This blood rite is an expiatory element present even in communion sacrifices. Across the spectrum of sin offerings, as they intensify in expiatory quality, the blood rite becomes more and more complicated.

In peace offerings only the fat, kidneys, and appendage of the liver are burnt on the altar. Part of the remainder is given to the priest, and all the rest reverts to the offerer to be eaten at a festive meal. In burnt offerings all but the skin is burnt on the altar. In all sin offerings the same portion as in peace offerings is burnt on the altar. The kind of animal used and what is done with it varies according to whether it is offered for the sin of the high priest, of the whole community, of leaders, or of ordinary persons. The flesh of victims offered for the sins of common people and leaders is eaten only by males of priestly families, for its sacredness spreads to anything it touches. The alimentary community it indexes (identifies) is likewise strictly distinguished from other groups. Except for this contagious sanctity, these "edible" sin offerings are almost indistinguishable from peace offerings for priests only. The only difference in the procedure is that a little blood is put on the horns of the outer altar.

In sin offerings for the high priest and for the whole community, blood is sprinkled seven times before the veil of the sanctuary and put on the horns of the most holy inner altar. Nothing is eaten of these more intensely expiatory sin offerings. Flesh, bones, skin, dung, all the remainder must be taken outside the camp and burnt there, and those who burn it become temporarily unclean (Lev. 16:28).

25

Burnt offerings and the burnt portion of peace offerings make "a pleasing odor for the Lord." The Lord himself referred to such sacrifices as "my food for my offerings by fire, my pleasing odor" (Num. 28:2). This alimentary connotation is absent from sin offerings. Even though the same portion of the victim is burnt on the altar as in peace offerings, it is not described as making a pleasing odor except once (Lev. 4:31) and then only in reference to "edible" sin offerings.[18]

In this way, most Israelite sacrifices can be located along a scale of increasing expiation, beginning with peace offerings, then burnt offerings, then "edible" sin offerings followed by non-alimentary sin offerings. Special sacrifices existed even further along the expiatory end of the continuum, and in these no blood was applied to the altar, nor any portion burnt upon it.

Numbers 19 gives the rules for the powerfully expiatory red heifer sacrifice: A red heifer is slaughtered outside the camp and the priest sprinkles its blood in the direction of the altar. The victim is then and there entirely burnt, and the priest throws cedar, hyssop, and a scarlet cloth into the fire. Afterward he must bathe and wash his clothes and even so he remains unclean until evening, as if he had touched a menstruating woman. The man who burns the heifer and the man who gathers the ashes are similarly unclean. But the ashes of this sacrifice are like a magnet for pollution: mixed with water from a running stream and sprinkled on persons and objects, they have the power to take away pollution from contact with corpses.

Still further along the expiatory end of the sacrificial continuum is the scapegoat (Lev. 16). Laden with all the sins of the people, it is too unclean to sacrifice, and is driven into the wilderness to the mysterious "Azazel." Another goat is sacrificed at the same time as a non-alimentary sin offering.

The Passover sacrifice is of different origin from peace, burnt, and sin offerings. It is a sacrificial whole, complete in both expiatory and communion elements. This is the sacrifice Moses taught the Israelites in Egypt, and required them to perform annually throughout their generations forever (Exod. 12). A perfect male lamb is slaughtered "according to their fathers' houses, a lamb for each household," and its blood is put above and on both sides of the door of the house where it is to be eaten. During the night that Yahweh slew the Egyptian firstborn, he passed over those houses marked by the blood. The whole lamb must be roasted, "its head with its legs and its inner parts," and eaten at one communion meal. Anything left over must be burned.

Consider one more sacrificial system, that of the Nuer during the first part of the twentieth century. Here, the occasion and purpose of the ritual, more than the way it is performed, distinguish expiatory from communion sacrifice: the same kind of animal may be killed in the same way whether it is killed for communion or expiatory sacrifice. What is done with the blood is not of special significance in either category of sacrifice. Victims or parts of victims are not rendered in smoke to God. God receives only the life, with no alimentary connotations.

Evans-Pritchard uses the term "piacular" for Nuer expiatory sacrifice:

> The purpose of Nuer piacular sacrifices is either to get rid of some preset evil or to ward off some threatening evil . . . The notions of elimination, expulsion, protection, purification, and propitiation cannot easily be separated out in these sacrifices, though in any particular sacrifice it may be possible to say that one or another notion is most in evidence. (1956: 2801)

Piacular sacrifices are performed for the benefit of individuals. For this reason Evans-Pritchard calls them "personal" sacrifices and contrasts them with "collective" sacrifices offered for an entire group. Piacular sacrifices "may be made on behalf of whole communities, as in times of epidemics, but then they are made for a great number of individuals." Collective sacrifices, in contrast, are "made on behalf of social segments, lineages and age-sets, which are conceived as whole groups, sometimes in relation to groups of like order." As personal sacrifice has "primarily a piacular intention," so collective sacrifice has primarily "a confirmatory one." Collective sacrifices are performed at rites of passage: initiations, various wedding rituals, rituals to end mourning, etc. "On such occasions sacrifice has generally a conspicuously festal and eucharistic character." Collective sacrifices, in short, are communion sacrifices. And, as is true of expiation and communion everywhere, "we cannot make an absolute distinction between the two sorts of sacrifice" (ibid.: 198–99).

The flesh of victims of collective sacrifice is distributed according to kinship relations and, like communion sacrifice everywhere, always eaten. In many sacrificial traditions, expiatory sacrifice is not eaten, or is eaten only in severely restricted ways. For example, Evans-Pritchard says that among the Nuer, "even a piacular sacrifice furnishes a feast" (1956: 215) but then notes that this feast is not part of the sacrifice. (See chapter 4 for more about this distinction.) When expiatory purposes are intensified, the form of the sacrifice changes:

> In sacrifices in which the idea of separation is strong, as in cases of incest, to sever kinship, and in one of the mortuary rites [to

separate the dead from the living], instead of the ox being speared and then skinned it is thrown on the ground and cut longitudinally in half. (Ibid.:216)

Only the right, good, male half is eaten by the sacrificing group; the "thrown away" left, evil, female half is eaten by unrelated persons. When piacular sacrifice is made for the whole community, to stop an advancing plague or enemy, victims are killed in the bush outside the village or camp, and the bodies are abandoned there uneaten.

All Nuer sacrifice is ultimately to God (spirit, *kwoth*), but sacrifices may be offered to him in one of his many refractions: personal sacrifices may be offered to air spirits as agents of disease, or collective sacrifices to totemic spirits associated with particular lineages. Collective sacrifices, because they concern lineage affairs, "involve the ghosts, who are usually little or not at all concerned in personal sacrifices" (ibid.: 201). But sacrifice is not offered *to* the dead, although it may be offered for the benefit of a dead person.

Personal sacrifices are ordinarily performed by the father of the family concerned; collective sacrifices require special lineage representatives to officiate, and sacrifices related to homicide must be performed by hereditary priests. There are no special places or times of sacrifice. A victim is called a cow, although it is almost never a real cow, but rather an ox (a bull must be castrated first), a castrated sheep or goat, or even a wild cucumber. The name is the same for all victims, but a cucumber, which might be adequate for a minor personal sacrifice, would never do for a collective sacrifice.

Logically analogous oppositions of communion-and-expiation are discernible in Greek, Nuer, and Israelite sacrifice, but the ways in which this opposition is represented in actual performances differ greatly. The significance of blood or other parts of the body, of fire, of various tools and weapons of sacrificing, of uncleanness; the choice of victim; rules about places and times for sacrifice; the role of the dead, of priests, of divinities and other transcendant beings, are all different.

There are two important ways in which Nuer, Greek, and Israelite sacrificial systems do resemble one another—and resemble many other traditions as well. In all traditions communion sacrifice is alimentary; in most traditions eating expiatory sacrifice is restricted or forbidden. In countless unrelated traditions, the distribution of the victim's flesh indexes the alimentary community, making social groups and distinctions between them recognizable to all concerned.

The second way these and other traditions resemble one another is an association of femaleness with what must be expiated. Among the Nuer,

The left side symbolizes evil as well as femininity; and here there is a double association, for the female principle is also associated with evil directly, as it were, and not merely through the convergence of femininity and evil in the concept of the left side. (Evans-Pritchard 1956: 233–34)

Among the Greeks, the pollution of childbirth and that of death were closely associated; both were consequences of Zeus's disastrous gift of the first woman. The Greeks were not very concerned about menstrual blood but childbirth defiled everyone in the house or in contact with the mother. For the Greeks, the pollution of childbirth "is none other than the defilement that estranges man from the gods" (Moulinier, 1952: 70).

Among the Israelites, pollution of childbirth and also of menstruation typified pollution in general. Ezekiel described the Exile as divine punishment for conduct "like the uncleanness of a woman in her impurity" (36:17). In the priestly rules, the very first illustration of occasions for expiatory sacrifices is after childbirth, when a woman must bring sin and burnt offerings. If she has given birth to a female child, her uncleanness is double that for a male child's birth (Lev. 12:8). I suspect that the "scarlet cloth" which must be burnt with the red heifer (notice that the victim is both female and red) is a euphemism for what the Hebrew Bible calls a "menstruous rag." By the intensifications of uncleanness, this sacrifice creates a pole of absolute otherness from cleanness that works like a magnet to draw away uncleanness. This is like the Ashanti *kunkuma* (see chapter 5), an unclean ritual object which takes away all kinds of evil, and which does contain menstrual blood at its polluted but powerfully expiatory core.

THREE

Sacrifice and Descent

FOR THE GREEKS, the essential features of their social world (those that distinguished it equally from the natural and the divine realms) were sacrifice, marriage, and agriculture.[1] In myth these all share the same origin: marriage and agricultural production were consequences of Prometheus's sacrifice ending the Golden Age. Turning from the myth to its social context, from Pandora to the world of young Greek brides, marriage takes on a more precise meaning: it is not a voluntary personal relation between two individuals, but a relation for and between family groups:

> Pleasure is not the object of marriage. Its function is quite different: to unite two family groups within the same city, so that a man can have legitimate children who "resemble their father" despite being the issue of their mother's womb, and who will thus be able, on the social and religious level, to continue the line of their father's house to which they belong. (Vernant 1980: 136)

The unfortunate defect of being "the issue of their mother's womb" is a quality children share with the beasts. Wild animals also have a mother, "to whom they are linked by the natural animal bond of childbirth; but they have no father. Without marriage there can be no paternal filiation, no male line of descent, no family, all of which presuppose a link which is not natural, but religious and social" (ibid.: 138). The sexual promiscuity of the beasts is precisely the absence of the patrilineal family, and the male purity of the Golden Age is the ideal principle of that family carried to a level of absolute perfection. Letting "P" stand for patriliny, the three-tiered structure can be written this way:

wild/natural level	social/religious level	Golden Age (divine level)
$-P$	$+P$	P^n
unregulated sex	regulated sex	male purity
death	social continuity	immortality

This structure encodes mortality just as it does sexuality. The social and religious continuity of the patrilineal family gives males an attenuated form of immortality in the institutionalized succession of fathers and sons. The beasts, recognizing no fathers, have no continuity at all to mitigate individual mortality. On the other hand, if children only resembled their fathers perfectly they would be identical younger versions, cloning younger exact duplicates in their turn, and the Golden Age of male immortality would have returned. It is only mothers, bearing mortal children, who dim this glorious vision of eternal and perfect patriliny. Remember Pandora: because of a woman, men are mortal.

Only in myth is the fatal flaw of having been born of woman overcome. Herakles was sacrificing bulls to his father, Zeus, when the fire ignited a poisoned shirt his wife had given him. In Ovid's account he bears his Latin name, Hercules:

> All that his mother gave him burned away.
> Only the image of his father's likeness
> Rose from the ashes of his funeral pyre . . .
> So Hercules stepped free of mortal being . . .
> And with an air of gravity and power
> Grew tall, magnificent as any god.

(the *Metamorphoses.* 1958: 248)

Purified by the fire (almost like bones and fat), Herakles became a heavenly god. As both mortal hero and immortal god, he received both chthonic and Olympic sacrifice.

That women destroy the ideal of perfect patrilineal continuity has a real foundation in Greek social organization. Women (who fail in such glaring ways to resemble the father) do not contribute to the continuity of their own family line. The above quotation from Vernant needs correction: it is not "legitimate children" but only legitimate sons who "continue the line of their father's house to which they belong." Women marry outside their own family and bear children for the continuity of a different family. Children are born not just of women, but of outsiders. For any boy, "all that his mother gave him" pollutes the purity of the paternal line.

The starkness of the Greek womb/tomb equation is probably unrivaled, but all over the world social structures idealizing "eternal" male intergenerational continuity meet a fundamental obstacle in their necessary dependence on women's reproductive powers. There are various ways to organize over or around this obstacle, to transcend it. Many societies value continuity flowing unilineally from father to son to son's son, and these are probably the most common contexts for intensively

31

sacrificial religions. But they are not the only ones. Even in settings where various kinds of descent through women are valued, and also in social organizations with no actual family base (such as the clerical hierarchy of the Roman Church), sacrificing produces and reproduces forms of intergenerational continuity generated by males, transmitted through males, and transcending continuity through women.

It is important to recognize that all the different ways people create enduring continuity between generations cannot really be sorted into categories like "patrilineal," "matrilineal," or "bilateral." Chapter 2 emphasizes that the terms "communion" and "expiation" do not actually describe any real sacrifice. They are only abstractions, lenses to look through. What is true of sacrificial traditions is true also of kinship traditions: they are so diverse that concrete general categories become impossible. There is not one real statistical typification "patriliny"; there are countless *different* normative ways in which people envision continuity between fathers and sons and value this intergenerational link as especially important for inheritance, political control, and other forms of social organization. There are also all the ways people do not conform to family norms. For example, Greek brides normatively married outside "the line of their father's house." But marriage inside the extended family did sometimes occur in Athens, especially in the case of an heiress, to keep the dowry in the family (Cantarella 1987: 45). When I use a term like "patrilineal" then, it is only an ideal type, not a real one, a lens for looking at a great variety of different ways of valuing father-son continuity, and of even more ways of leading real family lives.[2]

A century ago W. Robertson Smith recognized an affinity between patriliny and sacrifice. In *The Religion of the Semites* they are so closely linked that he could not err about one without simultaneously distorting the other. Following Wellhausen, Robertson Smith believed that all sacrifice was originally clan sacrifice (1972: 284). Rejecting his contemporaries' utilitarian theories of sacrifice as gift (or even bribery: *do ut des*), he claimed that the purpose of sacrifice was to create and maintain relationships of kinship between "men" and their gods. He did not consider that sacrifice might create and maintain kinship between men and men. He took that kinship for granted as "natural." Nor did he distinguish between the "principle of kinship" and the "tie of blood." There was no difference, for him, between consanguineal relatedness and the ordering of society according to the selective, normative systems that actual kinship groups create and maintain. By his "tie of blood" he meant only unilineal descent. But since this was, for him, "natural" kinship, he did not consider that biological descent had already been (socially and religiously) transformed into something else.

In common with most theorists of his time, he believed that originally everyone recognized only descent from mothers. The possibilities for sacrifice in such a society are limited, however, for "the children are of the mother's kin and have no communion of blood religion with the father. In such a society there is hardly any family life, and there can be no sacred household meal" (ibid.: 278). At some unspecified time, and in some unknown way, almost everyone but a few very primitive groups switched to patrilineal descent, still considered by Smith only as a natural blood tie, not as an achievement. It is on the father-son relation that the sacrificial relation of deity to worshiper is founded, although it was later expanded to include patron-client, master-servant, and king-subject.

Smith's lengthy treatment of relations between worshiper and deity was limited to consanguineal and derivative relations. He did not consider marriage as a possible model.[3] Nor did he mention relations between affines (persons and groups related to one another by marriage). Smith's kinship systems are so thoroughly unilineal that there are no affines anywhere, and consequently, no problems of affinal relations in unilineal descent.[4] In fact, "the members of one kindred looked on themselves as one living whole, a single animated mass of blood, flesh and bones" (ibid.: 274). Nowhere in *The Religion of the Semites* is there any indication of how these utterly united kin groups are related to, and differentiated from, other such groups.

For Smith, all kinship relations were entirely benign.[5] In spite of Cain and Abel, Jacob and Esau, Joseph and brethren, and many others, this Hebrew Bible scholar was serenely convinced that "those in whose veins the same life-blood circulates cannot be other than friends bound to serve each other in all the offices of brotherhood" (ibid.: 398). Kinship relations with deities are equally benign. "The habitual temper of the worshippers is one of joyous confidence in their god, untroubled by any habitual sense of human guilt . . . ancient religion assumes that ordinary acts of worship are all brightness and hilarity" (ibid.: 255, 257).

In identifying "natural" kinship with totally homogeneous, affineless unilineal descent, and in purging kin relations of all guilt, envy, hatred, and terror, Smith had already done all the work of sacrifice. His purifying process was so complete before anyone killed a victim that there was nothing left to expiate, to get rid of, from kinship structure or from religious life. The clean had already been wholly separated from the unclean. His preliminary atoning work was so perfect that there was no room left for atonement itself. As he himself said, "There was no occasion and no place for a special class of atoning sacrifices" (ibid.:

360). Atonement, expiation, sin offerings, and all the dark side of sacrifice was only a later, secondary development, a consequence of the "Assyrian catastrophe" and the despair that followed the Babylonian exile. As well as being historically inaccurate, this at-one-ment without atonement is logically and sacrificially impossible. Smith had created a Golden Age of his own among the Semites.

A peculiar mixture of error, erudition, and profound insight, *The Religion of the Semites* has been regularly denounced for the last seventy years. Smith has been condemned for leading astray biblical scholars, anthropologists, sociologists, psychoanalysts, and theologians. But bad scholarship is usually forgotten. If his work continued to trouble people, it was because his central idea was partly correct. He was right in linking sacrifice with kinship, even with kinds of kinship rather like what he described: clearly defined patrilineal descent systems, commonly excluding mothers and affines. Although his inattention to kin group differentiation, and to affinal relations, led Smith into absurdities, even his "single animated mass of blood, flesh and bones" has some real basis when the unity is conceived as social, religious, or moral, rather than as physical. (A corporate unilineal descent group, seen from the outside, says Meyer Fortes, "might be defined as a single legal personality.")[6] No matter how corporate, a patrilineage is never "a physical unity of life." Nor is unilineal descent natural, but social and religious. And sacrificing orders relations within and between lines of human fathers and sons, between men and men, at least as effectively as it does relations between men and their divinities.

Maintaining normative modes of family continuity through male or female lines ("unilineal descent")[7] glosses only some of the ways people may order social relations in terms of descent. Descent "systems" are all ideal ways of ordering the social relations of reproduction, and, as is true of all forms of social organization, unilineal descent is associated with specific kinds of economic production. The varieties of enduring intergenerational continuity such groups strive for may be glossed as "lineage" organization. Lineage organization is particularly efficient for control and transmission by inheritance of productive property such as farmland and livestock herds, and also of gainful monopolized skills, including priestly skills and political office. Such enduring descent groups (and blood-sacrificial religions too) are not of significance among people relatively unconcerned with inheritance of important productive property, such as hunter-gatherers, who have little durable property. Nor do they usually survive the introduction of a modern economy with occupational differentiation and monetary media of exchange. Like blood-sacrificial religions, such enduring family groups are concentrated among pre-industrial societies with some degree of technological development, in which rights in durable property are highly valued.[8] The symbolic structure in which the Greeks linked agriculture, patriliny, and sacrifice may be unique, but control of agricultural property by patrilineal descent groups as a material base of sacrificial religion is found around the world and across a wide range of societies. These range from extremely poor subsistence framers, with no central government at all, to highly sophisticated societies like pre-revolutionary China.[9]

Because these are all family groups, the control of the means of production is inseparably linked with the control of the means of reproduction, that is, the fertility of women. As Fortes says,

> I have several times remarked on the connection generally found between lineage structure and the ownership of the most valued productive property of the society, whether it be land, or cattle, or even the monopoly of a raft like blacksmithing . . . A similar connection is found between lineage organization and control over reproductive resources and relations. (1953: 35)

(For "reproductive resources," read "childbearing women.") "Rights over the reproductive powers of women," says Fortes, "are easily regulated by a descent group system" (ibid.: 30).

The social relations of production may be much the same whether intergenerational continuity through men or through women is more highly valued. But the social relations of reproduction will differ between "matrilineages" and "patrilineages," since matrilineages divide men's rights over women's bodies between brothers and husbands, who are ordinarily members of different lineages. In this sense the identity of the group controlling productive and reproductive property is always imperfect in matrilineages.

It should be recognized that although the different kinds of groups glossed as "patrilineages" are patriarchies, "matrilineages" are not matriarchies. Men ordinarily hold the major positions of authority in matrilineages as well as in patrilineages. It is the descent of authority, and of property, which differs: in patrilineages it is from father to son, in matrilineages from uncle to nephew, from mother's brother to sister's son. Both systems are ways of formally connecting men with women as childbearers, that is, ways of organizing intergenerational continuity between men and men in the face of the fact that it is women who give birth and with whom the next generation begins life already in close relation. Both systems are ways in which men regulate rights over women's reproductive powers, but in matrilineal descent systems these rights are divided: the man with rights of sexual access and the man and group with rights in the offspring are not the same.

Although obviously both types of unilineal descent, father to son and mother's brother to sister's son, are equally dependent on women's powers of reproduction for their continuity, this dependence is structurally recognized in matrilineal descent, but transcended in patrilineal descent. Rights of membership in a matrilineage may be determined by birth alone, providing sure knowledge of maternity. Paternity never has the same natural certainty, and birth by itself cannot be the sole criterion for patrilineage membership. No enduring social structure can be built only upon the shifting sands of that uncertain relation, biological paternity. Social paternity and biological paternity may, and often do, coincide, but it is social paternity that determines patrilineage membership. Some sacrificing societies, such as the Romans or the Nuer, distinguish between biological and social paternity in their vocabulary; for example, the Latin distinction between (biological) *genitor* and (social) *pater.* Only the *pater* was significant sacrificially.

Unilineal descent groups are not concerned merely with an existing order, but with its continuity through time, generation succeeding generation. When the crucial intergenerational link is between father and son, for which birth by itself cannot provide sure evidence, sacrificing may be considered essential for the continuity of the social order. What is needed to provide clear evidence of social and religious paternity is an act as definite and available to the senses as is birth. When membership in patrilineal descent groups is identified by rights of participation in blood sacrifice, evidence of "paternity" is created which is as certain as evidence of maternity, but far more flexible.

Consider patrilineal ancestor cults, whose powerful affinity with sacrificial ritual is widely recognized. Ancestral sacrifice ritually indexes patrilineage boundaries (keeps the difference between members and not-members) by distinguishing between those who have rights to participate and those who do not, and at the same time extends the temporal continuity of the lineage beyond its living members to include the dead.

Sacrificial ancestor cults are commonly features of corporate descent groups whose members are tied to a certain locality by inherited farmland, and also often by ancestral graves. Right of participation in sacrifices can also identify patrilineage membership even when the lineage is not a corporate group and is not clearly defined territorially, but in this case there may not be an ancestor cult, and sacrifice, more "spiritual" as the group is less corporate, may be offered to divinities. The Nuer and Dinka are examples. Sacrificing may be the exclusive privilege of only one descent group in a society: a hereditary priesthood, who may keep their own lineage boundaries absolutely clear while other, non-sacrificing descent groups in the same society lose such clearly defined identity. In this case the ideology of eternal genealogical continuity is also centered in the priesthood. The Israelite Aaronid priesthood is an example.

Sacrificing can identify, and maintain through time, not only social structures whose continuity flows through fathers and sons but also other forms of male to male succession that transcend dependence on childbearing women. Because it identifies social and religious descent, rather than biological descent, sacrificing can identify membership in groups with no presumption of actual family descent. This is the case with the sacrifice of the Mass, offered by members of a formally institutionalized "lineage," the apostolic succession of the clergy in the Roman Church. This social organization is a truly perfect "eternal line of descent," in which authority descends from father to father, through the one "Son made perfect forever," in a line no longer directly dependent on women's reproductive powers for continuity. (See chapter 8.)

Sacrificial ritual can serve in various ways as warrant of, and therefore as means of creating, patrilineal descent—as a principle of social organization, not as a fact of nature. When sacrifice works in this performative way it is what Thomas Aquinas called an "effective sign," one that causes what it signifies: in this case, patrilineage membership (*Summa Theologica*, III, Q62:1). For Thomas, as well as for tribal sacrificers, the effective work of symbolic action is, of course, reflexively dependent on the existence of other structures (social, religious, linguistic, legal, etc.). That is, sacrifice does not "cause" patrilineage membership where there are not patrilineages.

Sacrifice cannot be infallible evidence of begetting and therefore obviously cannot constitute biological paternity. It is the social relations of reproduction, not biological reproduction, that sacrificial ritual can create and maintain. Where the state and the social relations of production are not separable from patrilineally organized social relations of reproduction, the entire social order may be understood as dependent on sacrifice. "Not just the religious cult but the order of society itself takes shape in sacrifice," says Burkert of the Greeks (1983: 84). This is also true of other entirely unrelated societies, such as nineteenth-century West African city states like Benin and Dahomey and twentieth-century subsistence farmers or pastoral cattle herders, without urban development or centralized organization. The particular Greek elaboration of alimentary symbolism is surely unique, but Detienne's observation that "the city as a whole identifies itself by the eating of meat" (1979b: ix) accurately describes sacrificial maintenance of social organization in other traditions and other societies. The Israelite priesthood, for example, identified itself by eating of meat (the "edible" sin offering), and so did and do different kinds of patrilineal groups in Africa, Europe, Asia, and the New World.

When a form of social organization is dependent on sacrifice for its identification and maintenance, it can also be lost by failure to sacrifice, and improper sacrifice can endanger it. As Detienne says, "To abstain from eating meat in the Greek city-state is a highly subversive act" (1979b: 72). Georges Dumézil tells the sad story of the end of a Roman family. An official named Appius Claudius persuaded the family to sell its private sacrificial cult to the state for public use.

> According to Festus . . . Appius Claudius went blind, and within the year all members of the selling family died . . . Thenceforth it was the urban proctor who each year made the offering of an ox (or a heifer) in the name of Rome. (1979: 435)

According to Dumézil, "Some think . . . that we must understand [this account] by reversing the order of events." That is, the state only assumed control of the cult because the proprietary family had already died out. But the story's order of events (although not their speed) is quite possibly correct. Having lost its ritual means of identification, and with it the ritual entail of its property, the family line itself disappeared—not as a number of biological individuals but as the particular kind of social organization it was.

Consider a cautionary tale from M. Herskovits about the problems of maintaining patrilineal descent in the West African kingdom of Dahomey. Only certain ritual specialists could touch victims which had been offered to the ancestors and hope to survive the contact. Without these specialists there could be no sacrifice, but training them involved a long course of rituals in a specially constructed cult house for the dead. This course of training was undertaken as seldom as possible because of the great danger involved, both from the intensity of relations with the ancestral dead and also from the possibility of committing a fatal ritual error. The royal ancestor cult was the apex of the hierarchy of all ancestor cults in the kingdom, and consequently it was the duty of the king to officiate in the centralized training of the kingdom's ancestor cult specialists. After French colonizers ended the monarchy, the head of the royal patrilineal descent group, or sib, continued in the ritual position of the king. In the early thirties, when Herskovits was in Dahomey, the head of the royal sib had neglected to perform his ritual duty of building the cult house because, even if he did not die at once as a consequence of committing some ritual error, he would in any case die soon after from such prolonged and intense contact with the dead.

The last cult house for the ancestors of the entire kingdom . . . was established so many years ago that most of those who received this training are dead, and it is urgent that another soon be instituted, though it is believed that this will hasten the death of the head of the royal family. In the last one, it is said, some three thousand initiates came from . . . each sib all over the kingdom. . . . [When the last of these, now old] die, there will be no one able to touch a sacrificial animal, and thus will even greater evil befall all Dahomeans, and the entire royal family will die out. (1938, vol.1: 228)

This final prophecy of doom is not mere superstition. If the cult house were not built, if the prerequisite for continued sacrifice were not met, the royal sib might indeed die out. The biological individuals forming its membership need not die, but the royal sib, as a social organization constituted and maintained by sacrifice, dependent on repeated sacrifice for its "eternal" continuity, would decay with the end of sacrificing. Evils would befall all Dahomeans because all Dahomean kinship organization was sacrificially maintained and was organized in relation to the royal sib.

Only the Aztecs outdid the Dahomeans in volume, compulsiveness, and cruelty of sacrificing. Dahomean religion was not representative of sacrificial religion, it was an exaggeration of it, a concentration and intensification of many features which occur selectively and less starkly in many other sacrificing societies. In Dahomey, says Herskovits, a child "legally stands in no relation whatever to his mother's kin" (ibid. 153). This is certainly unusual, as is also the degree of continuity with the dead and the desperateness of dependence on sacrifice for maintenance of the social order. But all these are only exaggerations of what could be called a common sacrificial principle: that it is by participation in the rule-governed (moral, not biological) relatedness of father and son in a ritually defined social order, enduring continuously through time, that birth and death (continually changing the membership of the "eternal" lineage) and all other threats of social chaos may be overcome.

Man born of woman may be destined to die, but man integrated into an "eternal" social order to that degree transcends mortality. I use the word "man" advisedly, for in sacrificially maintained descent groups, "immortality," which may be no more than the memory of a name in a genealogy, is commonly a masculine privilege. It is through fathers and sons, not through mothers and daughters, that "eternal" social continuity is maintained. Daughters, who will marry out, are not members of the lineage in the same way as their brothers, nor do mothers have full membership in their husbands' and sons' lineage. Where participation in "eternal" social continuity is a paternal inheritance, mortality itself may be phrased as a maternal inheritance. (As Job said (14: 1,4), "Man that is born of woman is of few days, and full of trouble . . . Who can bring a clean thing out of an unclean?")

Exogamous patrilineal groups, whose members find wives from outside the group, are utterly dependent on alien women for their continuity. But if descent from these women were given full social recognition, the patrilineage would have no boundaries, no identity, and no recognizable continuity. The integration of any unilineal descent group, its continuity through time as the same, as one, can only be accomplished by differentiation from other such groups. There is necessarily an "either/or" about lineage membership (members must be distinguished from not-members), and for patriliny, this either/or requires transcending descent from women.

The twofold movement of sacrifice, integration and differentiation, communion and expiation, is beautifully suited for identifying and maintaining patrilineal descent. Sacrifice can expiate, get rid of, the consequences of having been born of woman (along with countless other dangers) and at the same time integrate the pure and eternal patrilineage. Sacrificially constituted descent, incorporating women's mortal children into an "eternal" (enduring through generations) kin group, in which membership is recognized by participation in sacrificial ritual, not merely by birth, enables a patrilineal group to transcend mortality in the same process in which it transcends birth. In this sense, sacrifice is doubly a remedy for having been born of woman.

FOUR

Creating Descent through Fathers and Sons

THIS CHAPTER DESCRIBES some varieties of sacrificially maintained patriliny in ancient Europe and twentieth-century Africa: in classical Athens and among the Tallensi, Lugbara, and Nuer (of the Gold Coast, Uganda, and Sudan, respectively). I have selected these societies from many possible candidates to show how patriliny is sacrificially maintained in different kinds of social settings. The Tallensi and Nuer are both included to show that even when forms of patriliny have been glossed as similar ("segmentary lineages"),[1] family organization may be very different. In ancient Greece[2] there were no "segmentary lineages." Greek, Tallensi, and Nuer religions are even less alike than are their social organizations. The Tallensi ancestor cult is the center of religious life; Nuer religion is monotheistic; the Greeks had many gods and heroes, and a cult of the dead as well, but no true ancestor cult.

Not only do these societies and religious traditions differ from one another, but access to them is through very different perspectives. In contrast to the multiplicity and fragmentation of Greek sources, each African tradition has been described in detail, at one historical period, by one good ethnographer—but with different interests. I include the Lugbara, although their religion and social organization resemble those of the Tallensi, because the ethnographer gives a closer look at ancestral cult sacrifice. Fortes focused on social organization and included sacrifice only because Tallensi society cannot be understood apart from it. Middleton focused on Lugbara religion itself, from a sociological perspective. Evans-Pritchard was more interested in theological than sociological aspects of Nuer religion. My account cannot adequately describe any of these societies, but it can and does demonstrate real similarities in the integrating and differentiating work of sacrifice across a range of different social organizations and religious traditions.

People in any society trace their relatedness to one another in a variety of ways. The Romans recognized two ways of figuring descent: *cognation* refers to descent relationships traced through both women and men; *agnation* to relation by descent through males only. Cognation (which is bilateral descent) branches out so rapidly that it cannot identify clearly defined groups enduring from generation to generation. Only agnation (which is patrilineal descent) gave Roman families and lineages "eternal" social continuity. And only agnation was inseparable from sacrificial religion.

For the Nuer, cognation (*mar*) is more important in daily life than is agnation (*buth*). But only *buth* organizes males in social structures enduring "throughout their generations for ever," and only *buth* is identified by rights of participation in sacrifice: only *buth* is identified by the eating of meat. The word *buth* means "to share the meat of sacrifices" (Evans-Pritchard, 1956: 287).

In such societies, cognatic ties may be of great personal importance, but personal relations between individuals do not endure through generations. The Lugbara of Uganda can trace a person's cognatic descent for only a few generations, but "patrilineal descent in the direct line can be reckoned for everyone back to the first men placed on earth by Spirit" (Middleton, 1965: 29). This is a sacrificial achievement.

Relations between sacrifice and agnation pose a chicken-and-egg question. For some theorists, social organization has a sure prior reality, secondarily represented in ritual; but this is only one side of a reflexive process. The "expression" of agnation in sacrifice is more than a symbolic reminder of a pre-existing descent relation because descent is defined not by birth, or even by begetting, but by sacrifice. (Among the Romans, wrote Fustel de Coulanges, "it was not by birth, it was by the cult alone that the agnates were recognized" [1956: 62].[3] Agnates are not people biologically related by descent in the male line who occasionally remind themselves of this sacrificially; agnates are instead people who sacrifice together—who know they are agnates because they sacrifice together.

"Agnates are people who share in the flesh of sacrifices," said Evans-Pritchard of the Nuer (1956: 287), but he did not think of sacrifice as constituting agnation. Nevertheless he remarked repeatedly that it is only observance of sacrificial ritual that maintains a lineage's identity and its differentiation from other social groups: "A lineage remains an exclusive agnatic group only in ritual situations" (1940: 228. See also pp. 202, 203, 210, 211, 226, 227, 230, 234; and 1951: 6, 24).

Meyer Fortes said that the Tallensi claim their patrilineal "clanship ties are a consequence of sacrificing together." But he did not believe them. According to him, their claim was merely "an *a posteriori* argument which is common . . . all over the country."[4] Nevertheless, he unavoidably shows sacrifice maintaining social structure: "The ancestor cult is the calculus of the lineage system, the mechanism by means of which the progressive internal differentiation of the lineage is ordered and is fitted into the existing structure" (1945: 33).

John Middleton's account of the constitutive work of sacrifice among the Lugbara of Uganda is unusually explicit:

> The essential purpose of sacrifice [is] to re-create ties of lineage kinship . . . It may be said that the distribution of meat may affirm these ties, but to say that it merely reflects a constellation of ties that are already in existence is a distortion. It is at those rites that changes in alignment are recognized, that, in fact, they actually take place. (1960: 90, 123)

The Greeks too recognized both agnation and cognation,[5] but there was no sacrificing associated with cognation. In contrast, participation in a sacrificial cult was the criterion of membership in all agnatic groups.[6]

> Thus it is for religion not just to embellish, but to shape all essential forms of community. The definition of membership is participation in a cult. This begins with the family, for which Greek has no special word: one speaks of house and hearth, thus consciously designating the domestic sacrificial site. (Burkert 1985:255)

What Burkert calls "all essential forms of community" were sacrificing agnatic groups. They included the family or household, *oikos;* the corporate named *genos,* an extended family line holding hereditary rights to priestly office and limited to the aristocracy; and even the state itself, including its subdivisions (tribe, phratry [or clan], deme, etc.).

Oikos membership was not a consequence of birth. Only some days later, when a sacrifice purified the household from the pollution of a child's birth, did its father recognize the child in the family cult, making it a family member.

Phratry membership was also determined by sacrifice. Once a year in Athens the phratries celebrated the three-day *Apatouria.* On each day a sacrifice was performed: on the first, for which the sacrificial victim was named *meion,* fathers presented male infants born that year; on the second, for which the victim was the *koureion,* fathers swore that initiates were their legitimate sons; on the third, for which the victim was the *gamelion,* a husband and his family "pledged" his bride as the daughter of a sacrificially legitimate family. For each, the sacrifice validated the act. Similar sacrifices took place elsewhere in Greece (ibid.: 255). If phratry members doubted the legitimacy of a candidate for initiation, they took the sacrifice away from the altar. If they participated in the sacrifice with him, he became a member and would refer to that sacrifice to validate his membership should it later be contested. For example, Demosthenes, defending a youth against a conspiracy to cheat him of his inheritance, claimed that the chief conspirator did not remove the victim from the altar, as he should have done had the introduction of this boy not been legitimate (XLIII 82; in 1964: 117–18).

Phratry membership determined Athenian citizenship and, with it, important economic and political privileges.

> Classical Athens defined the membership of its citizen body . . . rigorously in terms of descent. Citizens were those who were male; were sons of a citizen father; were born from a woman who was "pledged"; and had been accepted as members of their father's (phratry and) deme. (Davies, J. K. 1977: 105)

The state itself was still another sacrificially constituted descent group, with ritual validation of membership like that of family, deme, and phratry. "The young *epheboi,* candidates for admission to citizenship, sacrificed at the city hearth at the beginning of their two years military training, just as newborn children, brides and slaves were admitted to the *oikos* by a ceremony at *its* hearth" (Humphreys, 1983: 15). The Athenian state cult of Apollo Patroos was "a cult whose very name as well as underlying myth reflected descent as the dominating influence of the community" (Davies, J. K. 1977: 110).

Admitting an alien to the state cult (naturalization) was a rare and complicated form of adoption. It had to be confirmed by several thousand male Athenians in a secret ballot and could be contested by any citizen. One gets an impression of a xenophobic Athens, heavily defended against "alien pollution," always anxious about the purity of its cultic agnation. According to Demosthenes, these great precautions were needed to preserve the purity of the sacrifices (LIX 89–92; in 1988: 419–23). To preserve the purity of the sacrifices was also to preserve the purity of the exclusive group holding political and economic power.

In 509, Kleisthenes' reform established citizenship by residential areas, enfranchising may non-citizens.

> By setting up in the demes a route to citizenship alternative to the phratries, Kleisthenes inflicted what was, and was intended to be, the major defeat on cult power in its phratry aspect. (J. K. Davies 1984: 107)

The power of the aristocracy may have been diminished, but sacrificial agnation (cult power) was still alive and well. Although first created geographically, the demes were not municipalities but brand-new sacrificially maintained agnatic groups. After the original creation, change in residence could not affect deme membership, which was still transmitted from father to son. Kleisthenes organized the demes into ten equally fictitious tribes and gave to each new deme and tribe an eponymous hero "ancestor."

It was possible to create these "descent groups" because agnation was cultic rather than physiological. Sacrificing, not birth or begetting, maintained agnatic continuity. A purely physiological offspring, that is, a father's illegitimate son, was excluded from deme and phratry, and ordinarily from the family cult as well (Humphreys, 1974). If there was no legitimate male heir, law required that one be adopted by cultic initiation, since the family cult (and therefore the family, including its property and its dead) must be eternally preserved. Candidates for adoption must themselves be from sacrificially validated families. Physiological paternity was not entirely irrelevant: an adulterous woman, a terrible threat to agnatic purity, was excluded from sacrifices of every kind, under threat of terrible punishment from any and every hand (Demosthenes LIX 85–87; in 1988: 417–19).

Like the family cult, the state cult was celebrated at "ancestral graves" (of eponymous city heroes, like the Erechtheon on the Acropolis) as well as at a sacred hearth. But the state cult was not simply the family cult writ large; influences were reciprocal and probably there was an ongoing struggle between them. In some cases the cult of a particular *genos* was appropriated by the state and opened to all citizens, although the priest or priestess was still from the original *genos*. Eventually the state claimed a monopoly of cults (Burkert, 1985: 256).[7]

In Rome as in Greece, birth did not give family membership. Should the *paterfamilias* withhold his ritual recognition, legally the child did not exist. A name and paternal recognition were given on the "day of purification," *dies lustricus*, when sacrifice removed the pollution of childbirth. As in Greece, an illegitimate son (*spurius*) had no sacrificial rights in his *genitor*'s cult, but legal descent from a *pater* could be created ritually. An adopted man could no longer sacrifice with his original family, but the cultic continuity of the adopting family was assured, as law required.

Only those families organized around a *pater*, the patricians, were maintained sacrificially. Of course originally, only the patricians held political office or controlled important productive property, and until the end of the fourth century, only they could be priests. Within the family, the *paterfamilias* was both magistrate and priest, and on the level of the state, these two roles remained remarkably close. Almost every magistrate was also a priest. As the family and the family cult (*sacra privata* and *sacra gentilica*) were inseparable, so were the state and the state cult (*sacra publica*).

Unlike some African ancestor cults, neither Roman nor Greek family cults maintained named ancestors in "unbroken" genealogical lines for many generations back. Nor were the different agnatic groups, although sharing an ideology of eternal continuity and purity of descent, articulated with one another in terms of specific genealogical relations between named ancestors. The Greek agnatic groups (tribes, phratries, demes, *gene, orgeones,* etc.) all had founding hero "ancestors," as did the state, but the genealogical links that joined each member to the eponymous ancestor were neither known nor important.

Compared with the public cults, relatively little is known about the family cults of Rome or Greece. Neither of these was a true ancestor cult.[8] The contrast is sharp in turning from the clouded views of Greek and Roman family cults to twentieth-century African ancestor cults whose intricate workings have been described in detail.

Ancestor cults are not simply "worship" of the dead. They are ways of organizing relations among the living. Ultimately the dead are only important as they integrate and differentiate relations among their living descendants. Ancestral genealogies are not true records of biological descent. Instead, those selective ancestors who are ritually important are those that mark distinctions and alliances between groups of living persons; other ancestors are forgotten. Ancestors are a way of conceptualizing and recording social structure, which, like them, is an invisible force manifested only in its workings. They are also a way of regulating the inheritance of property. Like other articles of human manufacture, ancestors require continual maintenance, and sacrificing is the most effective means of maintaining them.

Tallensi social order depends on the continuity of the patriline. A lineage is a system in time: "Continuity in time is its fundamental quality" (Fortes 1945: 32). As a lineage grows, it continually branches, or segments, internally. Depending on the genealogical depth of any lineage segment, people are integrated into what Fortes calls a "maximal lineage" (of perhaps nine or more generations), or segmented into shorter and shorter "medial" lineages down to a "minimal" lineage of two or three generations. Any lineage comprises all the (recognized) descendants of a single named ancestor in a (putative) continuous agnatic line of descent. The founding, or apical, ancestor of each segment is the symbol of its unity (ibid.: 33). The more remote the apical ancestor, the greater the depth of the segment: if the apical ancestor is a grandfather, the segment is a minimal lineage; if he is a great-great-grandfather, a medial lineage, and so on.

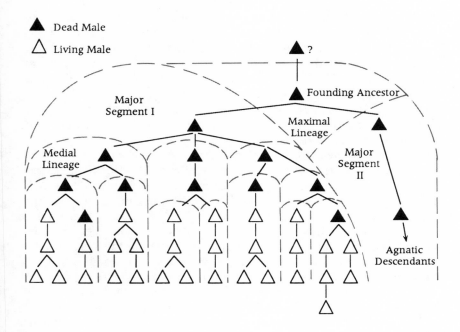

Fig. 1. Tallensi lineage structure (based on Fortes 1945: 34).

Fortes's diagram (fig. 1) does not include women because "women do not contribute to the continuity and perpetuation of the lineage" (ibid.: 152).

> "[A] woman does not build a house," says the natives in words reminiscent of the Roman formula, *mulier finis familiae est*. That is to say, a lineage is not perpetuated by its women members, but only by its male members. (Ibid.: 191)

Tallensi women marry out of their lineage and contribute nothing to its continuity. Women have no descendants. Because "women do not help to maintain the continuity of the lineage" (ibid.: 149) they can never sacrifice. Even if, as sole survivor of a lineage, a woman has nominal custody of its ancestor shrine, she cannot sacrifice at it because she cannot provide descendants to maintain the ancestors. Nevertheless, as Fortes says in a different context, "it is the reproductive power of the wives and the existence of children that secure the perpetuation of the lineage and the immortality of the ancestors" (ibid.: 229). This essential paradox of agnatic descent is invisible to many ethnographers: That those who produce children do not have social title to the product of their labor is an aspect of an alien reality not requiring explanation.

Unlike its Roman counterpart, Tallensi marriage does not deprive a woman of membership in her father's patrilineage, including rights to receive portions of meat at sacrifices. A lineage is obliged to inform its married daughters when a major sacrifice is to be performed. Accordingly, a Tallensi wife does not participate in her husband's ancestor cult, though she may be a "privileged spectator" at public and semi-public sacrifices (Fortes 1949: 99).

In comparing sacrificial systems, the relation of women to family cults is an interesting variable. In Indo-European sacrificial traditions, married women did participate in their husbands' family cults, sometimes in important ways. The center of Indo-European sacrifice was the sacred family hearth, tended by women. In Rome, the Vestal Virgins tended a hearth which was, in a real sense, the "family" hearth of the city (Dumézil, 1970: 311–26). At home, women used the sacred fire for cooking; perhaps this is why, unlike many sacrificial traditions, wives were incorporated into their husbands' family cults. In Greece, a bride's sacrificial initiation into the *oikos* cult allowed her to participate in it. In the Vedic tradition, a wife's assistance in sacrifice was so necessary that a widower could not perform it (Biardeau, 1976: 34). In her sacrificial role the wife was not a separate person (from a different agnatic family) but a part of her husband's own body. A Roman wife (*in manu*) participated in her husband's family cult as his legal and ritual descendant. At marriage, she ritually assumed the status of her husband's daughter (*filiae loco*). Her husband became her *pater* (legal and ritual father) although he was not her *genitor* (physiological father). Among the Tallensi, in contrast, a woman is sacrificially separate even from her children. After a woman's death, her son, wishing to sacrifice to her spirit, will ask her brother, or another man of her lineage, to do this for him, as he himself cannot sacrifice in her lineage.

Tallensi lineages are corporate groups; ties to farmland ensure territorial unity of the lineage. "Every unit of farm land corresponds to a unit of social structure" (Fortes 1945: 180), and every unit of social structure is defined by sacrifice. Each lineage has its own ancestor shrine, and he who has title to the shrine and control of its sacrifices also controls access to farmland. The prescribed and meticulous division of victims' flesh identifies lineage members' rights in the land as well as their formal social relations. Not only internal lineage order, but detailed relations between lineages, accessory lineages, subclans, and clans are maintained sacrificially. Like the Greeks, the Tallensi identify themselves by the eating of meat.

Sacrifices at lineage shrines are "the key mechanism for maintaining lineage cohesion." They also identify lineage political authority: "The role of a lineage head in corporate affairs, his duties and responsibilities, all arise from the fact that he has custody of the [ancestor shrine]" (ibid.: 227). Sacrifice maintains the formal relations between father and son:

A father's authority is irresistible because "he sacrifices for you" . . . You can only approach your ancestors through your father while he is alive, and if you do after his death it is always through the intermediation of his spirit. . . . The whole hierarchy of authority in the lineage rests on this ritual office. (1949: 189)

Purely personal relations between father and son cannot, by themselves, provide a ground for lineage structure. The social organization itself creates conflict of interest between father and son: "A man's social status, particularly in jural and ritual matters, but also in economic affairs, advances step by step with the dying off of his fathers" (ibid.: 156).

Tallensi are conservative in the unity required between *pater* and *genitor*. Fortes says that "true" paternity is always physiological, but he is one of those scrupulous ethnographers who describe events that undermine their own generalizations. A husband may delegate another man to act as *genitor* of his children; his ritual and social paternity is unaffected. Unlike Greece and Rome, a son born of an adulterous wife has full sacrificial rights in his mother's husband's ancestor cult. There may be friction between him and his "father," but he cannot be deprived of rights to participate in sacrifices. A purely physiological son, one born out of wedlock, has no sacrificial rights.

Rights of membership in the patrilineage being inalienable, Tallensi cannot be adopted. Slaves and illegitimate sons of lineage daughters are attached to a lineage and their descendants form an accessory lineage, but there is no adoption procedure to give them full membership. Even this, however, can be manipulated sacrificially. Fortes attended a major sacrifice in which accessory lineages took part. There were whispers of strangers being present, and Fortes thought at first that they meant himself, but as delays and acrimonious debate followed, he realized it was the presence of members of accessory lineages that was in question. The chief of the clan insisted on their inclusion. "It is I who really own the ancestral shrine," he said.

"And what if some people are of slave descent? . . . If a man has a slave he calls him to come and join in sacrifices to his ancestors; his slave is like his son. . . . Who are you to decide who is or who is not allowed to take part in sacrifices?"

Crest-fallen, the supporters of the *status quo ante* begged the chief's pardon. It was a victory for the forces of community integration and a personal triumph for the chief. (1945: 54–55)

Although the battle was not over yet, integration was possible because it is by sacrificing together that agnation is recognized.

As well as agnation, the Tallensi recognize cognation. Fortes calls these two the warp and the woof of the fabric of Tallensi society. The linear warp of agnation, uniting people into corporate groups and defining relations between such groups, provides both formal structure and enduring social continuity. Again and again Fortes refers to the temporal continuity provided by the lineage system and the ancestor cult: "The dynamic equilibrium of a lineage is an equilibrium in time" (1945: 224). "The social structure of the Tallensi is not intelligible if it is stripped of its temporal dimension. The essence of the lineage system is its continuity in time" (1949: 135).

The horizontal woof of cognation, lacking enduring intergenerational continuity, connects individuals in personal relations dispersed through many lineages. All wives live at their husbands' homes, and these exogamous marriages all provide ties among lineages.

Ties through women bring individuals together, but they divide lineages. The segmentation of lineages is at points of maternal origin. That is, segmentation of a lineage never occurs between the descendants of full brothers, but between the descendants of paternal half brothers. (As Evans-Pritchard said of the Nuer, lineage segmentation is the polygynous family writ large.) When a maximal lineage is visualized as a whole, it is in terms of pure patrilineal descent; but when it is visualized as a set of segments, of minimal lineages, the points of differentiation are not fathers, but mothers. "Maternal origin thus has significance only within the frame of patrilineal descent, as the polar opposite of paternal origin" (1945: 202). When a lineage segment wishes to set up its own separate ancestor shrine, some sediment from the ancestor shrine of the patrilineage of the differentiating progenitrix must be incorporated to distinguish it from the ancestor shrine of the maximal lineage.

The Tallensi also recognize a line of uterine, or matrilineal, descent which never forms corporate groups and is not maintained sacrificially. The "keynote" of such relations, unlike agnatic relations, is "mutual trust between equals" and institutionalized generosity. Neither ritual authority nor inheritance of property complicate such relations.

It is not by "the stain of her sex," but merely "by an accident of birth" (1949: 45) that Tallensi women are deprived of access to positions of any political, ritual, or economic authority. Perhaps it is partly because women, having no rights in the communities in which they live for all of their adult lives, are so thoroughly without social power that they are also without polluting power. There is no institutionalized menstrual taboo. Pollution of childbirth occurs only if a child is born at its mother's family home—which is never supposed to happen. Only in this case is an expiatory ritual of "removing the blood" performed (ibid.:29).

Fortes describes social organization in intricate detail but does not focus comparably on religion. Lugbara lineage organization and ancestral cult are somewhat similar to the Tallensi system, but Middleton's specific interest was the cult itself.

The eternal continuity of sacrificially maintained agnation holds at bay the disorder and change that otherwise threaten the Lugbara. Ancestors offended by "sin" (behavior that offends elders too) send sickness from which one recovers (no irreversible change has occurred), and then a communion sacrifice is offered. "Sin temporarily destroys the ideal relationship between the living and the dead. By sacrifice the parties restore this relationship, which is seen as a perfect, ideally unchanging and unchangeable one; after sacrifice order reappears" (Middleton 1960: 85).

Ancestors are concerned with lineage affairs, God with troubles beyond kinship.

> Every lineage has its own ancestors, but God is everywhere, in a relationship of equal intensity with all lineages. Since Lugbara never conceive of themselves as forming a single social unit they never come together to sacrifice to God, except that wide communities may occasionally unite to send a ram as a scapegoat to God. (Ibid.: 28)

In his immanent aspect, God is the source of evil, death, and change; in his transcendent aspect, he is benign but remote. The more expiatory a sacrifice, the more God-related it is likely to be. People know that an illness ending in death (and therefore irremediable change) was sent by God, and there is no point in sacrificing. God is concerned also with the recently dead, who have not yet become ancestors enshrined in "unchanging" relations with the living.

Lugbara ancestors are of two kinds: named "ghosts," and unnamed collective ancestors, including only begetters of males—no women because they have no descendants and do not sacrifice. Women, say the Lugbara, are things of the grass only "Women bear their children away from their natal lineage homes, and since they own no shrine they own no homes and are not full lineage members with full responsibility in lineage matters" (ibid.: 52).

Sacrificing is done at ghost shrines.

> A man places a ghost shrine only when his father is dead. Before
> that sacrifices on his behalf are made at his father's shrine. . . .
> Only the senior of a set of full brothers may put the shrines, his
> juniors using his shrines since they are under the ritual authority
> and protection that was formerly part of the status of their father.
> (Ibid.: 49)

In theory, descendants of younger sons are forever ritually subordinate
to descendants of the eldest son. But genealogical manipulation is the
heart of Lugbara politics, and since sacrifice, not physiology, orders agnation, impressive rearrangements of the "unchanging" ancestral order
are sometimes accomplished. (The genealogical skulduggery recorded
by Greek orators like Demosthenes appears almost amateurish when
compared to what the Lugbara can do.) Middleton describes the long
series of sacrifices through which one elder succeeded in raising an
ancestor up a generational notch: this ancestor, who had been a second
son, was sacrificially reconstituted as his own father's brother, greatly
improving his descendants' status in relation to descendants of the first
son, now his nephew instead of older brother (ibid.:134–211, esp. 209–
10).

Shrines inside a compound belong to a "minimal lineage." A number of these segments form a "minor lineage," a number of these latter,
a "major lineage." These larger segments share an external shrine, outside any family compound. "The sharing of the same external ghosts is
a sign that the group is a single ritual unit" (ibid.:62–63). These external shrines are far more sacred than internal shrines, and only lineage
elders may sacrifice at them. (To put it another way, sacrificing at an
external shrine is what indexes a lineage elder.) Not only lineage integration and amalgamation, but also lineage differentiation and segmentation are constituted at sacrifices at external shrines. In these sacrifices
"the elders may almost be said to be re-creating lineage structure"
(ibid.: 252). An external shrine is sometimes accompanied by a smaller,
less important shrine of an ancestress, "she by reference to whom the
minimal lineage is differentiated" (ibid.: 66).[9]

A Lugbara wife does not participate in sacrifices of her husband's
lineage, but neither does she have a part in sacrifices of her own lineage.
Only small girls and "old women past child-bearing who have returned
to their natal homes may take part" (ibid.: 118). At first sight, it looks
as if the only people who never receive any animal protein are childbearing women.

There are two parts to the sacrificial congregation: First, the true
agnates who share cooked meat with the ancestors. "By the sharing of
food an intimate relationship is affirmed, or rather re-affirmed, between

living and dead. Both are present not as two distinct groups but rather as members of a single community, the agnatic lineage" (ibid.: 86). The second congregational category, whose sacrifices are separate from those of the first, does not eat with the dead; it includes those same agnates as well as accessory kin and clients who have been sacrificially integrated as quasi-agnates. Raw meat is distributed to these according to genealogical segmentation, not according to numbers of people. Presumably, childbearing women receive some of this meat. The raw meat is taken home and redistributed according to the same agnatic principle:

> In each case the distribution of raw meat is according to lines of segmentation. The groups that give and receive raw meat are linked by one degree of lineage span in each case. The links are between a minimal lineage and its accessory lineages, the other agnatically related lineages of its minor lineage, and the other minor lineages of its major lineage. The links are seen in terms of the kinship ties between the apical ancestors of these groups. (Ibid.: 121–22)

That is, these links are not understood as being directly between living persons but between the ancestors who stand at the apex of each segment.

Lugbara social structure is identified by the eating of meat. The distribution of cooked meat identifies the lineage; distribution of raw meat, its ties with other lineages. The actual slaughtering and butchering is done by sisters' sons of the lineage because they are outsiders, not usually concerned in the lineage's tensions and quarrels. They do not share in the sacrificial meat and can be disinterested in its distribution.

Greek sacrificial flesh was also distributed to two distinct ritual congregations, a small restricted group who ate the internal organs at once, roasted on the sacrificial fire, and a wider group participating in the sacrificial meal cooked by boiling. Eating this meal "can be deferred and does not result in the same degree of bonding" (Detienne 1979b: 77).

Like the Tallensi and Lugbara, the Nuer are described as organized in segmentary lineages, but the similarity is an abstract one. In actual family life the differences are great, especially for women, who have far more autonomy than Tallensi women. Nuer lineages are corporate groups only in sacrificial ritual and there is no ancestor cult. Nor are the Nuer related to their god, *kwoth,* by any mythical descent. He is "father" in a moral sense and is so addressed, but like Yahweh, he does not beget. He is the ultimate recipient of all sacrifice.

The Nuer distinguish between agnation, *buth* (with which sacrifice is connected), and cognation, *mar. Mar* (which also means "my mother") has wider scope than Roman cognation: it refers to all ties between individuals, even between a father and son, when they are thought of as individuals; long-term affinal relations, especially when there are children, are included in *mar*. *Buth* refers to collectivities of agnates, to the principle of lineage structure, and to relations between lineages.

Everyday social relations are organized in terms of *mar*, not *buth*. The Nuer are Nilotic cattle herders, whose need for pasture prevents a permanently settled life. Nor are Nuer bound to specific localities by ritual ties: a cow dedicated to a spirit is a movable shrine. Village sites are owned by lineages, and there are always members of that lineage among the residents, but many, sometimes most, of the residents are connected to the dominant lineage through women. They are offspring of, or married to, daughters of the lineage. It is the village, whose members are all *mar* kin, which forms a corporate group. The dispersed lineages provide only "the conceptual framework of the political system" (Evans-Pritchard 1951: 5).

"The underlying agnatic principle is therefore in glaring contrast to social actualities. But the actualities are always changing and passing while the principle endures" (1945: 64). People do not live forever in the same village; after a while they move on with their cattle to another village, the home perhaps of a sister or a mother's brother, and when they move, the *mar* link which tied them to the old village loses its importance. Only the principle of lineage structure, *buth*, endures continuously. Evans-Pritchard writes,

> I suggest that it is the clear, consistent, and deeply rooted lineage structure of the Nuer which permits persons and families to move about and attach themselves so freely, for shorter or longer periods, to whatever community they choose by whatever cognatic or affinal tie they find it convenient to emphasize; and that it is on account of the firm values of the structure that this flux does not cause confusion or bring about social disintegration. It would seem it may be partly just because the agnatic principle is unchallenged in Nuer society that the tracing of descent through women is so prominent and matrilocality so prevalent. However much the actual configurations of kinship clusters may vary and change the lineage structure is invariable and stable. (1951: 28)

For the Nuer, there need be no congruence at all between *pater* and *genitor*. Anyone who has sufficient cattle for bride-wealth may marry a wife, even a woman—but ordinarily only a barren woman who counts "in some respects as a man" may take a wife (ibid.: 108). A man acts as *genitor* for her, but she herself is *pater*, and the children are members of her lineage.

A man may also marry a wife in the name of a relative who died without male *buth* descendants, and as many as half of Nuer marriages are such ghost marriages, "to ensure the survival of the dead in their names. . . . This is the only form of immortality Nuer are interested in" (1956: 163). Immortality, a feature of agnation, is a paternal prerogative.

If a man marries a wife in the name of his dead mother's brother (as *pater*), although the man lives with the woman and begets children (as *genitor*), he has no *buth* relation to his "own" children. If he is unable to marry another wife in his own name, he can count on a relative fulfilling the same duty for him as he has done for his mother's brother. The mother's brother himself may have been similarly married, a mere *genitor* leaving children but no descendants. If a husband dies, or if his wife refuses to live with him, she may move away and take other lovers. Her children, no matter who is their *genitor,* are still *buth* descendants of her original husband (whether he be a living husband or a ghost husband). Because the *genitor* is irrelevant in tracing agnatic descent,

> it follows that agnatic descent is, by a kind of paradox, traced through the mother, for the rule is that in virtue of payment of bridewealth all who are born of her womb are children of her husband and therefore paternal kin, by whomsoever they may have been begotten. (1951: 122)

Although *mar* joins people together, it does not do so permanently, and because it is more important in daily life, it threatens to obscure *buth* descent. The degree to which community of residence overrides differentiation of descent is remarkable.

> A lineage remains an exclusive agnatic group only in ritual situations. In other situations it is merged in the community, and cognation (*mar*) takes the place of lineage agnation (*buth*) as the value through which people living together express their relation to one another. . . . There must always be ritual distinctions or the clan and lineage system would collapse. (Ibid.: 228, 234)

Although Evans-Pritchard repeats and repeats that *buth* is made known only in sacrificial ritual, he rarely describes the process. In contrast to Fortes, who mentions the existence of Tallensi expiatory sacrifice but describes only communion sacrifice, Evans-Pritchard's interest was on the theological meaning of Nuer religion and he found that more accessible in "personal" expiatory sacrifice than in "collective" communion sacrifice: "We learn from the collective expression of religion more about the social order than about what is specifically religious thought. Its personal expression tells us more of what religion is in itself" (1956: 320). He was himself a theologically informed Roman Catholic convert who rejected a Durkheimian linking of religion and society almost as idolatrous (ibid).[10]

In most sacrificial traditions, including the Nuer's, the distribution and eating of sacrificial meat is a medium through which social organization is made known. But according to Evans-Pritchard, for the Nuer, "the cutting up of the victim, the preparation of its flesh, and the eating of it are not parts of sacrifice" (ibid.: 215). Eating the victims has no sacramental, but only a social, significance. This is so unusual that it raises questions about Evans-Pritchard's distinction. For example, he defines a term for adoption, *lath buthni*, as meaning "to be given shares (in sacrificial meats) and hence to be given agnation" (ibid.: 243). Commensality in this "collective" communion sacrifice seems very close to being a sacrament, in the sense of being an outward and visible effective sign (the eating of meat) of an invisible spiritual condition (*buth*). Evans-Pritchard does not specify what he means by "sacramental." He may have only wanted to reject Robertson Smith's notion of alimentary participation as mystical communion with divinities. Only *buth*, not divine life, is communicated to Nuer by alimentary participation.

Among the Nuer, expiatory sacrifice is almost always eaten, and perhaps (we are not told) shared with *mar* kin. Regular eating of expiatory sacrifice is unusual around the world but would be consistent with non-sacramental eating. In any case, Evans-Pritchard's own interest was not on alimentary aspects of sacrifice and he often did not even inquire about them; for example, "it may, I think, be assumed that in each case the animal was mostly consumed by the paternal kinsmen of the men who brought it to the sacrifice" (ibid.: 58). Certainly *mar* kin cannot all be excluded from sacrificial feasts, but just how they are included is not described, except that in some cases matrilateral relatives receive meat from the left side of the victim.

Among the Tallensi, living in corporate lineages, expiatory sacrifice is uncommon, and communion sacrifice is of crucial structural importance. Among the Nuer, "personal" expiatory sacrifice is more common than "collective" communion sacrifice. "The role of religion in the regulation of the social life, its structural role, is subsidiary to its role in the regulation of the individual's relation with God, its personal role" (ibid.:286). Evans-Pritchard understands "personal" expiatory sacrifice as unrelated to social structure, but it is most unlikely that its importance is unrelated to the dispersion of lineages, and to a need to differentiate individuals from their surrounding *mar* kin. Rather than being uniquely unrelated to social organization, this quality of Nuer religion was simply too familiar to need explanation.

Evans-Pritchard does describe the "collective" sacrifice by which a

Dinka captive is adopted into a lineage. (Nuer cannot be adopted, for their agnation is inalienable.) Dinka captives are raised as *mar* members of their captor's family, but adoption alone conveys *buth*. After the sacrifice, the Dinka "counts as a member of his captor's lineage and has a right to partake of the meat of its sacrifices and also to claim a portion of the meat of its sacrifices by any other lineage to which this lineage stands in a *buth* relationship" (ibid.: 287).

> A representative of the lineage invites the Dinka, now grown-up and initiated, to attend the sacrifice of an ox or sheep in his kraal. The head of the family provides the sacrificial beast and the representative of the lineage drives the tethering-peg into the earth at the entrance to the byre and walks up and down the kraal invoking the spear-name of the clan and calling on the spirits and ancestral ghosts of the lineage to take note that the Dinka is now a member of it and under their protection. He then spears the beast and the Dinka is smeared with the undigested contents of its stomach while the ghosts and spirits are asked to accept him. . . . The beast is then cut up, and a son of the house, or the representative of the lineage, and his new brother divide the skin and the scrotum, which the Dinka cuts . . . On all future occasions when animals are sacrificed by members of the lineage the Dinka will receive his share of the meat, for he is now a member of the lineage. The cutting of the scrotum is the symbolic act which makes the man a member of the lineage, because only an agnatic relative may cut the scrotum of a sacrificial beast. (1940: 222)

Adopted Dinka captives "trace their ascent up the lineage to its ancestor . . . The fusion is complete and final. The spirits of the lineage become their spirits, its ghosts become their ghosts" (ibid.: 233).

Girl captives are never adopted; they receive only *mar* kinship. By living with the family, "she has become a daughter to her captor and a sister to his sons, but she is not a member of their lineage" (ibid.: 222). Nor does she need to be, for

> a daughter does not carry on the lineage . . . Hence Nuer say "*Nyal, mo ram me gwagh,*" "A daughter, that is an unrelated person." As the Roman lawyers put it, she is *finis familiae,* the terminus of the family. But a man's name must continue in his lineage. (1951: 109)

Nuer women never sacrifice, and although Evans-Pritchard does not say why, presumably it is for this reason.

"When a woman joins her husband [some years after marriage], she comes under the protection of his lineage spirits and ancestral ghosts." She may therefore participate in lineage rituals. "But though a woman joins her husband's group and becomes part of it, she never entirely ceases to belong to her own family and lineage, under the protection of whose ghosts and spirits she remains" (ibid.:104). Uninterested in alimentary aspects of sacrifice, Evans-Pritchard doesn't specify, but possibly she may eat meat at sacrifices of both her husband's and her father's lineage.

Evans-Pritchard tells an anecdote involving the consequences of another kind of collective sacrifice, mortuary sacrifice to sever relations between the living and the dead.

> There was living [in a village in Western Nuerland] . . . an unhappy looking man of unkempt appearance called Gatbough. This man had some years before gone on a distant journey and had not been heard of for a long time. Then there came to his village news of his death and in the course of time the mortuary ceremony was held for him. He later returned home and was living in the village at the time of my visit. He was described as *joagh in tegh*, the living ghost. I was told . . . "His soul was cut off. His soul went with the soul of the (sacrificed) ox together. His flesh alone remains standing." His soul, the essential part of him, had gone and with it his social personality. Although people fed him he seems to have lost such privileges of kinship as pertain to the living and not to the dead. I was told that he could not partake of sacrificial meat because his agnatic kinship (*buth*) had been obliterated (*woc*) by the mortuary ceremony. A neighbor said to me, "He lives in our village with Baranyai but we do not count him a member of it because he is dead. The mortuary ceremony has been held for him." (1956: 153) [*Woc* is a term like the Israelite *kippur*, used of sin in the sense of "to wipe away."]

Greek sacrificial separation of the dead from the living was just as effective; even if done in error, the person was still "dead." Only after a special ritual pantomiming rebirth was created at Delphi could these outcasts be readmitted to society (Parker 1983: 61).

According to Evans-Pritchard, Dinka religion closely resembles Nuer religion. Most Dinka sacrifices are also both expiatory and alimentary, "personal" sacrifices performed in similar social contexts, local communities not organized as single agnatic groups. Lienhardt's accounts of distribution of meat at Dinka sacrifices (see fig. 2) may partially remedy Evans-Pritchard's omissions. For the Dinka, every victim demonstrates "the ordered social relations of the sacrificing group, the

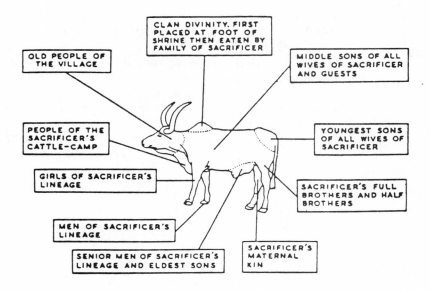

Fig. 2. Dinka "division" of sacrificial beast (Lienhardt 1961: 24).

members of which are . . . represented in their precise relations to each other in the meat which it provides . . . though their eating of the meat is not a communion meal or a 'mystical' communion" (1961: 23).

Dinka distribute meat in two ways: it may be "shared" or "divided." In sacrifices analogous to Nuer "collective" sacrifices, "the victim is not distributed to the territorial community. . . . [It is] consumed in its entirety by a single agnatic group amongst whom it is shared, but not divided" (ibid.: 234). At Dinka expiatory "personal" sacrifices, "the division of the flesh corresponds to the social differentiation of persons and groups taking part" (ibid). "Division" differentiates descent in community of residence. At the sacrifice Lienhardt describes in greatest detail, two bulls were killed—one "shared" by a single agnatic group and one "divided" among the residential community (ibid.:275). It is hardly surprising if sacrifice *differentiating* descent does not take the form of a communion meal.

I do not know how closely Dinka distribution practices resemble the Nuer's. They are not identical. The most important Dinka social distinction is between priestly and warrior clans, ideally related to one another through exogamous marriage as mothers' brothers and sisters' sons. Analogously, in the division of the victim, "the right hind leg, the most honorable part of the beast, is given to the classificatory and other maternal uncles of the sacrificing group" (ibid.: 24). Nuer, who have no such social distinction, apparently give only meat from the left side to matrilateral relatives.

The Dinka and Nuer are closely related and the Tallensi and Lugbara share common features. Otherwise the societies described here are not only very different but entirely unrelated. Nevertheless, in all of them, a similar principle of sacrificially maintained agnation is recognizable through all the different kinds of social context and ritual practice. In all of them, not physiological paternity, but an "eternal" agnatic principle maintained by sacrifice, transcends individual mortality and transitory relatedness through women, prevents general social chaos, and gives enduring continuity to their social world.

FIVE

Ashanti Sacrifice

S ACRIFICE IS NOT LIMITED TO SOCIETIES that emphasize descent from father to son. People also sacrifice in societies figuring descent through
mothers, but then sacrifice is quite differently related to family organization. Where intergenerational continuity through women is emphasized, instead of identifying and maintaining family organization, sacrifice may operate quite separately from it, or even in opposition to it.
For example, the West African Yakö organize themselves in both matrilineal and patrilineal groups (Forde 1962, 1964). Every Yakö belongs
to two distinct corporate lineages, whose members meet to perform certain rituals. One of these lineages includes only persons related through
their mother, their mother's mother, and so on; the other includes only
people related to one another through their father, his father, and so on.
Any lineage has both male and female members, but a woman cannot
hand on to her children membership in her patrilineage, nor a man
membership in his matrilineage. These lineages appear to be perfectly
balanced mirror images of one another—but only the *patrilineages* sacrifice.

Sacrificing has no regular relation to intergenerational continuity
figured through women. Matrilineages do not identify themselves by
the eating of meat, nor is bilateral organization identified by rights to
participate in sacrifices. This means that to understand the place of sacrifice in such societies each case must be examined individually and in
detail. Both the complexity of the topic and the inadequacy of the literature make a definitive cross-cultural study of the place of sacrifice in
matrilineal and bilateral family organizations impossible. Consequently,
in this chapter, I have chosen to focus on the place of sacrifice in one
primarily matrilineal society, the Ashanti of West Africa. The next chapter turns to Hawaii, where bilateral genealogical continuity was important. I have chosen these traditions because they are, by a very long
way, the most intensely sacrificial traditions I have been able to find in

societies figuring descent through women, or through women and men equally.

Before turning to a detailed examination of the Ashanti, a review of a range of societies emphasizing descent through mothers will show some of the problems in defining the place, and even the existence, of sacrifice within them. One obstacle is that sacrifice in such societies may have so peripheral a role that it is overlooked by ethnographers. Just because sacrifice is not mentioned does not prove its non-existence; even explicit denials of sacrifice are sometimes not to be trusted. The Crow Indians, says Lowie, "never worshipped their ancestors and made no bloody sacrifices" (1956: 237). Nevertheless he describes a sacrifice offered by a vision seeker fasting alone on a mountain peak, a sacrifice performed with reference to fathers' kin, not to mothers or mothers' brothers:

> As soon as the sun rose, he laid his left forefinger on a stick and chopped off a joint. This he put on a buffalo chip and held it out to the Sun, whom he addressed as follows: "Uncle (i.e., Father's clansman), you see me. I am pitiable. Here is a part of my body. I give it to you, eat it. Give me something good." (ibid.: 239–40)

Here sacrifice, ordinarily a social event involving a number of people and animals, is compressed into one individual's act, as if sacrifice could not spread out properly among the matrilineal Crow.

In contrast to Lowie's denial of sacrifice, a ritual may be given sacrificial interpretation that is questionable. The pangolin cult of the matrilineal Lele of Zaire is an example. The pangolin, a scaly anteater, is a tree-climbing mammal with scales like a fish that transgresses all the boundaries of Lele classification. That it is a non-domestic taxonomic anomaly is important for Lele religious symbolism and in the sharpest contrast to victims in sacrificial traditions throughout the world. The pangolin is not offered to gods, spirits, or ancestors. It is killed without ritual in a hunt quite separate from its ritual consumption. Says Luc de Heusch:

> The Lele believe [the pangolin] comes to offer itself of its own free will. . . . The hunter merely has to wait until it unrolls itself and lifts its head in order to kill it . . . It is thus in terms of sacrifice that one must interpret the killing and eating of this animal. (1985: 29)

Except for this, de Heusch recognizes that Lele religion is entirely without sacrifice (ibid.: 26).

Mary Douglas, on whose descriptions de Heusch's analysis is based, describes the pangolin cult without sacrificial interpretations in her ethnographic accounts (1954, 1955, 1957, 1963) and also in a later analysis of the cult (1975). There she says unequivocally that the Lele "did not perform sacrifice" (1975: 204). Douglas's only sacrificial interpretation is made without reference to the Lele's own sacrificial tradition, for there is none. "Like Abraham's ram in the thicket and like Christ, the pangolin is spoken of as a voluntary victim" (Douglas 1966: 169). Even leaving aside the cultural projection, the analogy is problematic: Abraham's ram was not voluntary but "caught in a thicket by his horns" (Gen. 22:13), and Christian sacrificial theology understands Christ not simply as victim but as high priest.

More typically, ethnographic literature indicates the existence of sacrifice in a matrilineal society, but because it is of peripheral importance even accounts of ritual may leave it undescribed. The Bemba of Zambia have been well described by Audrey Richards (1939, 1940, 1956), who includes extensive accounts of ritual. But she focuses on more regularly performed rituals and describes no sacrifices. She does mention infrequent sacrifice in connection with chiefs, but even at court, prayer, ritual sexual intercourse, and offerings of food and cloth are the usual forms of worship.[1] In her account of the ritual duties of chiefs, she mentions no sacrifice (1940: 105). Richards describes village ritual leaders performing ritual fire lighting, ritual sexual intercourse, prayers, blessings, divination, and building an ancestor shrine—but no sacrifice (ibid.: 104). She writes that a family head is "a priest of an ancestral cult," but mentions no sacrifice (ibid.: 83).[2]

Among the matrilineal Iroquois, there was no developed sacrificial tradition, although offerings of tobacco were common. Ritual torture and killing of captives were not clearly sacrificial (Tooker, 1964: 31–39). But in the nineteenth century, possibly earlier, the "white dog sacrifice" was performed during one of six major calendrical festivals (Tooker, 1965: 130). One or two white dogs were strangled, their bodies decorated, hung from a pole, and several days later, entirely burnt.

> As the body was consumed, a speech was recited and tobacco thrown on the fire. Among the Seneca, at least, the dog was burned so as to be sent as a messenger to the Great Creator. Among the Onondago, the burning of the dog was said to be in fulfillment of the dream of a deity termed in English "Upholder of the skies." (Ibid.: 129)

This looks like a non-alimentary sacrifice, but the details of its social context are lost. Even in 1936, "No informant now living has witnessed the White Dog Feast" (Fenton, 1936: 11). In any case, no Iroquois social organization was identified by eating white dog meat.

In some matrilineal societies, sacrificing is not separable from a world religion introduced centuries ago. In these cases there is no way to recover an indigenous religion and its social contexts to know what place sacrifice may have had in them. The "Sanskritized" Nayar in India and the Minangkabau of Sumatra, who have been Muslim for five centuries, are examples.

Fortunately there are some instances in which the social context of indigenous sacrificial ritual in matrilineal contexts has been described in meticulous detail, such as Victor Turner's descriptions of sacrifice among the Ndembu of Central Africa. According to Turner, "Ndembu do not have autonomous sacrificial rituals; sacrifice is always encompassed by a sequence of activities which includes many other ritual types." This is "in sharp contrast to" the patrilineal Nuer and Dinka, "for whom purely sacrificial rites are central in their religious practice" (1977: 192). Turner's analysis of the four-day Chihamba ritual identifies thirty-two separate procedures, only two of which resemble sacrifice (1975: 42–44). These are the symbolic slaughter of a male demigod, Kavula, involving the actual beheading of a real red cock, and the symbolic beheading of candidates, represented by the actual beheading of white hens. Turner writes, "Whether this symbolic slaughtering of Kavula and the subsequent symbolic beheading of the candidates are to be defined as 'sacrificial' acts is problematic." But he does identify the killing of the birds as sacrifice even though some expected features are missing. For example: "The fowls are *not* eaten in a communion meal. There *is* a communion meal but the sacred food eaten is not meat but beans and cassava" (1977: 193, 194. Emphasis in original). Apparently this is a non-alimentary separating sacrifice. There is no identification of social organization by the eating of meat.

The purpose of the Chihamba ritual is not to align participants with matrilineal structure, but the reverse. According to Turner, candidates are "being separated from" a matrilineal ancestress and dedicated to Kavula, who is not a matrilineal ancestor but is portrayed in the ritual as the husband of the ancestor and therefore in a paternal position. Turner describes this sacrifice as freeing participants from formal social structure and contrasts it to Roman sacrifice "to maintain the structured order." "One destructures, the other restructures," he says. Ndembu sacrifice releases participants from the "'deadly sins' of social structure"; Roman sacrifice is its opposite, "the very means of maintaining order and structure" (1977: 199, 212, 215, 197, 202).

Turner does not account for the difference between Ndembu and Roman sacrifice by reference to the contrasting family organizations, but only as a consequence of the greater wealth and complexity of Roman society (ibid.: 203). He discusses a number of other sacrificial religions, both of simple and of complex literate societies (all organized patrilineally) and suggests that sacrifice in the simpler societies is like Ndembu sacrifice. But in the simpler patrilineal societies he cites, such as the Nuer, sacrifice is never used to "destructure" descent organization, but rather to identify and maintain it. And in all of them sacrifice is "central in their religious practices" in a way it is not for the Ndembu.

Turner has also interpreted Ndembu circumcision ritual as sacrificial (1968: 276). In this ritual it is the father-son relation, not that between mother's brother and sister's son, that is significant both symbolically and in terms of the social organization of participants (ibid.: 12).

It is obviously impossible to do an exhaustive survey of the place of sacrifice in all matrilineal contexts, but an analysis of Ashanti sacrifice provides an ideal test case. Ashanti religion, kinship, and political organization have all been well described.[3] The Ashanti sacrifice animals in a wide variety of contexts, including an ancestor cult, and until the British conquest in 1896, practiced extensive human sacrifice. But Ashanti cultic ancestors have some unusual features: they are ancestors only of chiefs. A chief's paternity must be "impeccable," and his mother's mother's brother will also be his father's father. A close examination of the social contexts of Ashanti sacrifice shows not only that patriliny is entangled in the ancestor cult, but that other Ashanti sacrificial contexts are thoroughly patrilineal.

Ashanti was the greatest of the rich and powerful West African kingdoms that grew up around the slave trade (Wilks 1967: 211). All extensive West African human sacrifice can be understood as an added horror of the slave trade, in that those kingdoms that practiced it would not without the slave trade have attained the centralized political and military power to permit human sacrifice on such a scale. Given the demand for slaves in the New World, West African societies were either vulnerable to slavers or became slavers themselves. Defense against being sold in slavery was only possible with firearms, and these could be acquired in any number only by trading slaves to Europeans.

Two other important slaving kingdoms, Benin and Dahomey, resembled Ashanti economically and historically, but were rigidly patrilineal. A comparison with them will help clarify the social contexts of Ashanti human sacrifice. One important difference is that the kings of Benin and Dahomey regularly sacrificed humans in their patrilineal ancestor cults. In Ashanti, human sacrifice was never part of any, even royal, matrilineal ancestor cult rituals.

Benin and Dahomey both appear to have practiced more extensive human sacrifice than Ashanti, although accurate figures are not obtainable. Reports in the nineteenth-century British press of two thousand victims sacrificed in one Dahomean "Annual Customs" are exaggerated (Burton 1893: xiii). There is no reliable eyewitness account of more than forty victims at such events.

The occasions of most massive human sacrifice, in all three kingdoms, were the funerals of kings. But here again, in Ashanti such sacrifice was kept strictly separate from the matrilineal ancestral sanctuary. The victims chosen to accompany the king to the world of the dead were called 'kra, one of the patrilineal souls. Only certain members of the king's own household (killed without bloodshed and properly buried) and aliens (slaves, war captives, and criminals, whose bodies were thrown away) were sacrificed (Rattray 1927: 154).

In Dahomey, since the entire kingdom was an extension of the king's household, a man and woman from every single village and district and couples representing every craft and trade were sacrificed in order to duplicate the kingdom in the world of the dead, and all this was performed as part of the patrilineal ancestral cult (Herskovits 1938, I:394). The slaughter was not restricted to funerals; the king of Dahomey sacrificed a male and female slave daily to his ancestors, to carry to them his message of gratitude for another day of life (ibid.: 100).

Human sacrifice was certainly a method of social control in Ashanti. "If I were to abolish human sacrifice," the Ashanti king is reported to have said in 1848, "I should deprive myself of one of the most effectual means of keeping the people in subjection" (Wilks 1975: 594). But it was relied on far more heavily in Benin and Dahomey. In Benin, human sacrifice was the major defensive strategy, reminiscent of the Moabite king who turned back the Israelites by sacrificing his son on the ramparts (2 Kings 3:27). It didn't work against the British. A diary of a British surgeon describes the approach to Benin:

> As we neared the city, sacrificed human beings were lying in the path and bush—even in the king's compound the sight and stench of them was awful. Dead and mutilated bodies seemed to be everywhere—by God! may I never see such a sight again. Just before we came upon these horrors an old man appeared from behind a big tree which had fallen across the bush path we were following. He was using bow and arrow, and believed (as we were told afterwards) that he was invulnerable. He was, however, shot. (Quoted in Roth 1903: x)

This has no parallel in Ashanti, where the British saw no sacrifice victims along the way (Baden-Powell, 1896). (The Ashanti fought six wars against the British, some of which they won. The British conquest of Kumasi, the Ashanti capital, was a bitter fight against skilled military defense.)

Social structural features one expects to find in societies practicing extreme sacrifice were much more developed in Benin and Dahomey, and matrilineal descent is central in explaining why they were less so in Ashanti. Hierarchical distinctions which were elaborate and rigid in Benin and Dahomey were comparatively poorly developed in Ashanti. In Benin, the whole male population, even of villages, was and is ranked hierarchically according to order of birth (Bradbury 1973: 130). In the capital the ranking was even more pronounced. Women were lumped together at the bottom. In Dahomey, rigid "hierarchical organization applied not only to political institutions, but it did, and still does, deeply influence all phases of social and economic life" (Herskovits and Herskovits 1933: 9). Not only lineages, and within them, their members, but also all crafts and trades were ranked hierarchically.

Unlike Benin and Dahomey, Ashanti had always a strong egalitarian ideology. Ideally, members of a matrilineage were equals, and all residents of Ashanti shared a common civic status. This ideology existed even though there were sharp distinctions of rank, wealth, and occupation, especially between freeborn citizens and slaves. No matter how many generations passed, the matrilineal descendants of slaves could not escape their slave status, and in precolonial days were always potential sacrifice victims (Rattray 1929: 40). In spite of this conflict between ideology and social structure, sacrifice was never used as a means of incorporating slaves or others into the matrilineages.[4]

For neither Benin nor Dahomey was the social incorporation of slaves a problem. In Dahomey, Herskovits reports (1938, I: 99), slavery was a much worse state than "normal" African slavery, and was more like slavery in the New World. Most slaves, except concubines, were segregated by a caste-like, hierarchical distinction and forced to do continuous hard work. The offspring of slave concubines could, if desired, be fully incorporated into their father's lineage, since a child "legally stands in no relation whatever to his mother's kin" (ibid.: 153). A similar situation existed in Benin, where slave concubines were not markedly distinguished from wives, the same word being used for wife and servant, and "family groupings are conceived of in terms of a master-servant relationship" (Bradbury, 1957: 29).

Generational, and especially gender, hierarchy was actually, not merely ideally, much less pronounced in Ashanti, where authority over women and children by the maternal uncle was and is always limited by conflict with the husband and father. Rattray writes that formerly men preferred slave wives because "over slave children a father has more authority than the uncle does over free children" (1929: 40). Slave wives and children could at any time be sold or sacrificed. "Pawning" was common: a woman's matrilineage borrowed money from her husband, and she and/or her children became his "pawns," a kind of temporary (if the debt were repaid) slavery. "The lower the status of the wife the more desirable from the husband's point of view and the more in conformity with European ideas of marital authority did his position apparently become" (Rattray 1929: 48). Such devices also made domestic power relations more like those in Benin and Dahomey.

Benin and Dahomey were stable, almost monolithic monarchies with markedly patrimonial characters, the whole kingdom being conceived as an extension of the king's household. Ashanti was an alliance of nine matrilineal chiefdoms, and even at the height of its power this alliance was somewhat unstable. In the eighteenth century a centralized administrative structure unaligned with any matrilineal chiefdom was established to remedy this situation.

Beginning around 1700, the kingdom expanded rapidly by conquest, trading slaves and gold for European firearms and manufactured goods, until it controlled much of what is now Ghana. The early kings created the new centralized system of administrative officials in charge of the elaborate military and paramilitary organizations as well as of finance, tribute, trade, law enforcement, human sacrifice, and many lesser duties. Unlike the old aristocracy, succession to office in the new "bureaucracy"[5] was patrilineal. The first posts were held by male patrilineal descendants of previous kings; as the system developed, appointments were made from among sons of previous officeholders. Says the historian Ivor Wilks, "The power of the king was greatly increased by the emergence of the new bureaucracy . . . Unlike the older [matrilineal] aristocracy . . . the bureaucracy was totally subservient to the king"[6] (1967: 225). But even in the bureaucracy, material property was still inherited matrilineally, consequently "only skills and not capital, tended to accumulate within the patri-group," limiting its power (ibid.: 214).

The rapid development of the bureaucracy was possible because secondary patrilineal organization already existed in Ashanti. There still are these patrilineal groups, loosely organized and lacking the social structural importance of the matrilineages. Since the conquest, these patrilineal *ntoro* (literally "semen") transmit not political power, but only spiritual goods: names and souls are inherited patrilineally. The matrilineages (*abusua*) control and transmit the attributes of *this* world: material wealth and political office.

The Ashanti state was conceived as an alliance of stools, the material symbol of office. The matrilineal chiefs were held together by common allegiance to the Golden Stool, "the stool of stools," "revered by the whole people as the shrine of 'the soul of the nation'" (Fortes 1969:

42; Busia 1954: 191). More sacred than any chief's stool, the Golden Stool is[7] not matrilineal, but has strong patrilineal connotations. Members of the patrilineal bureaucracy were "sons and grandsons of the Golden Stool." Their posts were known as "sons' stools,"

> and were vested in patricentric residential groups, within each of which existed an accumulation of particular administrative skills, and the conditions necessary for their transmission from generation to generation. (Wilks 1967: 214)

One such patrilineal group, the "executioners," performed all human sacrifices and capital punishments. These two were not distinguishable, since the number of "condemned criminals" was not determined by the number of crimes committed, but by the number of victims required by the king. The number was a large one, and slaves and certain others filled up the quota (Wilks 1975: 307). The executioners' patrilineal descent was ritually celebrated in the one killing which is described in detail (Rattray 1927: 89). They were apparently numerous; a reliable nineteenth-century observer described "two parties of executioners, each upwards of one hundred" (quoted in Rattray 1927: 122).

The major annual occasion for human sacrifice was the annual meeting of the national council when all chiefs were required to visit the capital to reaffirm their allegiance to the king (Wilks 1975: 388–89). This event was important in developing a national ideology distinct from any matrilineage, even the king's. "It was at customs and rites such as these that the many loosely bound and often hostile factions, which owed nominal allegiance to the Ashanti king, came for the time being to think themselves part of a nation, rather than branches of a family or clan" (Rattray 1927: 132).

This annual ceremony, says Rattray, cannot be understood apart from "those exogamous divisions on a patrilineal basis known as *ntoro*" (ibid.: 136). The Golden Stool and various symbols of the paramount *ntoro*, to which most kings belonged, were ritually purified. All kings performed the rituals in which the paramount *ntoro* was first ritually polluted by blasphemous sacrifice, and then purified by correct sacrifice.

During the ceremony, humans were sacrificed by the executioners to serve the ghosts of dead kings, but *not* as the king's matrilineal cult ancestors. These sacrifices took place in the royal mausoleum, never in the sanctuary of the royal ancestral cult. The symbols representing the dead kings were not blackened stools, as in the matrilineal cult, but brass pans like the shrines of the patrilineal gods, and apparently the patrilineal souls of the dead kings were believed to receive the sacrifices.

These sacrifices were very like the Dahomean "Annual Customs," the "watering of the graves" of the royal patrilineal ancestors, and unlike any Ashanti matrilineal ritual.[8]

Colonization put an end not only to human sacrifice, but to the whole patrilineal administrative system within which it had been practiced (Wilks 1967: 213). Unlike the executioners and other specialized groups of the patrilineal bureaucracy, *ntoro* today are not corporate groups and are exogamous only within known genealogical connections.

I turn now to the two main categories of sacrifice that survived the conquest: sacrifices for individual protection, and ancestral cult sacrifice. Sacrifices for individual protection are made, not to ancestors, but to the patrilineal gods or to fetishes (*suman*). As spiritual beings, Ashanti gods reproduce entirely without female assistance. In ancient times, the supreme sky god sent his sons to earth where they became the major bodies of water. These produced sons and grandsons who are associated with the various *ntoro*. The word for gods (*obosom*) is often used synonymously with *ntoro* (Rattray 1927: 155). A priest once said to Rattray, "As a woman gives birth to a child, so may water to a god" (1923: 146).[9]

The distinction between fetishes and gods is not a clear one, some fetishes having become gods and all fetishes drawing their power ultimately from the sky god (Rattray 1927: 137). The Ashanti have many kinds of fetish, most of which come and go as they are effective, none of which are tied to any matrilineal descent group (Goody 1957). Fetishes are clearly distinguished from matrilineal stool shrines, even if a fetish happens to be in the shape of a similar stool (Rattray 1923: 95, n.1). The most powerful of them all, the *kunkuma*, must never, for any reason, be brought into a matrilineal ancestor shrine. The chief of the patrilineal executioners was also called the *kunkuma* (Wilks 1975: 249).

For most fetishes contact with menstrual blood is disastrous.

> Contact with [a menstruating woman], directly or indirectly, is held to be negative and render useless all supernatural or magico-protective powers possessed by either persons or spirits or objects (i.e., [fetishes]). Even by indirect contact, therefore, an unclean woman is capable of breaking down all barriers which stand between defenseless man and those evil unseen powers which beset him on every side. (Rattray 1927: 75)

The *kunkuma* is invulnerable to this danger, but exposed to a contrasting one: it must never be sprinkled with water to purify it. It is made of an old broom, chosen because it has been in contact with every kind of filth, and hidden in it is a piece of fiber polluted with menstrual blood.

Not content with thus defiling it, the owner had taken every ta-
booed object that concerned him in any way and brought each
in turn into contact with the *kunkuma* . . . "The *kunkuma* can
save you," said the priest, "it takes on itself every evil." (Ibid.:
13)

The salvation offered by this fetish is of a special kind. It can do no
active good, neither heal nor grant fertility, for it has only apotropaic or
expiatory power. It is a kind of moral "black hole," able to draw down
into itself all kinds of sin and sacrilege.[10] Before the conquest, the uses
to which the executioners put the *kunkuma* were all expiatory. Spilling
the blood of human victims on it ensured that no vengeful ghost could
return. Human victims killed on such a fetish were not buried but
thrown away; they were distinguished from victims called by the name
of one of the patrilineal souls and intended to serve another human
spirit after death. The victims of fetish execution were banished even
from the spirit world (Rattray 1923: 100; 1927: 154). The *kunkuma* is a
means of dealing with evil as that which must be made absolutely other,
like menstrual blood.

There remain those sacrifices connected with the matrilineal ancestor cult. Ashanti do not sacrifice to ordinary ancestors, nor are their
ancestral cults family affairs. In contrast to Benin, Dahomey, Tallensi,
Lugbara, and other patrilineal ancestor cults, only those men who die
in a chief's office become sacrificial ancestors; destoolment during a
chief's lifetime disqualifies him (Fortes 1969: 188). The chief's office,
says Fortes, "belongs to the whole community, not to any one lineage.
The man is, ideally, so merged in the office that he virtually ceases to be
a member of his lineage, which always has an independent head for its
corporate affairs" (1953: 32). Ashanti cult ancestors do not represent
kinship in any family aspect, but only in its political aspect (Fortes
1965: 130).

The symbol of office of an Ashanti chief is a white stool. At his death
this stool is ritually blackened, consecrated with sacrificial blood and fat
of animal victims, and placed in the ancestral stool house, taking its
place with other blackened ancestral stools of previous officeholders. A
lineage sister of the chief holds the office of "queen mother." She too
has a stool of office and this too is blackened at her death and placed in
a separate stool house, but sacrifice is never offered to such stools. Vegetable food, sometimes fish, and, rarely, antelope meat is offered to them
(Rattray 1923: 105). In Ashanti, as is usual throughout the world, only
domestic animals and humans are proper sacrifice victims: game and
fish are specifically non-sacrificial offerings. There is just one exception

71

to the rule that stools of male ancestors only receive sacrifice: the stool of a mythical ancestress who was not born of woman, nor came out from the female earth with other mystical ancestors, but sprang direct from the sky god—an Ashanti Athena (ibid.: 111).

Ancestral cult sacrifices were and are performed only at regular lineage festivals, at enstoolment and death of a chief, and for purging the lineage of unusual sacrilege, such as incest, affecting the lineage as a whole (Fortes 1969: 189). The rarely performed purifying sacrifices are not described. The regularly performed sacrifices are described in great detail by Rattray, and all succeeding ethnographers support his descriptions.

These are strictly alimentary communion sacrifices, in which food, drink, and the cooked meat of animal victims are offered to ancestral stools and shared among participants. Rattray once asked about the possibility of human sacrifice to ancestral stools, and was asked in return "how I could ask such a foolish question when I knew well that the flesh of the sacrifice was afterwards partaken of" (1923: 95, n. 1). The chief, in particular, *must* eat of it. Blood and fat of victims are also applied to the stools. Human blood, both menstrual and sacrificial, is strictly excluded. Even the water used in such a sacrifice must be drawn by a woman past menopause. "In olden times," writes Rattray, "if any menstrous woman entered the room where the stools were kept she would have been killed instantly" (1923: 96). The queen mother cannot enter her own stool house if she is menstruating. According to Fortes (1963: 68) it is specifically the menstrual taboo that prevents women from holding political office other than queen mother, since such office requires performing regular stool rituals.

Both patrilineal and matrilineal descent figure in the office of chief. Busia describes the two sacrifices performed at an enstoolment. The first sacrifice, similar to regular ancestral sacrifices, was performed in the stool house. The second, performed outside the stool house, was for the sky god.

> The oldest of the sons of the chief . . . killed the sheep. It was cut up and shared amongst the sons of the chiefs and the younger royals . . . It was taboo for any other person to eat of the meat. (1968: 13)

To be eligible for succession to a stool vacancy, a man must be a father (Fortes 1969: 197). A candidate's paternal origins must also be "impeccable" (Fortes 1963: 59). Unknown, irregular, or slave paternity disqualifies him. In Fortes's time, beliefs and rituals associated with the *ntoro* had become less important among younger people; "on the other hand, the *ntoro concept* retained its older significance for holders of high office. No chief of superior rank, let alone the king, could have held office were his *ntoro* not known" (1969: 198 n.12).

This prerequisite of "impeccable" paternity, when lineage membership itself is inalienable simply by birth from a lineage woman, becomes more intelligible by trying to grasp just what quality of a deceased chief is attached to his consecrated stool. A perfectly clear understanding of this is elusive. Says Fortes,

> as to what constituent of the living person is transmitted into an ancestor, our authorities are vague and I myself never succeeded in getting a coherent account from my informants. An ancestral "spirit" is not thought of as a kind of nebulous being or personified mystical presence, but primarily as a name attached to a relic, the stool (1965: 129)

If Fortes is correct that names are what are attached to cult stools, these are *patrilineal* ancestral spirits, since names are inherited only patrilineally. The *ntoro,* says Rattray, is "the all-important matter in naming a child, for, first only a person of the child's *ntoro* could name it, and, secondly, it might not be named after anyone who had not during life belonged to the same *ntoro*" (1927: 318). To name a child is to reincarnate a patrilineal soul. "This reincarnated *ntoro* soul . . . was and still is, the important and only real factor in personal names"[11] (1927: 62–63, 319).

Inquiring into the nature of Ashanti souls does not exactly shed clear light on ancestral stool spirits, but it is instructive nevertheless. There are three different words for patrilineal souls: *ntoro, sunsum* (usually synonymous with *ntoro*), and *'kra.*[12] A woman is "for all practical purposes . . . soul-less, because she cannot transmit any kind of *sunsum*, but only her blood" (Rattray 1927: 318). The matrilineal, or blood, spirit, "which gives persons their bodily form, becomes on death a *saman* (ghost, spirit ancestor), retains its bodily form, and goes to live in the spirit world to await reincarnation through some woman of its own clan" (Rattray 1927: 319). Rattray uses this word *saman* frequently when referring to stool ancestral spirits. But he also uses a word for patrilineal soul, *sunsum:*

> The stool, which during the life-time of its possessor was so intimately bound (literally and metaphorically speaking) with its owner's *sunsum* or soul, thus becomes after death a shrine into which the departed spirit may again be called upon to enter on certain special occasions. (1923: 92)

The Golden Stool is associated only with the *sunsum* of the Ashanti nation; in the mythical time of the first king, the national *sunsum* was attached to the stool in an *ntoro* ritual (ibid.: 289). The Golden Stool does not have matrilineal associations. But we are left in the dark about what kind of spirit, matrilineal ghost or patrilineal soul or name, *saman* or *sunsum,* is attached to an ancestral stool.

We can lighten the darkness only by reference to cross-cousin marriage, a topic dear to anthropologists but likely to be tedious to others. It is cross-cousin marriage that makes a chief's father's father also his mother's mother's brother. Ashanti practice both matrilateral cross-cousin marriage (a man marries his mother's brother's daughter) and patrilateral cross-cousin marriage (a man marries his father's sister's daughter).[13] In Rattray's day the preference for patrilateral cross-cousin marriage was so strong that his questions about reasons for cross-cousin marriage in general were answered with reasons for patrilateral marriage only (1927: 322). Parallel cousin marriage (with the daughter of the mother's sister or the father's brother) is incestuous. Although cross-cousin marriage is declining among non-chiefs, it is still preferred, since it can reconcile conflicting inheritance interests (Fortes 1950: 282). For example, a man must leave his property to his sister's children, but if his own children are their spouses his children will benefit from the inheritance.[14]

Patrilateral cross-cousin marriage is very rare around the world, compared with the matrilateral form (Lévi-Strauss 1968: 438). The two forms produce different genealogical structures: matrilateral cross-cousin marriage results in a continuous outward move of affinal connection, but the patrilateral form doubles back again every other generation, so that a man's father's father and his mother's mother's brother will be the same person. In other words, patrilineal and matrilineal descent converge. Lévi-Strauss has illustrated this with the diagrams in figures 3 and 4 (1968: 443). The arrows show the movement of women. Notice the reversal in the patrilateral diagram.

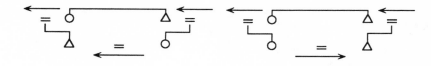

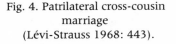

Fig. 3. Matrilateral cross-cousin
marriage
(Lévi-Strauss 1968: 443).

Fig. 4. Patrilateral cross-cousin
marriage
(Lévi-Strauss 1968: 443).

Lévi-Strauss, whose theory of cross-cousin marriage is based on the notion of exchange of women holding society together, has a low opinion of the patrilateral form:

> It constitutes an abortive form . . . because it precipitately closes the cycle of reciprocity and consequently prevents the latter from ever being extended to the whole group. . . . It represents the Cheap-Jack in the scale of marriage transactions. (1968: 448–49)

For Lévi-Strauss, both forms of cross-cousin marriage regulate access to that supreme value and object of exchange: women. The Ashanti had a different value in mind. In Rattray's survey of reasons for cross-cousin marriage,

> about 80 per cent of the answers took the form, "It is because of names," with such variations as "because of great names," "to get back great names," "because if my niece bears a son, I can name him after myself or my ancestors." (1927: 321)

These ancestors are patrilineal. The "niece" is a father's sister's daughter to his son, her husband; her uncle, who is her husband's father, will be her son's paternal grandfather as well as his maternal great-uncle. Only patrilateral cross-cousin marriage can recover "great names" and, with them, patrilineal descent. Even when names did not figure in the answers, a similar principle was expressed: "'in order that my niece may bear a *Kra pa* (that is, a 'pure reincarnation' or 'a pure soul,' someone who is of the same *abusua* (blood) and *ntoro* as an ancestor) . . . (that we wish beyond all)'" (ibid). What the Ashanti valued most was the fusion of patrilineal and matrilineal descent achieved only in patrilateral cross-cousin marriage.

In the same discussion, Rattray says that cross-cousin marriage "is necessary" for kings and chiefs.[15] If patrilateral cross-cousin marriage is prescribed for chiefs and kings, then the confusion in Rattray and obscurity in Fortes[16] over the nature of ancestral stool spirits disappears: patriliny and matriliny, *sunsum* and *saman* are fused in these stools, for those who hold stool offices have fused paternal and maternal lines in their own descent. The ancestral stools themselves are addressed with a kinship term, *nana*, which is translated as "grandfather" but which actually refers indiscriminately to father's father and mother's mother's brother, a congruence only actually occurring with patrilateral cross-cousin marriage. Conversely, a chief is called the "grandson" of the stool ancestors, a reciprocal term fusing son's son and sister's daughter's son (Busia 1968: 12).

In the conditions for succession to office, in the rituals of enstool-ment, in the names attached to ancestral stools, and in their spirits or souls, patrilineal descent always figures in all ancestral stools involved in sacrifice. It is safe to conclude that there are no forms of sacrifice in Ashanti that bear a direct relationship to matrilineal family organization as such.[17]

Hawaiian Sacrifice

THIS CHAPTER IS DIVIDED in two sections. It begins with a description of Hawaiian sacrifice and its social context, written in the ethnographic present tense to conform with quotations from the only systematic account of it, Valeri's excellent *Kingship and Sacrifice* (1985).[1] The chapter concludes with a historical account of the sudden end of Hawaiian sacrifice in 1819, and of the important parts played by women in bringing that about.

For Hawaiians, descent from women is just as important as descent from men. Even though their bilateral descent system is hierarchically ranked, within it women are fully equal to men and sometimes hold ranks higher than any of their male contemporaries. But this bilateral genealogical system is not supported by sacrifice; rather, it is opposed by a sacrificial system that maintains political power in an exclusively male hierarchy. Says Valeri, "The global inferiority of women relative to men in the sacrificial system contrasts sharply with their equality to men in the genealogically determined hierarchy" (1985: 113). The opposition between the genealogical and sacrificial systems is conceived as a gender polarity "between sexual reproduction, which is primarily associated with the feminine pole, and the sacrificial reproduction of social units . . . associated with the masculine pole" (ibid.: 123–24). The word "reproduction" here refers not only to practices ensuring continuity of a social and economic system, but also has a more literal and culturally specific sense: for Hawaiians, sacrifice is "man's childbearing," and women are as rigidly excluded from it as are men from bearing real children (ibid.: 114).

Men's childbearing is superior to women's childbearing, that is, sacrificial reproduction of social and political order is considered superior to sexual reproduction of individuals. The inferior genealogical system, in which the sexes are joined, is impure; the sacrificial system, in which the sexes are separate, is pure. (The blood of menstruation and childbirth is the quintessence of impurity.) In association with impure women, men lose purity. Separated from women, they regain it, or rather, they can be purified by sacrifice. The whole sacrificial system rests on this opposition of male and female as pure and impure, and the ranking of males within the sacrificial hierarchy is an elaboration of the gender hierarchy. "The whole system," says Valeri, "is summarized by the following proportion: pure: impure:: male: female:: male superior: male inferior" (ibid.: 128).

The gender hierarchy is made most evident in the alimentary separation of the sexes. Since all eating by men is sacrificial, women and men can never eat together. Their meals cannot even be prepared on the same fires. This separation is reflected in the architecture of dwellings. All households have three separate buildings: an eating house for men, a separate eating house for women, and a sleeping house in which the sexes come together. The men's eating house is sacred, a domestic sacrificial temple.

Since cooking involves sacrifice, it is an exclusively male occupation. Men prepare one oven for the women, cook the food in it for them, and prepare a second oven for themselves, using a much wider range of edible species. The gods are the origin of all nature, and all natural species are divinized. Only those kinds of food stuff that can be completely desacralized can be eaten by women. The desacralization is done by men in sacrifices that separate the foods into two parts: one sacred and reserved for men, the other profane and for women. "The existence of the profane part is made possible by the ritual concentration of the sacred character of the entire species in the gods' part, which itself is inseparable from the part belonging to the men" (ibid.: 120). Those foods that are most important in alimentary sacrifice can never be made profane enough for women. These include pigs, coconuts, bananas, and many others. Since pigs are the most important sacrificial victims, pork especially is forbidden to women. The penalty for breaking food taboos is death. The foods that are permanently taboo for women are those especially important in the alimentary sacrifices that index social units—in other words, those foods most important in the sacrificial reproduction of the male hierarchy.

Alimentary sacrifice also indexes distinctions between hierarchically ranked groups of males. Eating is separated not only by sex, but also by rank among men: "The position of inferior men approaches that of women, in that the most sacred species (pork, coconuts, etc.) are only rarely consumed by them, being eaten most often by high-ranking men in temples to which male commoners are not admitted any more than women" (ibid.: 127). Even those men permitted in the temple "eat together separately": portions of alimentary sacrifices are distributed according to relative rank (ibid.: 38, 306). The male eating hierarchy is ranked according to purity, that is, according to proximity to the gods. Small boys not yet initiated in the men's house eat with women, except for the sons of high-ranking chiefs, who are too pure ever to eat profane female food, and pass straight from their mother's breast to initiation in the household temple. The higher a man's position in the sacrificial hierarchy, the more elaborately sacrificial are his meals. The more sacrificial his meals, the more effectively do his eating practices maintain his hierarchical position.

The hierarchical relation between chiefly and commoner men duplicates that on a lower level between commoner men and women, a distinction maintained by male commoners' sacrificial eating in their domestic temples. Male commoners are "at best spectators of the state cult, at worst its victims," but in their own homes they are "domestic chiefs" (Sahlins 1981: 52).

Commoner women have no part at all in the sacrificial system, which defines them only negatively, as *im*pure, *not* men (ibid.: 46–47). The exclusion of women from worship of the major gods is so complete that, according to the oldest Hawaiian source, "the majority of women . . . had no deity and just worshipped nothing" (Malo, quoted in Valeri 1985: 113). But this sounds like the perspective of male chiefs, for whom women are so profane, such antitheses of the sacred, that they are by definition without religion. What women may have done in purely female contexts is unknown. Religious dimensions of common women's lives are as absent from the accounts—all from males—as are the women themselves from the sacred male community of Hawaiian sacrifice.

Young boys are initiated into the domestic temples by their fathers, but this de facto father to son continuity does not lead to ritual celebration of patriliny. Similarly, priestly skills are handed on from father to son in the priestly "lineages" (ibid.: 132) without patriliny becoming the symbolic focus of sacrificial ritual. The crucial male to male intergenerational link for the sacrificial hierarchy is that between the king and the male gods, and the king's divine descent is represented in sacrifice not by patrilineal symbols, but by symbols of "man's childbearing," such as an "umbilical cord" produced by males only, representing the sacrificial bond. The sacrificial hierarchy is constructed around the sacrifices by which the king reproduces his own divinity: his descent from the male gods. Without these royal sacrifices there is no continuity of the exclusively male political hierarchy.

The gods themselves are hierarchically ranked. Consequently, by performing a sacrifice, "one [a male person] puts oneself in a given hierarchical category. Of course . . . the choice is not free: one can sacrifice only to the gods that correspond to one's hierarchical position in society. Thus, sacrifice ensures that the hierarchy of gods is translated into a social hierarchy and reproduces it" (ibid.: 109). A man has access to major gods only through his hierarchical superiors (ibid.: 134). At the top of the hierarchy, the king, assisted by his high priest, offers sacrifice to the highest and most masculine god of all, Ku. In Ku is represented "the whole of divinized masculine attributes" (ibid.: 13), and he also perfectly represents the human species, since "the human male . . . stands for the entire human species because he is its superior form" (ibid.: 270).

As well as being less pure than the gods, "goddesses are few and have a marginal position in the Hawaiian pantheon. This corresponds to the marginal position of women in the ritual system" (ibid.: 19). The goddesses represent "typically feminine attributes . . . everything that is associated with the begetting [sic] of children, beginning with seduction . . . and ending with childbirth" (ibid.: 18). Although high-ranking women may sometimes bring offerings to the goddesses, the actual sacrificers are male priests.

An entirely different category of divinities represents the polar opposite of the pure divinities. These sorcery gods are opposed to the great gods as evil is to good. Sorcery gods are impure, and sacrifices to them may be performed by priestesses, the sex of the sacrificer depending on the impurity of the god. "Pure goddesses require male sacrificers as mediators between them and women, while impure gods may in certain cases be approached by men through female mediators. This happens because purity is an essentially masculine property, while impurity is essentially feminine" (ibid.: 112). Priestesses sacrifice only to the impure gods even so, and they must be either consecrated unmarried women or women past menopause.

Victims too are hierarchically ranked. "In the main temples, where only masculine deities are worshipped, only male animals may be offered in sacrifice. Even the vegetable offerings, such as coconuts or bananas . . . have a masculine connotation" (ibid.: 46). The more closely a victim is identified with the man who offers it, the more valuable it is, the most valuable being a human victim, always male. Pigs are almost human: piglets may be breast-fed by women, and a favorite pig is closely identified with its owner.

Like the gods, the numerous temples are also hierarchically ranked. A male commoner may have a domestic temple, but a chief has two sacrificial temples: "As head of a household, he sacrifices and eats in his domestic temple; as head of a social segment, he sacrifices and eats in the company of his nobles and clients in his 'official' temple"(ibid.: 174). The hierarchy of temples corresponds to that of the major gods: each major god subsumes a class of particularized gods just as each official temple subsumes all those of inferior chiefs and all domestic temples within its district (ibid.: 184, 13). At the top of this hierarchy are the temples reserved exclusively for the king, where human sacrifice is performed. The king's temples have the same relation to society as a whole as do domestic temples to individual households and chiefs' official temples to their own districts (ibid.: 174). Just as the highest god, Ku, represents the entire human species, so the king, assisted by the high priest, offers the most sacred victim to him for the entire society. The king's monopoly of human sacrifice "means that this sacrifice, which encompasses all the others, can only be made for the benefit of the collectivity"(ibid.: 49). The exclusive right to offer human sacrifice is the index, the primary identifying sign, of kingship. It is consequently an effective sign, causing what it signifies: he who offers human sacrifice successfully is king.

Rights in land are determined by the sacrificial system, not by inheritance through the genealogical system. Each right to a piece of land is contained in a more encompassing right above it in the sacrificial hierarchy. The ultimate right to all land is vested in the king, who sets aside some for himself and divides the remainder among the high-ranking nobles who are his main supporters. The recipients, in turn, keep some land for their use and distribute the rest among their own main supporters. Each of these does the same with his own portion, and so on, down to the bottom of the sacrificial hierarchy; "every land right rests on a relationship of subordination"(ibid.: 154–55). Land is distributed to men only, for control of an area is exercised through control of the temple connected with it. Land is of divine origin and women are almost entirely excluded from its agricultural use, from food production as well as from food preparation. "At most, [women] are given the task of appropriating some secondary foods—which in a way are 'residual,' like the women themselves: shellfish, mollusks, seaweed, small crustaceans, and so on" (ibid.: 123).

The chain of land rights and the chain of the temple hierarchy are made manifest (indexed) in firstfruit sacrifices. The most important requirement for legitimating a man's land rights is for him to make offerings of its produce, especially of its firstfruits, to his overlord as to a god. These offerings move up the hierarchy until they reach the king, who consecrates them to the major gods. "At each point in the chain the human recipient of the firstfruits of a land segment is only the representative, through his own overlords, of the major gods. The higher one [a man] is in the hierarchy, the more closely one represents these gods" (ibid.: 156). The final sacrifice, that of the divine king as the gods' closest representative, makes all the lower offerings it encompasses not merely tribute, but sacrifice.

The entire political and economic system is organized around the king. In sacrificing, "he is the veritable creator of society as a coherent whole" (ibid.: 158)—or at least he is the "veritable creator" of the sacrificial hierarchy as a coherent whole, for he is the link with the gods on whom the whole hierarchy depends. At his death, the sacrificial system, that is, the political order, collapses. Without the king and his sacrifices, there are no property rights. Anarchy is so extensive that women eat taboo food and even enter the temples. Order is restored when a new king is sacrificially installed. This does not happen immediately, for "there are not clear or automatic rules of succession" (ibid.: 159). Succession, like everything else in the political system, depends on royal sacrifice.

The genealogical system by itself does not determine the king's successor. There are a number of reasons for this. One is that if intergenerational continuity of office were determined by genealogy alone, the king could be a queen. Another is the incredible tangle of chiefly genealogies, a consequence of a number of factors: bilateral descent; the extreme frequency of noble unions between siblings, half siblings, uncle and niece, etc.; the high number of marriages contracted by each noble, male or female; the coexistence of polyandry and polygyny, and so on (ibid.: 159). As a result, when the king dies, there are always a number of pretenders with nearly equal claims. The victor in the ensuing violent conflict is identified by sacrifice: "He who succeeds in sacrificing all the others becomes the only king" (ibid.: 161). (A human victim may be killed outside the temple, in combat or execution, and offered in sacrifice after his death. The sacrifice is the consecration rather than the killing.) Of course the victor must also have enough support to defeat the other pretenders, but this by itself is not enough:

> The victory that transforms one of the high-ranking pretenders into a divine king . . . implies the elimination of the other pretenders. . . . But these rivals are not simply killed; they are sacrificed, hence incorporated into the god, reduced to him. Moreover, they are not only enemies, but also close relatives of the victor. Hence they are his doubles. Thus, by sacrificing them the victor is indirectly incorporated into the god, given a divine status. In sum, he becomes a divine king. (Ibid.)

By sacrificing his close male relatives, a king reinforces his divine descent, his direct link with the male gods. The body of a king who dies in office is also sacrificially processed, including cooking to separate flesh and bones. "These rites enshrine the dead ruler as the ancestral spirit (*'aumakua*) of his successor " (Sahlins 1981: 25), a successor who may not be his actual descendant. The sacrificed body of Captain Cook was similarly ritually processed to make him an ancestral god of the reigning king (ibid.: 26). That is, Hawaiian sacrifice constitutes purely male divine *ascent,* the royal genealogical link with the gods, rather than human intergenerational *descent.* As Sahlins says, "Hawaiians in fact do not trace *descent* so much as *ascent*" (1985: 20).

Sacrificial reproduction and sexual reproduction are both ways of reproducing divinity. Hawaiians' original ancestors were divine, and this genealogical connection is preserved among the nobility. In a bilateral system exogamous marriages would rapidly dissipate the divine heritage, but incestuous unions, especially between full siblings, keep it in the family. "Royalty would reproduce only itself; it would be characterized by a lineal narcissism, so to speak" (Valeri 1985: 150). Having sacrificed all his brothers, a new king proceeds to marry all his sisters (ibid.: 165–66). Consequently, in spite of bilateral descent, Valeri refers to "the royal lineage" (ibid.: 142). This extreme endogamy "allows a couple to produce a child who is a replica of the god as ancestor" (ibid.: 114). Such marriages not only preserve hereditary divinity, they recreate it, because incestuous union "is itself a divine behavior, a positive sign of divinity" (ibid.: 147). Low-ranking nobles are not allowed these incestuous unions because they create, as well as preserve, divinity.

Sexual reproduction of divinity is powerful, but the divine child may be a little girl who outranks all her relatives. Sacrificial reproduction runs no such risks. Sacrificial relations to the gods are direct, active, and masculine; relations through sexual reproduction are indirect, passive, and feminine (ibid.: 114). In his sacrifices, especially those of his installation, the king ritually controls his divine genealogy and reproduces himself and the god without dependence on women's reproductive powers. This "man's childbearing" includes cutting an umbilical cord, one produced not sexually, but sacrificially.

> The "umbilical cord" that makes the god be born, that gives him life, . . . symbolizes society itself and the continuity of its life. It also symbolizes the king as the "cord" that mediates between gods and men and insures the conversion of the life of the one in the life of the others. This is why the reproduction of the god, the reproduction of society, and that of the king all coincide in the same ritual. (Ibid.: 316)

The king's temple rites, as well as some human sacrifices performed outside the temple, are called by a word meaning "cord": *'aha.* This word also means: "(1) a group of persons gathered or associated for a given purpose; (2) sacrificial rites accompanied by prayers" (ibid.: 294). The sacred cord represents both the sacrificial social bond and the king's genealogical tie with the gods.

Three relationships coincide in the cord: that between the king
and the god, that between the king and his followers, and that
among the followers. . . . The bond between the king and god is
capable of symbolizing the other two bonds but not vice versa.
This is because the god, and the king immediately after him, embodies the concepts that are the presupposition of all social relations. (Ibid.: 297)

All *sacrificially constituted* social relations, that is. Maleness is foremost
among these concepts.

Before his sacrificial installation, the king does not always hold the
highest rank in the genealogical system itself, but his sacrificially constituted link with the gods nevertheless becomes the measure of all
noble genealogies. (A noble is one who can trace a genealogical connection to the king within ten generations. Commoners are not allowed
to trace ascent beyond their grandparents [ibid.: 157]). The sacred cord,
the king's sacrificial genealogical link with the gods, is

the genealogy that binds together all other genealogies, since it
is their reference point and the locus of their legitimacy or their
truth. Hence, the king's "cord" (*'aha*) is in fact also the "association" or "congregation" (*'aha*) of nobles. The cord becomes the
community; the link that connects the king with the god becomes the social bond itself. (Ibid.: 296–97)

This social bond, created in sacrifice, is limited to males. The sacred
umbilical cord created in "men's childbearing" contains all the ties that
bind the male sacrificial hierarchy, but it transcends the ties indexed by
ordinary physiological umbilical cords: those binding mother and child.

The king's sacrifices construct a sacred male community, based on
his genealogical link with the gods. Direct sacrificial transmission of divine genealogy is kept separate from indirect sexual transmission of divine genealogy. The sacred cords are not inherited through the bilateral
descent system. At the king's death, his sacred cords are unraveled and
their strands woven into caskets to enshrine his bones (ibid.: 298). The
undoing of the king's sacred cords coincides with the anarchical disso-
lution of all sacrificially created social order after his death. The sacred
cords of the new king must be made anew in his own sacrifices, for the
social bond, the genealogical link with the gods created by each king in
sacrifice, "is contingent on him and must be entirely recreated by his
successor" (ibid.).

As in other sacrificial traditions, the Hawaiian calendar is ordered
by a series of sacrificial festivals. These rituals divide the year in two
parts, which involve different kinds of sacrifice. Four months are de-

voted to Lono, the god of fertility, both human and agricultural. The important sacrifices during this period are those that desacralize the staple foods that women may eat. Human sacrifice and war are forbidden; they take place only during the eight months that focus primarily on the worship of the highest god, Ku.[2] As well as human victims, sacrifices to Ku involve the foods (pigs, coconuts, and so on) that are taboo for women and central in the sacrificial reproduction of the male hierarchy. The sacrifices installing the king are the climax of this latter period, and because a king's installation is never permanent, they must be repeated regularly. "The hierarchical chain must be constantly renewed" (ibid.: 160).

The new year begins with sacrifices of pigs, coconuts, and bananas, after which the king's human sacrifice temples are closed for the four months of Lono worship. At the heart of the New Year festival are the firstfruit sacrifices. In these sacrifices, a sacred portion of various staple foods, such as taro, is given to the gods; none of these are eaten, but the rest of the foods are freed for human consumption, even for women. These non-alimentary separating sacrifices take place mostly during the ritual clockwise circuit of the island by Lono's image. Later, a second image of Lono as god of play is offered mock sacrifices, in which people take back all of Lono's share, and nothing is left on the altar (ibid.: 224). These mock sacrifices initiate four days of sexual orgies, dancing, play, and feasting—but the feasting is minimally sacrificial. Sacrifices of pigs, coconuts, and bananas, all the foods for regular temple sacrifice, are forbidden (ibid.: 206). In the absence of the violent sacrifices that maintain hierarchical distinctions, the distinctions themselves fade. The king and his nobles stay away.

> The high priest is secluded in a consecrated place . . . ; he is blindfolded so that he does not see the people violating the normal taboos of which he is the custodian. Also, he is forbidden to eat fresh food . . . probably because it would not be consecrated, since the temples are closed. (Ibid.: 207)

Hierarchical distinction is not entirely lost. Women and men still do not eat together and there is no violent anarchy such as there is after the death of the king. According to Valeri, "the festival does not negate the social order but substitutes for the normal order founded on the king's sacrificial violence an order that springs from the pure pleasure of being in society, of love and good fellowship" (ibid.: 221). But this sociability "will not survive the festival except as transformed into hierarchy" (ibid.: 226).[3]

When the king returns, Lono is captured and brought into the king's temple. Then there is a *real* sacrifice: a pig for Lono and one for the king and his men."This sacrifice has the air of a true communion . . . the sacred meat that is the index of the community [of male nobles] it reproduces cannot be eaten in private, . . . by eating . . . the king and his followers absorb and take possession of the elementary social bond, the sociability that Lono represents" (ibid.). This sacrifice must be performed after the New Year festival "in order to resume the consumption of pork, and therefore sacrificial contact with the divine. Its performance is motivated by the necessity for separating the pure people who enter into sacrificial contact with the gods from the impure (women, commoners)" (ibid.: 258). Finally, Lono's image is put away until his return the following year (ibid.: 226).

A similar purifying sacrifice, separating men and women, is performed before beginning the great cycle of sacrifices in which the king reproduces the god and himself as a divine king. In this cycle, a transubstantiation is accomplished: a tree becomes a god. The cycle itself begins in the forest with cutting down a tree that will become of the image of Ku. The tree must be of a particular species known for its marked masculine characteristics: it is upright, hard, red, and so on. A human victim is killed by beheading at the base of the tree. In later human sacrifices in the temple, no blood is shed; later still, the victim must be killed outside the temple, his body must be washed and purified by priests before consecration in the temple. This progression, from impurity (bloodshed) to purity, from disorder to order, also characterizes the transformation of the god, from wild tree to transcendent god, and of the king, from "wild" individual to ordered "representative of the collectivity," a legitimate divine king (ibid.: 271).

Seven days of sacrifices follow, including human sacrifices and much sacred umbilical cord ritual, culminating in ritual that "has the aim of reestablishing a genealogical connection with the god" (ibid.: 397, n.184). From the time the tree is felled until it is installed in the temple as the completed image of Ku, two priests, representing Ku as a baby, eat only baby food—banana flower nectar (ibid.: 305). Finally Ku's image and images of other gods are ready. That night a special priest goes fishing for the hard-to-catch *ulua* fish. Usually he catches a human victim instead. This victim may be the adversary the king has already defeated, or may be a transgressor, representing the adversary the king intends to defeat after the sacrifices are completed. On the following day, Ku's "final and definitive 'birth'" takes place, his umbilical cord is cut, he receives a number of sacrifices, and he is girded in his loincloth (ibid.: 306). "This birth rite and the rite for putting the loincloth on the god that follows it are identical to those performed for any male child to transform him fully into a social being" (ibid.: 314). Then there is a great sacrifice of four hundred pigs, bananas, coconuts, and other offerings, including some human victims. These are distributed according to rank among the different categories of gods and men. The gods' share is cooked separately, including broiling the human victims. The climax of the cycle is the great sacrifice, performed when the loin-cloth rite "signifies that the gods have become adult, complete men" (ibid.: 318). The meal is a hierarchical communion, indexing the hierarchy of men and gods, and causing what it signifies. "This hierarchy is represented and effected by the order in which the sacrificial shares are received and by their value" (ibid.). Following the meal, the *ulua* victim is sacrificed: the king's adversary sacrificed as a fish, or a fish sacrificed as the king's adversary. This is a non-alimentary separating sacrifice; none of it is eaten. According to Valeri, the preceding communion meal has made men and gods too close. "This is probably why it is followed by a sacrifice that is *entirely* abandoned to the gods and that can there-fore represent their separation from men" (ibid.).

The following day, a priest representing a god eats an eye of a hu-man and one of a pig victim. The participants, except for the king and high priest, turn away from the divine images, which they may no longer look at, seeing only the victims piled on the altar, mediators be-tween men and gods. Valeri interprets this final temple ritual as the removal of the gods to the invisible realm, distancing them from all but the king and high priest, whose power is thereby increased. Following this, all move outside the temple to an area where images of goddesses are kept. (Goddesses are too impure for the temple.) Here a desacraliz-ing ritual is performed.

> As it was necessary for men to separate from impure women in order to establish contact with pure male gods, now, in order for them to reenter the profane world, it is necessary for them to be relatively polluted by contact with the feminine principle embod-ied by the goddesses. (Ibid.: 326)

The day after the men have been desacralized, the king's female relatives bring a long loincloth to offer to the goddesses. (Tapa cloth is women's only important product, except for children.) The priest who makes the sacrifice announces, "'They will not live, the women with the guilty mouth' [who eat taboo food] . . . your goddess will make them die'" (ibid.: 330).

> Thus, only after women have been reproduced as a separate cat-egory can men effectively reunite with them without fear of com-pletely losing the mana acquired in the temple.
>
> This . . . will make it possible to reproduce concrete individ-uals (children) after the abstract reproduction of the ideal indi-

vidual (the god, who embodies the species) has been accomplished. In other words, the "pure," that is, nonsexual, reproduction of the species as a concept is the sine qua non for the "impure" (sexual) reproduction of the species incarnated in concrete individuals, in new children. (Ibid.)

According to Valeri, "the superiority of sacrificial links over genealogical ones is the superiority of action over passivity, of direct relations over indirect ones, and ultimately, of political relations over kinship" (ibid.: 114). By sacrifice, men born of women overcome the gender equality of their bilateral genealogical system to create a purely male political hierarchy. They accomplish this not by maintaining a system idealizing patrilineal descent, but by bringing under sacrificial control a single, purely male genealogical link, that between the king and the male gods, and making this link the basis of social continuity. In this way, sacrificially constituted divine ascent transcends bilateral descent. But the price of transcending dependence on women's reproductive powers by this particular sacrificial method is a degree of dependence on royal sacrifice so extreme as to make the entire system vulnerable. The best evidence of this vulnerability is the final collapse of the sacrificial system. To examine this, I turn to history (and the past tense).

The first encounter between Hawaiians and Europeans was in 1778. Cook's "discovery" of the islands happened to take place during the four months of Lono's annual return. According to Sahlins, the astonished Hawaiians mistook Captain Cook for Lono. The following year Cook returned, this time to the island of Hawaii, just as Lono's ritual circuit of the island was about to start, and, ignorant of this, Cook proceeded to circumnavigate the island at the same time, in the same clockwise direction. When he finally anchored, it was near an important Lono temple where he was worshiped by prostrate crowds, and, draped in the mantle of Lono's image, was made the recipient of sacrifices. Thousands of singing Hawaiians brought all kinds of agricultural bounty to his ships. Just before the end of Lono's allotted time, Cook sailed away, promising to return next year. A few weeks later, a storm having damaged a mast on one of his ships, he decided to put back to the harbor where he had received such extraordinary generosity. Alas, since Ku was now in the ascendancy, he was no longer welcomed as Lono, but was perceived as a threatening divine rival of the king. Hostilities followed, during which Cook was killed and then, in sacrifice to Ku, his cooked long bones were consecrated as an ancestral god of the reigning king (Sahlins 1981: 25).

Before this king died, he made known that he intended to leave the right to offer human sacrifice to his son Kiwalao and to leave his god, Ku-island-snatcher, signifying "the warlike side of kingship," to his nephew Kamehameha. After the king's death, Kiwalao began to distribute land to his followers in kingly fashion, but Kamehameha attacked and Kiwalao ended up on the altar (Valeri 1985: 161–62). The bones of Captain Cook now became Kamehameha's own ancestral god. After defeating and sacrificing a number of other rivals, Kamehameha, aided by arms from the British, finally became the first king to rule over all the islands.

The years of Kamehameha's reign were marked by increasing contact with foreigners. Exchanges with them, begun as sacrifices to Lono, became secular trade, especially in reprovisioning ships and in sandalwood, immensely valuable for trade with China. Sahlins identifies two important ways in which these contacts changed class and gender relations in Hawaiian society. Before the Europeans came, commoners had labored to supply all the material wants of the chiefs; as the commoners said, "A chief is a shark who travels on land" (Handy and Pukui 1972: 199). After contact, chiefly oppression increased. Great numbers of commoners were rounded up in corvee labor to bring sandalwood logs down from the rain forests. The king and his nobles used the taboos of the sacrificial system to keep control of such trade in their hands alone, and they did not allow the laborers time to work their family gardens. As commoners of both sexes began to go hungry, their loyalty to the chiefs weakened.

Sahlins points to relations between commoner women and European seamen as the other major source of change. Traditionally, commoner women, encouraged by their families, sought sexual encounters with male chiefs, and offspring of such unions greatly improved the lot of their mothers' families. If chiefly offspring are desirable, those of gods are even more so, and when Cook's ships arrived, great numbers of young women hurled themselves at the crew. "'No women I ever met with,' Cook wrote, 'were less reserved. Indeed, it appeared to me, that they visited us with no other view than to make a surrender of their persons'" (quoted in Sahlins 1981: 39). Even at the height of hostilities, after Cook was killed, women continued to visit the ships, swimming out at night at the risk of their lives. The British seamen relied on their own traditions to interpret the women's motives, and gave (at first unsolicited) payment for sexual services rendered. These gifts included not only costume jewelry and mirrors, but iron adzes and nails, greatly desired by commoner men. In this fashion, large amounts of foreign goods passed through women to common men: a second level of exchange developed, separate from that between chiefs and European traders.

This kind of exchange was not controlled by sacrificial taboos. Especially subversive was that the seamen expected the women to eat with them at the same table, sharing their pork, coconuts, and bananas, and these men were neither sacrificed as transgressors, nor struck dead by the gods. The commoner women, who had no positive reason for loyalty to the male chiefs' religion, accepted the invitations to dine with pleasure. As Sahlins says, "By eating with men—their sailor "husbands"—of foods reserved to the gods, Hawaiian women violated the sacred restrictions that had defined them as women" (1981: 52). Commoner men did not condemn such blasphemies because they benefited from the material rewards of this exchange system. The effect of both levels of trade was to undermine the ground on which the sacrificial hierarchy was built, by unifying the interests of common men and women in opposition to the chiefs.

The foreigners, once gods, were profaned by eating with women. But since they did not die from violating the taboos, they increased their power even while losing sacredness (ibid.: 54). To keep them away from his temples on the island of Hawaii, King Kamehameha moved the center of trade to Honolulu, and delegated the jobs of dealing with the foreign traders to his male affines, especially the relatives of his favorite wife. This woman, Kaahumanu, was also his most astute political advisor. Her brothers gained unusual political and economic power from the appointments, but they were not a danger to Kamehameha in the same way as his male collateral relatives, fellow members of the royal "lineage" who were potential rivals. Kamehameha kept his collateral relatives busy with temple affairs. He appointed a relatively low-ranking chief, a classificatory brother of his favorite wife, to supervise all trade and relations with foreigners. This man became known to foreigners as the "prime minister," and took the name "Billy Pitt."

Kamehameha's primary wife, Keopuolani, was the highest-ranking person (genealogically) on the island of Hawaii. Her father was Kamehameha's first sacrificed rival, his cousin Kiwalao; her mother was Kiwalao's full sister. Keopuolani was so high-ranking that wherever she went, everyone had to fall flat on the ground on pain of death. Her oldest son, Liholiho, was of higher genealogical rank than his father the king, and Kamehameha addressed him as "my god."

Before he died, Kamehameha, like the king who preceded him, gave his highest-ranking son the right to consecrate human sacrifice, "to show that he had chosen Liholiho as his successor," but he gave his god Ku-island-snatcher to his nephew Kekuaokalani (Valeri 1985: 333, 163). Some years later, in May of 1819, Kamehameha died, having created a new post, "regent," and appointed to it his wife Kaahumanu—or at least so she successfully claimed.

In traditional fashion, Liholiho went into seclusion for ten days after the king's death, while the sacrificial order was in chaos. When he returned, Kaahumanu tried to persuade him to end the food taboos on which the sacrificial order rested. His own mother supported her and, to prove it, ate forbidden food with his younger brother in Liholiho's presence (Kuykendall 1938: 67). Liholiho went back into seclusion. He has been called "weak, dull-minded" by those who knew him (ibid.: 61), but he was in a difficult position. He could either side with his cousin Kekuaokalani, owner of Ku-island-snatcher, who was defending the sacrificial system and who certainly intended to sacrifice Liholiho, or with his mother and stepmother, who would not sacrifice him, but were demanding the end of the sacrificial system.

When Liholiho returned for his installation in October 1819, his stepmother Kaahumanu took "the occasion to pronounce before the assembled Hawaiian notables the purported will of the deceased king that she rule jointly with his heir" (Sahlins 1981: 63). She and Liholiho's mother, with the support of Billy Pitt and other allies, had arranged a banquet at which Liholiho was to eat the gods' food with chiefly women. He did so, in great agitation, and immediately ordered the destruction of temples and divine images all over the kingdom. Says Valeri, "Henceforth the hierarchy survived only in its genealogical form and consequently in its female-centered mode of reproduction. It is no accident, then, that female, not male, chiefs played the most important political roles after the abolition of the Old Regime" (1985: 128).

Liholiho's cousin and rival, Kekuaokalani, owner of Ku-island-snatcher, began organizing to restore the sacrificial system and sacrifice Liholiho. But Kaahumanu urged her supporters, led by Billy Pitt, to attack at once before Kekuaokalani was well organized. Billy Pitt's forces, with better access to European arms, defeated and killed Kekuaokalani. He was not sacrificed, however, "since Liholiho had put an end to the sacrificial system, and therefore to the king's divinity" (ibid.: 163).

Not until the following year did the first missionaries set foot on the islands. When these Calvinists from Massachusetts arrived, they found a powerful champion in Kaahumanu.

The end of the Hawaiian sacrificial system has been a topic of some controversy among anthropologists. If women's roles are unrecognized, the collapse becomes strangely abrupt—"so it has seemed to students of Hawaiian history: a whole religion destroyed in a day, the 19th of October 1819" (Sahlins 1981: 55). Kroeber attributed the events of that day to "cultural fatigue," like metal fatigue, an unpredictable instantaneous disintegration (1948: 403–5).

Accounts of the sudden death of "Hawaiian religion" construe the state cult as the religion of the people, and its demise equally a loss for women and men, commoners and chiefs. "Until the arrival of the first Christian missionaries . . . the people of the archipelago were left without a shade of religious restraint or guidance" (Kalakaua 1888: 438). So wrote the last king of Hawaii. But Sahlins quotes a European living in Hawaii some years before the fall: "'The common people know nothing more about their religion than a stranger who never saw the islands.'" That a king should see the state cult as the religion of "the people" is understandable, but what is the motive of late twentieth-century scholars for doing likewise? "A people's abandonment of their traditional religious practices—not in favor of a new cult, but in exchange for nothing—is a highly unusual event" (Webb 1965: 21). Indeed, it is so unusual that it cannot be said to have happened even in Hawaii.

With the exception of Sahlins, most scholars (in true Hawaiian fashion) completely leave out of their analyses the commoner women who violated the food taboos for four decades before the end of the sacrificial system. Even Davenport's otherwise excellent account (1969) claims that contact with Europeans was mostly limited to chiefs, by which he means, of course, *male* contact with Europeans. Apparently Kaahumanu (and maybe many chiefly women, aware that common women survived their transgressions) had privately rejected the sacrificial food taboos for a long time. A Scotsman who lived in Hawaii from 1809 to 1810 wrote, "The women very seldom scruple to break [the taboos], when it can be done in secret . . . I once saw the queen [Kaahumanu] transgressing in this respect, and was strictly enjoined to secrecy, as she said it was as much as her life was worth" (Campbell, quoted in Sahlins 1981: 49).

Western males have been reluctant to recognize the extent of Kaahumanu's power. Early European sources credited Billy Pitt with being the real power. Hawaiian sources are clear that he was only her agent. Three years after the end of sacrifice, what is probably the first text written in Hawaiian described her as the "owner" of all the kingdom (Sahlins 1981: 56). Scholars too have discounted her role, and that of Keopuolani. For Webb, "the whim of a pair of even very powerful women" is not enough to account for the end of the sacrificial system. But Kaahumanu's motivations were no "whim." Had the sacrificial system remained intact, a new king, having sacrificed Liholiho, could end Kaahumanu's regency and redistribute the great tracts of land allotted to her brothers by Kamehameha. With sacrifice abolished, her power, and her brothers' land, would stay in the family. The end of sacrifice "had the effect not only of secularizing the Hawaiian polity, but also of making succession completely hereditary. . . . This served to stabilize . . . the central government" (Levin 1968: 425). The central government was mostly under Kaahumanu's control, and after her death, her regency was inherited by her sister's daughter.[4] Like a dike holding back the sea, the sacrificial system had kept women from access to political power and prevented that power from being inherited through women. Now the dike was broken.

SEVEN

Sacrifice, Descent, and the Patriarchs[1]

THIS SOCIOLOGY OF SACRIFICE has focused on ethnographic and historical accounts of traditions that are remote from American experience of organized religion. I want now to look through this same lens at something closer to home: the sacrificial literature of the Hebrew Bible. I shall ask the same questions about relations between sacrifice and family continuity that have been asked of ethnographic sources.

I do not propose to untangle Israelite sacrifice historically, but rather to look in detail at relations between sacrifice and descent in the biblical ancestor myths, the stories of the Patriarchs. I shall leave aside the question, dear to biblical scholars, of whether these stories provide historical information about actual society at the time of the Patriarchs.[2] Instead I shall identiy the three major Genesis sources and show how their very different sacrificial interests are consistent with their equally different interests in descent. This leads to a new understanding of the stories. (Readers unfamiliar with the stories of the Patriarchs will find this chapter easier to follow if they consult the genealogy following page 111 (fig. 5) and read Genesis 11:24–29:33.)

The biblical accounts of sacrifices and rules for sacrificing are the work of different authors, from different historical periods, themselves drawing on separate ancient oral traditions. These authors were not "objective" historians, nor were they interested in pure description of their own practices (Rogerson 1980: 45–49). What they say—and do not say—about sacrifice is shaped by their own particular interests. More complicated still, all of the various authors have conflicting things to say about sacrifice. It was just these conflicting accounts of sacrifice that allowed the great nineteenth-century biblical scholar Julius Wellhausen to conclude that the first five books of the Bible are not all from the hand of a forgetful and self-contradictory Moses, but are from four different major authors.

Wellhausen observed that the author of Deuteronomy (known to scholars as "D") recognizes that sacrifice at local sanctuaries and "high places" was once legitimate, but insists on a reform in which sacrifice may be offered only at the temple in Jerusalem. Two other authors know nothing of this centralization, so they must be earlier than D. These two take their names from their different names for the divinity: the Yahwist, "J" (from the German spelling, Jahweh), and the Elohist, "E." A fourth source, the priestly author, "P," takes centralization for granted as eternal tradition. Consequently, although he tells stories of earlier times than D, he must be later. Wellhausen dated J and E in the ninth and eighth centuries, D in the seventh, and P in the fifth century, and most scholars still generally agree, although perhaps making them, especially J, a little earlier. Wellhausen's account of the development of the priesthood followed similar lines: an early stage when there was no priesthood and sacrifice was a family or clan celebration, as in the stories of the Patriarchs; a second stage, at the time of the monarchy, when a Levitic priesthood began to emerge; and finally the post-exilic theocracy, in which the Aaronid priestly descent group ruled the nation and Levites in general were temple servants.[3]

These authors differ not only in their accounts of the location of sacrifice but also in the kinds of sacrifice they describe. J and E ignore sin offerings but they do describe the joyful meal before Yahweh, the peace offering, a communion sacrifice. For P expiatory sacrifice is primary and the peace offering has faded away. Wellhausen explained the shift from communion to expiation as, at first, following from centralization itself: as worship became separated from daily life, sacrifices not connected with a meal became more important. (As in most traditions, Israelite communion sacrifice was eaten, but eating expiatory sacrifice was restricted or forbidden.) Wellhausen understood the full development of sin offerings as a consequence of guilt: the Exile and the disasters preceding it created such despair that "the whole of the past is regarded as one enormous sin" (1885: 279). Although Wellhausen's account of the evolution of Israelite sacrifice has received considerable criticism,[4] this psychological explanation has been accepted for over a hundred years. A sociological explanation is more illuminating.

Just as the priestly descent group became more sharply differentiated from other groups, and especially when the Aaronids became an exclusive ruling group, so Israelite sacrifice became more expiatory. (A similar expiatory development occurred in the sacrifice of the Mass as the Christian priesthood became differentiated from the laity. See chapter 8.) According to P, the ordinary sin offering was almost identical in performance to the peace offering. But while the meat of the peace offering was shared among all present, the sin offering could be eaten *only* by males of the priestly lineage: an expiatory sacrifice for the general population and a communion sacrifice for priests only. The peace offering could join together all participating Israelites, but the sin offering indexed (identified and integrated) only the priestly descent group, sharply differentiating it from the rest of the population. Before the Exile (in the times of the peace offering) when priests were mere royal appointees, it was not nearly as important for them to differentiate their lineage as it was after the Exile when they ruled the country. And of course, J and E, who provide accounts of peace offerings, were relatively unconcerned with purity of priestly descent.

The sacrificial interests of the biblical authors have received much scholarly attention; their interests in descent have been comparatively ignored. Of all the sources, P is the most concerned with sacrifice and cult; J is the least sacrificial. The prescriptions for how to do sacrifices of various kinds are all P's work. P is also by far the most concerned with a pure and eternal patriline; J is the least concerned. It is P who repeats the phrase "Throughout your generations for ever" (e.g., Lev. 3:17; 10:9; 17:7; 23:31, 41; 24:3). Not all the genealogies in Genesis are P's, but all those long lists of "begats" are his. A comparison of J's genealogy in Gen. 4 with that of P in Gen. 5 shows that J's genealogy is not strictly unilineal: it includes named women who conceive and bear children. J begins this way: "Now Adam knew Eve his wife, and she conceived and bore Cain, saying 'I have gotten a man with the help of the Lord'" (4:1). P's account of the first generation goes this way: "When Adam had lived a hundred and thirty years, he begot a son in his own likeness, after his image and named him Seth" (5:3)[5] P's genealogy is perfectly patrilineal. No women are named; wives are not even mentioned as existing.

A respected biblical scholar has written:

> The term that is most typical of this source—one might call it P's signature—is *toledot,* etymologically "begettings", and hence also genealogy, line, family tree, . . . and by extension also story, history; . . . P's frequent recourse to the term *toledot* . . . is a correct reflection of the writer's abiding interest in genealogical detail. There must be no break in the chain of transmission through which God's dispensation has been handed down; hence it is essential to trace the pertinent line all the way back to Creation. . . . P's constant preoccupation with the purity of the line through which God's purpose has been implemented leads at times to motivations that are not found in the parallel versions. (Speiser 1964: xxiv–xxv)

Israelite priestly office, as described by P and later priestly sources, was always inseparable from pure patrilineal descent.[6] After the Exile, issues of descent had a unique urgency, for there was an immediate problem of deciding who among the returning exiles was a descendant of Abraham with rights in the community. It is typical that the priesthood clung to patrilineal descent as the only way to legitimate this inheritance. Ezra 2:59–63 refers to this time: "Those who could not prove their father's house or their descent . . . were excluded from the priesthood as unclean." In contrast, the prophet author of the last part of Isaiah, writing just after the Exile, ignored descent and claimed that the true heirs of Abraham were the righteous (Isa. 56:1–8).

Some biblical scholars, especially Protestants, seem to feel a kind of distaste for P's obsession with purity and continuity of descent and for his valuing the details of ritual exactness over moral concerns of a wider kind. J, who is everyone's favorite, is considered by some scholars to have been non- (or even anti-) sacrificial: "The J author disclosed his dislike for ritual acts of worship by omitting from the traditional [Genesis] stories all accounts of sacrifices" (Pfeiffer, 1947: 173). This view of J as radically anti-sacrificial is exaggerated, but not without grounds.[7]

The J material was probably written during the time of David and Solomon by a supporter (supporters?) of the early monarchy (Soggin, 1976: 102–3). Unlike priestly political interest in patriliny, no supporter of David could claim continuity of descent as the prerequisite for succession to royal office, since David excluded Saul's sons from succession.

The world that is disclosed in the stories of the Patriarchs (or in any narrative) is not permanently fixed in the text itself, but will vary with the context of meaning, including academic training, that the reader brings to the text (the situatedness of the interpreter). The stories as recounted below are read with reference to relations between sacrifice and descent, and therefore yield an interpretation which differs from that of orthodox biblical scholarship. And if an interpretation is judged by its power to make intelligible that which had been unintelligible, by how much it opens to understanding, this interpretation has validity, for it provides a single coherent context of meaning that illuminates more than one issue that is problematic for biblical scholars. (E.g., How can we understand the wife/sister stories? Why is Isaac such a shadowy figure?—or why was Rebekah's father so marginal? What is the significance of Isaac's taste for game?—or of Rachel's theft of her father's household gods? And so on.) Biblical scholars consider a number of confusing passages to be scribal errors or additions: Gen. 24:50; 25:19; and especially 49:26a. In the context of meaning presented here, all these passages can be understood to mean exactly what they say.

Throughout the stories of the Patriarchs, there is a continuing tension between descent from fathers and descent from mothers, which is treated in consistent and individually different ways by the three authors. P mostly refuses to acknowledge that such a problem exists. He cannot use sacrifice to remedy it because he excludes accounts of sacrifice from his own stories of the Patriarchs: It is not in his interest to legitimate sacrifice without priests. E, and especially J, recognize the descent problem, but J is willing to let it be, while E corrects it sacrificially. All accounts of sacrifice in the patriarchal stories are from E, and all remedy the descent from mothers (from Sarah, Rebekah, and Rachel) that threatens unilineal descent from fathers. Only J tolerates "bilateral" descent and consequently needs no sacrificial remedies. P and J both exclude sacrifice from their Genesis stories, but for different reasons.

J's regular recognition of descent from women presents a real threat to "eternal" patrilineal continuity. As an illustration of how such recognition destroys the continuity of the patriline, consider P's genealogy of Abraham in Gen. 11. In the tenth ascending generation only the name of Noah is needed for perfect continuity. But had bilateral descent been consistently recognized, for perfect continuity one thousand and twenty-four ancestors would have had to be named in Noah's generation—a task beyond even P's ability.

Some societies protect unilineal continuity by denying one parent's role in procreation. There was, for example, the firmly accepted idea in ancient Greek society (and still current in Western society despite modern embryology) that only the father is the real parent, the mother being just the nurse for the seed (*Eumenides* 658, in Aeschylus 1926: 335). (Conversely, there are examples in societies stressing descent through mothers of the strongly held idea that only the mother counts in procreation [Cf. Malinowski 1948: 220–31].)[8] Israelite tradition did not deny descent from women and consequently faced the dilemma: How is a pure and eternal patriline to be maintained if descent from women is not denied? Endogamy appears to be a solution; marriage to a woman of the same patrilineage ensures the offsprings' patrilineage membership even if it is figured through the mother.

Close agnatic endogamy (marriage within the patriline) is extremely rare except in Semitic traditions. In a way reminiscent of the Patriarchs, throughout the Arab world families have preferred men to marry their father's brother's daughters.[9] The descent line of the Patriarchs continued only through endogamy: Isaac and Jacob (but not Ishmael) married endogamously. Joseph married exogamously but his sons were adopted by Jacob, correcting this, and other, irregularities of their descent. Agnatic endogamy does seem to solve the dilemma of how to maintain unilineal descent from fathers while recognizing descent from mothers. But notice that it also conceals a conflict: it is unclear about which is the "real" parent through whom unilineal descent flows.

Some Semitic societies still face similar difficulties. According to the American anthropologists R. F. Murphy and L. Kasdan, agnatic endogamy "produces a latent bilateral structure that is the very antithesis of the patrilineal ideology." In Bedouin genealogies, as in P's, "patrilineality is maintained by the suppression of female names—indeed of the very fact of marriage. . . . The patrilineality of endogamous descent groups is an untruth that can perdure only through a suppression of truth" (1967: 13).[10]

In the stories of the Patriarchs there are three superintensive representations of agnatic endogamy, three accounts in which husband and wife are presented, or present themselves, as brother and sister (Abraham and Sarah twice, Gen 12:10–20 and 20:1–18, J and E; Isaac and Rebekah once, 26:6–11, J). Biblical scholars, who are burdened with the requirement that the Patriarchs be respectable, have long wrestled with these embarrassing wife/sister accounts, which appear to portray the Patriarchs as either liars or incestuous. All three accounts tell of a Patriarch in a foreign land who, fearing that he would be killed by those coveting his beautiful wife, claimed she was his sister. The king of the country took her into his harem, was beset with catastrophes, recognized his error and restored her. E's account states that Sarah was an actual half sister of Abraham, having the same father but a different mother. Such a marriage would be impossible in any regular patrilineal descent system. Unless we reject E's account (thereby making the Patriarchs liars) we must see here a recognition of descent from women so pronounced as to be almost "matrilineal," for if Abraham and Sarah had the same father but different mothers, it is *only* as their mothers' offspring that their marriage was not incestuous. There is no way P would have told such a story.

These accounts (none in P, one in E, two in J) are exactly consistent with the various authors' willingness to recognize ambiguity of descent between fathers and mothers. J even allows uncertainty about Isaac's paternity: only E says Sarah was untouched by the king (20:4).

The archaeological discovery of the Nuzi texts, cuneiform legal documents from a city in Haran (an area in Mesopotamia which was Abraham's original homeland and the home of Rebekah, Rachel, and Leah) spurred on biblical scholars' longing to ground the Patriarchs in a real historical society. Some of these texts record a marriage in which the wife was adopted as the husband's sister. Drawing very general conclusions from these texts, Speiser believed he had finally solved the mysteries of the wife/sister accounts:

In Hurrian society the bonds of marriage were strongest and most solemn when the wife had simultaneously the juridical status of a sister, regardless of actual blood ties. . . . The practice was apparently a reflection of the underlying fratriarchal system, and it gave the adoptive brother greater authority than was granted the husband. (1964: 92)

Speiser believed this was a general practice of upper-class Hurrian society. The "underlying fratriarchal system" on which his explanation depends presupposes "survivals" of an original "matriarchal" system in which brothers, rather than husbands or fathers, would possess what family authority a man might have. In actual matrilineal systems the mother's brother is, of course, the head of the family.

Speiser's explanation has been powerfully undermined by Greengus (1975) and others.[11] Greengus shows that of thirteen texts concerning Nuzi sister adoption only three also include a marriage, and all involve those at the very bottom of Nuzi society. The adoptive sisters were commonly slaves, and in one case the adoptive brother was given the right to make the woman work as a prostitute. Greengus has no alternative explanation to offer, and although the failure of Nuzi sister adoption to fulfill the respectability requirement for Patriarchal antecedents is a devastating argument against Speiser's theory, no one has yet suggested a better one. According to Cazelles, the Nuzi contracts are still the best background for the wife/sister accounts. "Greengus is far from contradicting Speiser on this point" (1978: 241).

Constructing an entire historical society from the impoverished medium of three cuneiform texts is precarious work. It seems more useful to think of the wife/sister accounts as symbolizing genuine social issues rather than as recording actual social practices. Speiser's theory depends for sense upon an "underlying fratriarchal system," that is, an underlying system of matrilineal descent. He did not see that positing such a system endangers patriarchal descent. Imagine a society in which wives are regularly adopted as sisters: the practice can best be understood as a solution to a conflict between patrilineal and matrilineal systems. A man is at the same time the father and the mother's brother of his children. His son is also his nephew and can inherit both patrilineally and matrilineally from his father-uncle. This would solve all kinds of inheriance problems, but concealed within it is still the potential conflict: Whose is the son?—the mother's or the father's? Is the line of descent really through fathers?—or is it through women? A similar conflict can be identified in the patriarchal narratives. The Patriarchs themselves are represented as figuring (or wanting to figure) descent through fathers, but J and E represent the families of their wives as figuring descent through mothers. (When I use the phrase "mother's son" below, I mean that a son's descent from his mother is recognized to a degree that threatens patriliny.)

The patriarchal narratives tell the story of the resolution of this descent conflict, a resolution in which sacrifice plays a crucial role. A reading in these terms reveals a steady development of an increasingly tense "plot": Will Isaac's loss of control over his descent line destroy the patriarchal line? Will Laban, the mother's brother, triumph and succeed in claiming Jacob's sons as his own? Of course hope for the final resolution is held out from the beginning in the meaning of Abraham's name: "The father is exalted."[12] Biblical scholars have not recognized this descent conflict in their interpretations of the patriarchal narratives because they bring to the stories a presupposition of established certainty of patrilineal descent not to be found in the text, except in P.

J, E, and P naturally differ in their account of Abraham's descent problems. For P there is almost no such problem. There is a hint of trouble in Sarah's initial barrenness (16:1) but it is solved without conflict. Sarah gave Abraham her maid Hagar, who bore Ishmael (16:15–16).[13] Chapter 17 is pure P. "And I will establish my covenant between me and you and your descendants after you throughout their generations for an everlasting covenant" (17:7) said God Almighty (P's special term) to Abraham. God Almighty's blessing of Sarah is certainly problematic for patriliny: "I will bless her, and she shall be a mother of nations; kings of peoples shall come from her" (17:16b). There is also some related obscurity, for some versions of 17:16, including the Septuagint, read "he" and "him," meaning Isaac, as the source of the issue. Only these passages suggest descent conflict in P. Isaac was born and circumcised with no reference to strife in the home.

J and E, on the other hand, tell stories full of conflict over issues of descent. Sarah, in offering Hagar, said, "It may be that I shall have children through her." But Ishmael, although he was Abraham's son, turned out not to be Sarah's. Ishmael was the offspring of an exogamous union (Hagar was an Egyptian) and descent from Abraham alone was not enough to make him the true heir. Ishmael was only a "father's son"—insufficient for continuity. Only Isaac could be the true heir, for he could trace his patrilineal descent through his mother (who, according to E, had the same father as Abraham).[14]

When Sarah demanded that Hagar and Ishmael be sent away, J's Abraham was putty in her hands. E (21:10–13) tried to save the patriarchal image: Abraham obeyed not Sarah, but God, who told him to do whatever Sarah said since his line of descent would be through Isaac.[15] In J's story, the angel of the Lord said directly to Hagar, alone in the wilderness, "I will so greatly multiply your seed that it cannot be numbered for multitude" (16:10). This is too much for E. His version cleans things up patrilineally: God said to *Abraham*, "I will make a nation of the son of the slave woman also, because he is your seed" (21:13).[16]

The barrenness of the Patriarchs' wives always indicates descent problems. J accents Sarah's barrenness by reporting that the wife and concubine of Abraham's brother Nahor have borne him twelve sons. (A winner in the patriarchal descent struggle must beget twelve sons.)[17]

J leaves Isaac as much a "mother's son" as a "father's son," but E's story (22:1–19) of the near sacrifice of Isaac restores him to patriliny.[18] At the last minute Abraham's hand was stayed and he offered a ram in place of Isaac. By this act, Isaac, on the edge of death, received his life not by birth from his mother but from the hand of his father as directed by God (Elohim); and the granting of life was a deliberate, purposeful act rather than a mere natural process, a spiritual "birth" accomplished without female assistance. Abraham received, at this sacrifice, assurance of countless descendants. J has no parallel to this story.[19] (In Islamic tradition, the Arabs being descendants of Ishmael, it was Ishmael and not Isaac who was nearly sacrificed and who carried the important line of descent. See Combs-Schilling 1989 for an account of Ibrahim's near sacrifice of Isma'il as transcendent male childbirth.)

The story of Isaac is a patriarchal cautionary tale. Isaac is a transformation of the same theme as Abraham, but *without sacrifice*. Like Abraham, Isaac married a patrilineal classificatory sister. Like Abraham, his brother had twelve sons while his own wife was barren. Like Abraham, Isaac claimed his wife was his sister and she spent a time in a foreign king's harem. Like Abraham, he had two sons, the older a "father's son," the younger a "mother's son," who also carried the ambiguous line of descent. The outside/inside contrast, which in Abraham's generation was a feature of the two women (one exogamous, the other endogamous), has shifted to the two sons: Esau was a man of the outdoors, "a skillful hunter, a man of the field, while Jacob was a quiet man, dwelling in tents" (25:27). The stories of both Abraham and Isaac tell of conflict about descent, but Abraham saved patrilineal descent by sacrificing, and Isaac never sacrificed. In the Isaac stories the descent conflict latent in the Abraham narratives is played out to its full disastrous consequences.

Even P, who typically ignores most of Isaac's crisis of descent, does not pretend that things were otherwise. Gen. 25:19 begins, in P's usual style, "These are the generations of Isaac: . . ." (literally "the begettings of Isaac"). When P does that elsewhere a long list of patrilineal descendants follows, but here P begins and ends, "Abraham begot Isaac." That is, P records *no* begettings of Isaac. "Abraham begot Isaac" is a "generation" of Abraham. This is so unlike P that scholars conclude it is a scribal error:

> "Abraham begot Isaac" gives the appearance of being a gloss by a scribe who missed a heading, "These are the generations of Abraham." To have Isaac's birth mentioned in his own genealogy is quite without parallel. (Cross, 1973: 303–4)

But P may have intended just what the text says: Isaac was begotten but did not perpetuate his patriline. P says nowhere that Isaac begot Jacob and Esau. He only tells us that Isaac married Rebekah," sister of Laban the Aramaean"—and this is also the key to the problem.

The story begins in Gen. 24, J's well-known account of the quest for Rebekah. Abraham, concerned that Isaac not marry exogamously in Canaan, instructed a servant to return to his native Haran for an endogamous bride for Isaac. Aware of the dangers of Hurrian (Aramaean) "matriliny," Abraham twice warned the servant on no account to take Isaac (24:6,8). Rebekah's father, Bethuel, was doubly a patrilineal nephew of Abraham. (See figure 5.) For agnatic endogamy, Rebekah should have been a perfect bride. But, strangely, J describes her family as organized around descent from her mother instead of her father. J presents kinship relations at Rebekah's "mother's household" (24:28) as so consistent with matriliny that to make them conform to patriliny requires supposing, on no other grounds, that there is an error in the text. Biblical scholars accept this solution, but it is more faithful to the text to conclude that J meant what he said. Speiser comments,

> Rebekah's father Bethuel, however, presents some difficulties in the present context . . . In vs. 50 . . . the text states that "Laban and Bethuel spoke up in reply." The listing of the father after the son is irregular enough; what is worse, no gifts for the father are mentioned in vs. 53, although the recipients include Rebekah's "brother and mother" as well as the young woman herself; similarly in vs. 55 it is once again "her brother and her mother" who ask that Rebekah postpone her journey, while nothing is said about the father. Hence there can be little doubt that Bethuel was no longer alive at the time, which is why Laban was free to exercise his prerogative as brother. . . . The inclusion of Bethuel in vs. 50 is due either to a marginal gloss inspired by the genealogical references, or to some textual misadventure. (1964: 184)

All these "difficulties" vanish if the family was "matrilineal," or rather, if J wished to recognize descent through women. In a matrilineal system, Laban, as Rebekah's brother, would be in a position of authority concerning her marriage; quite likely only he, his sister, and their mother would receive gifts or be in a position to decide the date of Rebekah's departure. That Rebekah's own consent was required for her marriage and departure (24:38) is inconsistent with ordinary patrilineal virilocal marriage, and so surely is her family's final blessing: "Our sister, become thousands of ten thousands, and may your seed possess the gate of those who hate them" (24:60).

J's well-known story tells how Rebekah, after years of barrenness, finally gave birth to twins. Esau the hunter, the older, was a hairy "father's son," and Jacob was a smooth-skinned "mother's son": "Isaac loved Esau because he ate of his game; but Rebekah loved Jacob" (24:28). Isaac's taste for game must be understood in sacrificial terms; in the Bible the difference between game and domestic animals is a sacrificial difference. All over the world game is ordinarily unsuitable for sacrifice.[20] Among the Israelites, only domestic animals and sometimes birds or humans were suitable victims, never game. According to the Holiness Code, domestic animals once were slaughtered only sacrificially (Lev.17:3−4). D, in calling for centralization, allowed domestic animals to be slaughtered without sacrifice as if they were game, "like the gazelle and the hart" (Deut. 12:15). Although J (typically) never listed rules for sacrificing, it is safe to conclude he was aware of game as specifically non-sacrificial meat. J's Isaac did not merely fail to sacrifice, like Hawaii's Liholiho, he explicitly avoided doing so, with consequences (but for Jacob's saving sacrifice) nearly as disastrous. Isaac's refusal to sacrifice led to his loss of control of his line of descent.

J's Gen. 27 tells how the failing and nearly blind Isaac commanded Esau to go out to hunt for game "such as I love," to prepare and serve it in order to receive his father's blessing as the heir. Rebekah, who overheard, ordered Jacob to kill two kids of the flock (domestic animals), to prepare and serve them to his father, and receive for himself the blessing. Jacob protested, but was told to do as his mother said. She disguised him with the skins of the "victims" so that blind Isaac, feeling for his hairy son Esau, was deceived and gave Jacob his irrevocable blessing. When the deception was discovered to the rage and dismay of Isaac and Esau, Rebekah ordered Jacob to flee to her brother's home in Haran.

Descent flows through this blessing (Westermann 1985: 444), as it does throughout the Genesis blessings (including Rebekah's family's blessing). Blessings from God are similar in that they are primarily the granting of descendants (e.g., 15:5; 16:10; 17:5ff.; 22:17; 26:4,24; 28:14; 35:11). In conveying descendants, all these blessings also convey a line of descent.

This entire story is from J. P tells it otherwise (27:46; 28:1−9): there was no deception, no descent conflict, no "mother's son" opposed to a "father's son." Isaac himself, well and uninterested in game, sent Jacob off, but only to get a wife in order to become fruitful and multiply. Laban is called the son of Bethuel. In J's version he is only Rebekah's brother. In P's account there has been no threat to the paternal line. In J's account all appears lost, and Jacob, the sister's son, fleeing his paternal relatives, has gone to the mother's brother in "matrilineal" Haran, taking with him the blessing of the heir, the line of descent.

Jacob's arrival in Haran (J) repeats the themes of Abraham's servant's arrival there in quest of Rebekah. Also at a well, Jacob recognized Rachel. She brought him to her father, Laban, Jacob's mother's brother, who said (ominously), "Surely you are my bone and my flesh" (29:14). Now we see why Abraham was so adamant about not allowing Isaac to go to Haran, for Jacob, entangled in the local "matrilineal" scene, a sister's son working for his mother's brother, married uxorilocally and avunculocally[21] to his mother's brother's daughters, could not escape for twenty years. Now, when descent through mothers appears to have triumphed, the repeated theme of two siblings, the younger carrying the important line of descent, becomes for the only time two sisters: Leah and Rachel.

The discussion among biblical scholars (see Van Seters 1975: 78–85) as to whether Laban did or did not adopt Jacob becomes superfluous if Laban's family is seen as figuring descent through women. In matrilineal systems, the sister's son is regularly the mother's brother's heir. Looked at this way, the uncertainty about whether Jacob was or was not recognized as Laban's heir becomes a feature of the uncertainty about whether Jacob's descent is to be figured through women as Laban's sister's son, or patrilineally as Isaac's son.

Jacob wanted to marry Rachel in return for seven years service to Laban, but, J tells us, Laban gave him Leah instead and Jacob served seven more years for Rachel. Leah bore six sons (her share of the twelve needed to win) and the sisters' two maids each bore Jacob two sons. The two maids are structurally necessary since Rachel, in whom the descent conflict centers, must bear only two sons, but nevertheless Jacob must end up with twelve sons. Rachel, like Sarah and Rebekah, was barren for some years, indicating that she, not Leah, is the one to watch for developments in the descent conflict. Finally she gave birth to Joseph. Jacob now had eleven sons—still one short. (Meanwhile, back in "patrilineal" Canaan, Jacob's brother Esau had, of course, begotten twelve sons.)

Laban was a paradigm of the authoritarian mother's brother, except that he acted alone in decisions about his daughters' marriages. But Rachel and Leah appear to have had neither mother nor brothers; even in an actual matrilineal system, under such conditions, a father might well have similar authority. What is important is that J and E not only describe Laban's family as one in which there was no descent of authority from father to son,[22] but on the contrary as one in which Laban himself insisted on the principle of descent through women. For example, when he overtook the fleeing Jacob, Laban claimed that "the daughters are my daughters and the sons are my sons" (31:43)—these "sons" being the ones everyone else thinks of as Jacob's sons, and whose relation to Laban can only be traced through women.

Genesis 31 begins the resolution of the conflict in favor of patriliny. It is mostly E's work,[23] but even J (31:3) says the Lord told Jacob, "Return to the land of your fathers . . ." According to E, Rachel and Leah encouraged the departure, saying that Laban regarded them "as foreigners," as not members of his family (31:15). E's account makes even Jacob's right to the flocks he took with him a matter of the animals' divinely ordained paternity (31:10–12), while for J their breeding is ambiguous to say the least (30:25–43). E cleans up Jacob's morality but leaves Rachel's in bad shape: She stole and took with her Laban's "household gods."

Rachel's theft has almost as long a history of attempted interpretation as the wife/sister accounts.[24] Like them, an interpretation based on the Nuzi texts has been widely accepted. This claims that "possession of the house gods could signify legal title to a given estate" (Speiser, 1964: 250); and therefore Rachel stole them to legitimate Jacob's possession of the flocks he took with him. Greenberg has criticized this interpretation:

> What is determined by bequeathal of the gods is not title to an inheritance share but, rather, who is to carry on as paterfamilias . . . Hence Rachel's desire to possess the gods of Laban, if it meant anything in this connection, could mean only that she wished Jacob to be recognized as paterfamilias after Laban's death. (1962: 242)

But Jacob had no desire to be "paterfamilias" in Laban's family, says Greenberg, and even had he so desired, possessing the gods must condemn him as a thief. The only way "the regnant view of Rachel's motives" can be accepted is if Rachel "acted irrationally, or under gross misapprehension of the legal effect of the theft" (ibid.: 244).

Greenberg's own interpretation is based on an anecdote by Josephus about a Parthian woman, a "millennium and a half" after Rachel, who took her gods along when going abroad. Like her, according to Greenberg, Rachel took Laban's gods to continue her customary worship. That Greenberg is willing to turn to an unrelated society fifteen hundred years later to support his interpretation is indicative of the lengths to which competent and erudite biblical scholars will go rather than recognize descent through women.

Greenberg cleared away the obscuring idea that possession of the gods legitimated rights in property alone, and recognized that what was legitimated was control over a line of descent, that is, control over a social structure organized around property. But for him this must mean Jacob's right to be "paterfamilias," and because he did not see that Laban's line of descent was through women, he was obliged to reject that whole scheme of interpretation.

From the point of view of the continuing conflict of descent, Rachel's theft, which only became necessary when she was going to Jacob's father's home, was to legitimate her claim to Joseph as a "mother's son," as her descendant in her family's line of descent through mothers. Her possession of the gods would make Jacob not a "paterfamilias" but a mere husband in a system of descent through women.

Rachel's theft is the reverse of Jacob's theft from Isaac and Esau, and her theft is necessary to balance and correct his. Jacob stole a paternal line. Rachel stole a maternal line. Jacob's departure for "matrilineal" Haran was a consequence of his theft. Rachel's theft was a consequence of her departure for "patrilineal" Canaan. Both used deceit to gain control of a line of descent and both thereby lost it. But Jacob's loss was only temporary, for Rachel's loss is like a double negative, canceling out his. Rachel's theft is E's antidote to J's chapter 27.

The interpretation that Rachel had stolen her family's line of descent through women makes increasing sense as E's story continues: Laban pursued and overtook Jacob, and was angry about the theft of his gods, daughters, and grandchildren, but didn't even mention the flocks. Jacob, unaware that Rachel was the thief, told Laban to search: Anyone found with the gods would die. Laban searched first Jacob's tent, then Leah's, then the two handmaidens', but did not find them. Rachel, meanwhile, had hidden them under a camel saddle, and when Laban entered her tent to search, she was sitting upon it. She apologized for not rising, "but the way of women is upon me." (E here presupposes the Levitical Law, according to which anyone who touched what a menstruating woman was resting on became unclean.)

The deliberate, purposeful use of menstrual blood (that polluting "opposite" of purifying sacrificial blood) occurs nowhere in the Bible except in this story of a woman's struggle for control of a line of descent. Just as J's story of Jacob's theft opposed the killing of domestic animals to that of killing game, so E's story of Rachel's theft is told in terms of an even stronger sacrificial opposition. From a patrilineal perspective, both are tales of shocking actions by women from the same dangerous

line of descent through mothers. In E's story the blasphemy has esca-
lated—but not the threat to patriliny. J's Rebekah deceived her husband
Isaac. Had it been Jacob whom Rachel defeated by her deliberate use of
menstrual blood, this would surely have been patriliny's darkest day—
but it was only Laban, a father, it is true, but one from the "matrilineal"
side. Before E's story is finished, the sentence of death Jacob foretold for
the thief has been carried out and Rachel has met a final defeat.

Failing to recover his ancestral idols, Laban admitted defeat and
proposed a covenant between himself and Jacob. In J's account, Jacob
and Laban made a mound of stones and concluded their covenant. But
E does not leave it at that.[25] Once again he restores patriliny by sacrifice.
Laban invoked "the God of Abraham, the God of Nahor, the God of
their father" to keep peace between them, and Jacob swore by the
"Fear"[26] of his father Isaac. Then he sacrificed (his first sacrifice) and
invited his "brothers" to eat.

Sense requires that Laban must have shared the sacrificial meal, yet,
as one biblical scholar writes, "Laban is not said to partake, but the
'brethren' of Jacob," and Jacob had no brethren with him (Thompson
1963: 67). Interpreted in terms of relations between sacrifice and patriliny, this obscurity vanishes. Jacob and Laban's resolution of their descent conflict was to rephrase their relationship, by means of sacrifice,
in terms of patrilineal descent. This is why the invocation was to "the
God of Abraham, the God of Nahor, the God of their father." Nahor,
Abraham's brother, was Laban's patrilineal grandfather, just as Abraham
was Jacob's patrilineal grandfather. The father of both Abraham and
Nahor was the ancestor who represented the point of patrilineal alliance
between Jacob and Laban. This common great grandfather is what anthropologists call an "apical ancestor."[27] (In ancestral cults, the ancestors who are ritually important are just those that mark alliances and
distinctions between lineages.) In terms of this sacrifice, Laban was no
longer Jacob's mother's brother, but one of his "brethren," his patrilineal
classificatory brother. Jacob had sacrificially reconstituted (had at-oned)
their descent relations: they had become agnates sacrificing together.

E's story continues after sacrifice has restored patriliny. Rachel bore
a second son, and following a hard labor, died in childbirth. The same
birth that killed Rachel made Jacob the father of the necessary twelve
sons. "And as her soul was departing (for she died) she called his name
Ben-oni, but his father called his name Benjamin" (35:18). There are
two others accounts of name changes in the patriarchal narratives:
those Patriarchs who restored patriliny by sacrifice, Abraham and Jacob, also changed their names. Those who did not sacrifice and who
lost control of their line of descent, Isaac and Joseph, did not change
names.[28] Benjamin's name change surely indicates that he too has

crossed over into patriliny. The name Benjamin means literally "son of the right (side or hand)." For evidence, also from E, that the Israelite tradition, like other sacrificial traditions, associated the right side with the proper line of paternal descent, see Gen. 48:13–19. The name Ben-oni, "son of my sorrow," reflects Rachel's post-sacrificial defeat, for Benjamin was not a "mother's son." Only one of the twelve sons, Joseph, born before the sacrifice, was a "mother's son."

P ignores all this. For P, Jacob acquired wives without conflict with Laban, begot twelve sons uneventfully in Paddan-aram, including Benjamin, who never had another name (35:26). Jacob departed in peace with all his wives, sons, flocks, and possessions "to go to his father, Isaac" (31:18b). There was no theft of Laban's gods, no sacrificial reconstituting of kinship with Laban (nor any need for it), no death in childbirth, and Isaac was still alive when Jacob returned to him.

Rachel's sons, Joseph and Benjamin, are another version of the two siblings theme. Ishmael and Esau, as father's sons, were excluded from the patriarchal line of descent. Joseph, as a mother's son, also could not directly carry the line of descent, for the Patriarchs' underlying line of descent through mothers needed to be decently veiled by patriliny.

The story of Joseph belongs to a separate literary tradition from the rest of the patriarchal narratives, almost certainly much later than J or E. Certain portions of the text, however, are not part of the original Joseph narrative, but are more consistent with the other patriarchal narratives. The evidence that Joseph was a "mother's son" is found only in these portions. There are two such indications. The first, and less important, is in P's account of Jacob's adoption of Joseph's sons (48:3–6). Being P's account, this passage naturally does not recognize descent from women, or indicate positively that Joseph is a "mother's son." It simply wipes out any remaining problems of descent from Rachel. Jacob (who, in E's parallel account of this final restoration of patriliny, had thought it wise to sacrifice again before setting out) has arrived in Egypt and been reunited with his lost son. Prefacing his demand with a reference to God Almighty's appearance to him when he was promised countless descendants, he said to Joseph: "Ephraim and Manasseh shall be mine, but progeny born after them shall remain yours." He explained this as consoling him for Rachel's death, but nevertheless, he adopted them as *Leah's* children, ensuring that their descent was uncomplicated by Rachel's theft. Joseph's own "progeny" could not be direct descendants of Jacob. (Manasseh and Ephraim, to put them in the order of their birth, are the final version of the theme of two siblings.)

The second justification is far more significant. Once again it is a matter of taking at face value a passage that scholars reject as meaningless because they do not recognize descent through women. The passage is in the "Blessing of Jacob" (Gen. 49). This ancient poem is older than the work of J, E, or P, although it was probably incorporated by J. It is the testament given by the aged and dying Jacob to his twelve sons, one by one. As in other Genesis blessings, descent flows through the blessing. All twelve sons were blessed, but only Joseph received a blessing of the mother: "blessings of the breasts and the womb" (49:25). Biblical scholars who try to explain this blessing of the mother do not ask why only Joseph was so blessed, nor do they consider that a social issue of descent may have been involved.[29]

The next verse (49:26a) continues Jacob's Blessing and is a lucid and explicit expression of the conflict and resolution of patriarchal descent: It condenses the whole story into a single phrase. But scholars are in universal agreement that it is an untranslatable scribal error. Back in 1611 when this passage was still being translated, the King James Version rendered it this way: "The blessings of thy father have prevailed above the blessings of my progenitors unto the utmost bound of the everlasting hills: they shall be on the head of Joseph, and on the crown of him that was separate from his brethren." The obstacle is the word translated as "my progenitors" (*horay*). The Hebrew word is "conceivers," otherwise found in the Bible only in the feminine singular, meaning "mother" (Hos. 2:5; Song of Sol. 3:4) Here it is masculine plural, a form scholars find "incomprehensible" (Westermann, 1985: 241); "hopeless" (Speiser, 1964: 368); "v. 26a is obviously corrupt and cannot be restored" (Vawter, 1955: 16).

In Hebrew, as in French, the masculine form takes precedence over the feminine whenever the referent includes both males and females. The ancient poet needed a word referring to Rebekah and to Laban and probably also to their whole family, including Rachel. (Jacob's struggle was with Laban, not with Rebekah.) Not having access to terms like "matrilineal descent group" the author sensibly, grammatically, and aesthetically chose "conceivers," in the masculine plural. The passage is to be understood this way: The blessings of (and therefore descent from) your father (Jacob, who restored patriliny by sacrifice) have prevailed over the blessings of (descent from) my conceivers (my mother's family: Laban and his line of descent through mothers) unto the utmost bound of the everlasting hills.

That 49:26a should remain unintelligible for hundreds of years is a vivid example of how the situatedness of the interpreter limits the possibilities of interpretation. Having taken patrilineal descent for granted, scholars cannot see its establishment as an achievement, and consequently they cannot ask how it is achieved.

I have discussed these stories not as records of patriarchal history, but to identify the different positions of the three authors on issues of descent and sacrifice. J, whose characters build altars but never sacrifice on them, reveals the ambiguity of patriarchal descent most fully. The entire story of the disastrous course into "matriliny" is his, from the quest for Rebekah through Jacob's integration into Laban's family. J's resolution covers this with a decent patrilineal veil, but leaves ambiguity underneath. E recognizes the ambiguity of patriarchal descent as a menace to be remedied sacrificially. Just as all the accounts of sacrifice are his, so also are all the high points of the achievement of patriliny. He tells nothing about Isaac's loss of his line of descent, but the whole cycle of stories restoring patriliny are his, beginning with Rachel and Leah's complaint that Laban had cast them out of the family, through Rachel's theft, Jacob's sacrifice, Rachel's death in childbirth, Benjamin's name change, and finally, the adoption of Joseph's sons.[30] Except for this final patrilineal triumph, P does not tell any of these great stories. Since he can recognize only priestly sacrifice, he relies on denial rather than sacrifice to defend patriarchal descent. He (almost completely) ignores the danger and gives a bland account of an (almost) unchallenged eternal continuity of patrilineal descent.

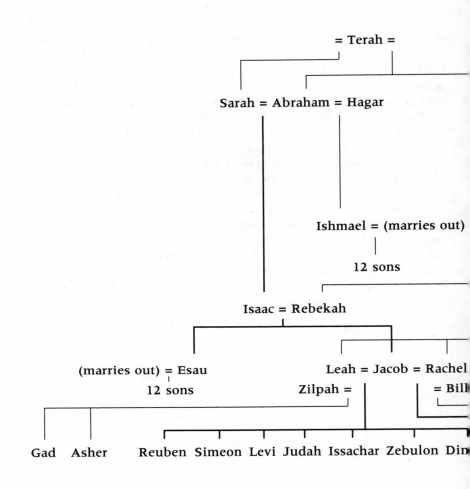

Fig. 5. Terah genealogy. (Endogamous marriages, and descent from them

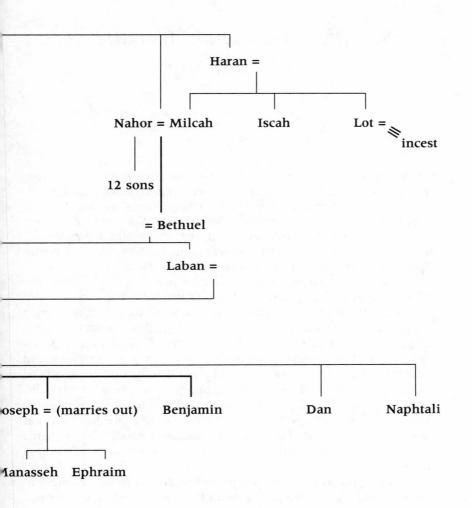

Haran =

Nahor = Milcah   Iscah   Lot = ≡ incest

12 sons

= Bethuel

Laban =

oseph = (marries out)   Benjamin   Dan   Naphtali

Manasseh   Ephraim

narked in heavy lines.)

EIGHT

Sacrifice and Social Structure in Christianity

TURNING TO CHRISTIAN SACRIFICE, our interest is still in relations between social organization and the performance of sacrificial ritual, just as it was in examining the Greek, African, Hawaiian, and Israelite traditions. In the Roman Church, where the sacrificial cult has historically been most elaborately developed, regular sacrificial practice has never been separable from clearly defined hierarchical social structure organized in unilineal "eternal" continuity of descent between males: the Apostolic Succession of the sacrificing priesthood. Historians describe changes in eucharistic practice and theology, and they also describe changes in Church social organization, but they do not describe them as features of one another.[1] Nevertheless, all major developments of sacrificial practice and theology have involved corresponding developments of Church social organization. One of the most striking and consistent of these correspondences is that throughout the sacrificial tradition, precisely as the one line of priestly descent became more differentiated from the laity, so did the eucharistic sacrifice become more expiatory, an increasingly non-alimentary separating sacrifice. And after Vatican II, as clerical-lay distinctions diminished, so did the Eucharist become less expiatory, including a renewed extension of alimentary communion.

This chapter focuses on changes in liturgy and related changes in social organization in the post-Vatican II Church; the many other important changes of Vatican II will be left aside.[2] Because Christian positions on sacrifice are themselves interpretations of the Church's sacrificial history and cannot be understood apart from it, a discussion of the historical background is unavoidable. Similarly, because Christian sacrificers have understood themselves to be acting not as ordinary humans but as participants in divine action, even a strictly sociological account must acknowledge a range of theological positions or distort sacrificers' understandings of their own actions beyond recognition.

For Christians, there is ultimately only one sacrifice, in which Christ is understood to be both priest and victim. But because sociology is concerned with human rather than divine action, we reverse the theological order of precedence and focus, not on the death of Christ, but on the regularly repeated sacrificial rituals. Historically, the Eucharist has been sometimes a sacrifice and sometimes not: an effective, actual sacrifice for some, and most explicitly not one for others. Christians have been willing to die for each of these opposed interpretations.

Because there is only one sacrifice, for the Eucharist itself to be sacrifice, bread and wine must become body and blood of the one victim, and so also must the offering be made by the one priest. In sacrificing, a priest acts not as an ordinary man, but super-naturally, in the person of Christ, as mediator between God and the faithful. This exclusive power to sacrifice is the basis of priestly hierarchical authority. Church hierarchy is not analogous to a secular ranked social structure, such as an army: to secularize Church hierarchy is to destroy it. The fundamental hierarchical distinction, underlying all secondary ones, is between God and nature, between supernatural and natural.[3] The hierarchy presides "in place of God over the flock," says Vatican II (*Lumen Gentium* 3:20; Abbott 1966: 40). The supernatural base of this hierarchy is absolutely dependent on sacrifice. Supernatural ranking among Christians comes into being only with the sacrificial cult and disappears with it. In hierarchical order, the principle of unity is subordination: *unus grex sub uno pastore,* one flock under one shepherd. This principle of unity allows the continuity of descent of the episcopate to sustain continuity of the Church as a whole. Because the hierarchical structure is dependent on sacrifice, to question the eucharistic sacrifice has been to question the social structure, and to reject the social organization has been to question or reject the sacrificial practice. Consequently, to take a theological position on whether the Eucharist itself is or is not an actual sacrifice is simultaneously to take a political position.

The post-Vatican II Church offers excellent sociological insight into the difficulty of maintaining a sacrificial cult and a sacred hierarchy in an industrialized, democratic, pluralistic world where structures of domination are not organized as descent systems, a world that, especially since the French Revolution, has increasingly lacked social structures that allow sacrificial ideology to be taken for granted. Agrarian feudal society was itself a plausibility structure for sacrificial religion. Life in late twentieth-century industrial cities offers little to support it and much to undermine it.

The end of the Middle Ages was also the beginning of threats to the Church's established sacrificial practice that could no longer be successfully overcome. The Protestant reformers agreed with one another on nothing about eucharistic theology except to deny that the Eucharist

was an actual sacrifice and to reject the inseparable corollaries of eucharistic sacrifice: the clergy as a sacrificing priesthood mediating between
God and man, and the organization of that priesthood in unilineal
"eternal" descent. At the Council of Trent, (1545–63) the Roman
Church responded polemically, defending with anathemas the eucharistic sacrifice and the exclusive sacrificing power of those indelibly ordained in the one line of apostolic succession. In 1570 Pope Pius V made
obligatory[4] a liturgy based on Trent's conservative sacrificial position:
the Tridentine Mass.[5] From Trent until Vatican II, the Church systematically protected its sacrificial practice and hierarchical organization,
but at a price of liturgical rigidity and an increasingly defensive posture
toward the modernizing world (McSweeney 1980).

Especially since the mid-nineteenth century, sacrificing effectively
maintained the supernatural basis of hierarchy only in an increasingly
isolated ghetto of the sacred. Declared Pius IX in 1864, "If anyone says
that the Roman Pontiff can and should reconcile and accommodate
himself to progress, liberalism and modern civilization, let him be
anathema" (*Enchiridion Symbolorum* 2980; Denzinger 1976: 584). Leo
XIII imposed orthodox Thomism as the *only* system of ideas that could
be taught in Catholic seminaries (McSweeney 1980: 67–73). This defensive posture was maintained until Vatican II. Even in the 1950s theologians who questioned traditional hierarchical differentiation between
clergy and laity (Congar) or between supernatural and natural (de Lu-
bac) were disciplined.

Vatican II undertook the gigantic task of calling the Church to be
relevant to its contemporary world while at the same time preserving
its traditional heritage, to change without breaking with its past, to keep
one foot in the Middle Ages, as it were, while setting the other down in
the late twentieth century. The immensity of this distance is made evident in many of the conflicts and tensions of the post-conciliar Church.
For example, the principle of hierarchy in the Church is not reconcilable
with a modern, secular ideology of democratic equality, nor can the
profane "nature" transcended by the supernatural be reconciled with
the "nature" investigated by science.[6] Especially in changing the liturgy,
Vatican II undermined the supernatural basis of hierarchical structure.
Because the essential difference between priesthood and laity was constituted and maintained in sacrifice, to change the liturgy was to change
not just eucharistic theology, but the identity of the priesthood and the
social structure of the Church (Dinges 1987).

Some scholarly interest in liturgical reform had developed since the
late nineteenth century, but the Tridentine Mass stood essentially unchanged from 1570 until December 1963, when the first official docu-

ment of Vatican II, *The Constitution on the Sacred Liturgy (Sacrosanctum Concilium)*, was promulgated, to be followed in 1969 by documents specifying the New Order of the Mass (Vatican Council II 1975). When the Vatican II liturgical changes came, not only were they sudden, they were structural and profound. These changes were presented as restoration more than as modernization, a return to an earlier, more essential, form of the Mass, without some of the accretions of the ages. Most of the "new" liturgy is taken directly from the earliest known eucharistic liturgy. But the Mass had become more and more exclusively and literally sacrificial over the centuries, and such a reform necessarily diminished the emphasis on eucharistic sacrifice, thus undermining the priesthood, which had been identified by its exclusive sacrificing power, and its social organization, separated from the laity in its own eternal line of descent. Conservative "traditionalists," unalterably opposed to the Vatican II changes, pointed out analogies to earlier Protestant liturgical changes, which they saw as also "characterized not so much by new prayers making heretical doctrine explicit as by the elimination of sacrificial language" (M. Davies 1977a: 5).

Liturgical practice and theology must draw on some combination of three sources: the Bible, the Church's historical tradition, and the world experienced by liturgists and contemporaries in their own lives. The difficulty is to reconcile these three in terms of sacrifice, when the contemporary world offers few supports for sacrificial ideology, and the tradition defended at Trent has departed from scripture especially in the development of sacrificial practice and social organization. Nowhere in the New Testament is the Eucharist described as being itself a sacrifice, nor is there any indication of a special office for celebrating it. The New Testament refers to Jewish and pagan priests, but nowhere to Christian priests, except the universal priesthood of all believers. There is not only no mention of an institutionalized apostolic succession, but by implication there can be no successors to the apostles as such (R. Brown 1970: 55).

Only one New Testament book is about priesthood and sacrifice, but it is about the end of all sacrificing, whose ultimate goal of transcending "bodily descent" (having-been-born-of-woman) has been finally attained. For the author of the Letter to the Hebrews, the entire system of Levitical (Aaronid) sacrificing is obsolete, superseded by the eternal priesthood of Christ. Christ is "a priest not according to a legal requirement concerning bodily descent but by the power of an indestructible life" (Heb. 7:16). Even the antecedent for Christ's priesthood is not Aaron, but Melchizedek, who "is without father or mother[7] or genealogy, and has neither beginning of day nor end of life" (7:3). There is now only one sacrifice and one priest: "The former priests were many in number, because they were prevented by death from continuing in office but . . . he continues for ever" (7:23–24). The "Son who has been made perfect for ever" (7:28) has achieved eternal continuity with the Father, and there is neither need nor possibility of future sacrifices (7:27; 9:25–26; 10:5–10, 12, 14, 18, 26). The author of Hebrews mentions neither the Eucharist nor church offices.[8]

By the second century (as the Second Coming was delayed) the Church, threatened by persecution, heresy, and schism, faced the major problems of continuity and succession, problems for which sacrifice is a particularly useful solution. Owner of a valued spiritual property, the Church developed a sacrificially maintained social structure well suited to preserve and transmit its enduring heritage. The Eucharist became *the* Christian sacrifice, increasingly identical with that on Calvary; the bishops who celebrated it became unilineal successors to the apostles; and clerical office became sacrificing priesthood, not charismatic ministry. Intensification and centralization of sacrifice and sacrificially maintained social organization became the essential means of routinization of charisma.[9]

Already in the early second century the Eucharist was called *thysia* and was celebrated by the bishop for the congregation (Didache 1912, 14:1–3, *in The Apostolic Fathers*), but it was still an offering only of praise and thanksgiving, not yet of body and blood (Daly 1978: 313). By the middle of the third century, Cyprian, Bishop of Carthage, had become the first to refer to the body and blood of Christ as the object of sacrifice by Christian priests (Cyprian 1964: 204–5, 213–14). He was the first to call the bishop *"sacerdos,"* "priest," and the first to make a fully explicit transition from a universal apostolic heritage to a single line of apostolic descent attached to the episcopate (ibid.: 85–86, 228–29).[10]

The interdependence of sacrifice and social organization of clerical-lay differentiation and expiatory emphasis, is especially evident at times of sudden intensification of sacrifice. When Christianity became the established religion of the Roman Empire in the fourth century, sacrificing and sacrificially maintained hierarchical social organization simultaneously took great leaps forward. Said Chrysostom in his *Treatise on the Priesthood,*

> For though the priestly office is discharged on earth, it ranks among heavenly ordinances . . . For, when you see the Lord, sacrificed, and laid upon the altar, and the priest, standing, and praying over the sacrifice, and all the people empurpled with his most precious blood, do you then fancy yourself among men, or continuing upon the earth? Are you not instantly transported

into the heavens, so as, discarding every fleshly sentiment from your mind, to look around with naked soul and disembodied spirit on celestial objects? (Book III, 4; tr. Marsh 1844: 59–60)

The Roman administration had always been legitimated by sacrificing; now the bishops, and especially the Bishop of Rome, were integrated into that administration (Emminghaus 1978: 63). As parishes expanded outside cities, bishops governed whole territories. Christianity, which had begun as a religion of individual, mostly urban, converts, became an established sacrificial religion of landowning extended patrilineal families and agricultural workers. Lay synagogue terms for church office were replaced by priestly terms and presbyters became sacrificing priests. Deaconesses, who in the East had received the laying on of hands, were declared to be not clergy but laity.

The term "laity" had been used without pejorative connotation; now it took on a "derogatory sense of 'unsanctified, profane'" (von Campenhausen 1969: 89), and explicit ideas of the Eucharist itself as expiatory and propitiatory appeared. Ritual purity, as distinct from moral purity, became crucial for priests, and the reproductive powers of women were specifically polluting. Celibacy became an ideal for the priesthood, much later a requirement.[11] Celibate women, transcending their own profane nature, could be classified up one supernatural hierarchical rank, as male. Wrote Jerome, "As long as woman is for birth and children she is as different from man as body is from soul. But when she wishes to serve Christ more than the world, then she will cease to be a woman and will be called man"—*vir*, as in "virile," not *homo* (Jerome 1884: 567). In the sixth century, the Council of Auxerre banned women from receiving the host in an uncovered hand lest they profane the sacred victim; later still, only priests could handle the host or drink the wine.

By the early Middle Ages, the priesthood was formally identified by its exclusive sacrificing power. Other functions receded into the background. "The accent was shifted to one single function . . . that of offering the Eucharistic sacrifice. The priesthood was then defined as *potestas in corpus eucharisticum*" (R. Brown 1970: 99). The participation of lay persons correspondingly shrank until they were silent spectators at the elevation of the host, communicating only once a year, and then receiving only bread. The laity no longer understood the Latin liturgy, but they were not meant to understand: the most important parts of the Mass were said so quietly they could not be heard by the people. The priest, his back to the congregation, addressed only the Father and the sacred victim.

By the ninth and tenth centuries, private masses with no congregation at all became common. Private masses were to appease and pro-pitiate God, especially for the benefit of the dead. They were commonly non-alimentary sacrifices, even for priests. In them the eucharistic sac-rifice had become entirely expiatory. Just as with the Aaronid priest-hood, the sacrifice that identified the Christian priesthood was a sin offering, eaten by the priests alone or not even by them.

Since the fourth century, sacrificial realism had raised theological problems about the precise relation of the elements of bread and wine to the body sacrificed in the Mass and on the cross. These problems were unresolved until the sacrificial tradition reached its full development in the thirteenth century, simultaneously with the peak of centralized po-litical power of the clerical hierarchy. In 1215 the Fourth Lateran Coun-cil accepted the doctrine of transubstantiation, and later the Eucharistic sacrifice was given its classic doctrinal expression by Thomas Aquinas. Thomas states explicitly that the sacrifice of the cross is repeated in the Mass: The body and blood of the same victim are offered by the same priest (*Summa Theologica*, III, Q83:1).

This is the sacrificial tradition defended from Trent to Vatican II. But in the somewhat precarious balance between scripture, tradition, and contemporary experience achieved by the liturgical reforms of Vatican II, sacrificial aspects of tradition can be said to have suffered. This was not a consequence of explicit rejection of tradition. Consistent with Trent, Vatican II affirmed that "both sacred tradition and sacred scrip-ture are to be accepted and venerated with the same sense of devotion and reverence" (*Dei Verbum*, 9; in Abbott 1966: 117). Likewise, a tra-ditional understanding of the priesthood was affirmed, e.g., "The min-isterial priest, by the sacred power he enjoys, molds and rules the priestly people. Acting in the person of Christ, he brings about the Eu-charistic Sacrifice . . ." (*Lumen Gentium* 10; in Abbott 1966: 27). The apostolic succession of the priesthood was also explicitly affirmed: "The apostles took care to appoint successors in this hierarchically structured society. . . . Among those . . . the chief place belongs to the office of those who, appointed to the episcopate in a sequence running back to the beginning, are the ones who pass on the apostolic seed" (*apostoli seminis*—Latin for "seed" is *semen*. *Lumen Gentium* 20; in Abbott 1966: 39). Only bishops have the power to generate descendants in this ge-nealogical line; priests, who cannot ordain, are immature members of the apostolic descent system.

While affirming, in some texts, a traditional theology of the Church as sacrificially maintained hierarchy, Vatican II nevertheless marked a shift to a theology of the Church as community, based more on the New Testament than on traditional sources such as Trent. Vatican II still in-sisted that the universal priesthood of the faithful (that is, the laity) and the hierarchical, ministerial priesthood "differ from one another in essence and not only in degree" (*Lumen Gentium* 10; Abbott 1966: 27). But just what that essence is became less clear. The laity, after centuries of being "strangers or silent spectators" at the Mass, were called to "that full, conscious and active participation in liturgical celebrations which is demanded by the very nature of the liturgy. . . . this full and active participation by all the people is the aim to be considered before all else" (*Sacrosanctum Concilium* 48, 14; in Abbott 1966: 154, 144). The whole traditional sacrificial structure, built on the exclusive sacrificing power of the priesthood, was shaken by this call for active lay participation in liturgy. Priests everywhere were plunged into a crisis of identity, and a "crisis of liturgical reform" developed (Vilanova et al. 1969), in which some carried liturgical change far beyond the official position of Vatican II, and others, holding fast to sacrificial tradition, rejected the Council's reforms.

The complex position of Vatican II and the post-conciliar Church on sacrifice is ambiguous, often deliberately so for the sake of compromise. What is said and done in one context is not always in perfect accord with what is said and done in another, and what is left unsaid is just as important as what is spelled out. Rather than try in vain to specify the full range of the Church's stated and unstated positions,[12] I will describe two opposed theological positions from western Europe that were officially rejected by the Vatican in the years after Vatican II. In rejecting these, the Church defined its boundaries. On one hand is a non-sacrificial, ecumenical position, most clearly represented by Hans Küng, whose writings on priesthood led the Vatican to revoke his mandate to teach as a Catholic theologian. On the other hand is a conservative cultic position represented by the excommunicated Archbishop Marcel Lefebvre and his "traditionalist" followers. In between is the range of theological positions endorsed or tolerated by the Church. These two theological positions do not strive toward even a precarious balance between scripture, tradition, and the contemporary world. Lefebvre and his followers defend the sacrificial tradition unmoderated and at all costs, while Küng explicitly rejects it. I shall let them speak for themselves, by quoting from their publications.

Traditionalists ignore scripture wherever it does not accommodate tradition. The Council of Trent is the rock on which they stand. Trent itself actively defended not a biblical base—that was where the Protestant reformers stood—but the sacrificial tradition as it had been institutionalized especially since the late eleventh century. A traditionalist spokesman comments, "The Tridentine Mass is the most fitting expression of the traditional Faith, the Faith expressed with such clarity by the Council of Trent. The Tridentine Mass expresses clearly . . . a solemn sacrifice offered to a transcendent, omnipotent God; the exalted role of the priest at the altar as mediator between God and Man" (M. Davies 1979: 333). In contrast, "The New Mass has been constructed in such a fashion that it can be celebrated in a form containing hardly a reference to the sacrificial nature of the Mass . . . The changes have served to obscure the nature of the unique priestly role" (ibid.: 329–30). Whether one endorses or rejects the theology of Trent, this aspect of the traditionalist complaint makes sense sociologically.

For Lefebvre, liturgical change is the root of all Vatican II's undermining of hierarchy. According to him, these de-sacralizing reforms "have contributed and are still contributing to the demolition of the Church, the ruin of the priesthood, the destruction of the Sacrifice" (quoted in M. Davies 1977b: 4). Says Lefebvre, "The Church since the council . . . has chosen to have a new Sacrifice of the Mass, or rather let us say a new Eucharist" (1979b: 223). Traditionalists share Lefebvre's conviction that there were "time-bombs," concealed by "orthodox padding," in the *Sacrosanctum Concilium* (*The Constitution on the Sacred Liturgy*). For them, "the demand that the full active participation of the congregation 'be considered *before all else*'[13] is a time bomb of virtually unlimited destructive power" (M. Davies 1977b: 4, 229, 239).

The Tridentine Mass contains prayers in the first person, legacies of the private masses: "Receive, O Holy Father, almighty eternal God, this spotless victim which I, thy unworthy servant, offer unto Thee, my living and true God, for mine own countless sins." To the great distress of traditionalists, all first-person prayers have been removed from the New Mass. But Archbishop Lefebvre, still celebrating the Tridentine Mass, insists that "the priest, when he is alone, offers the Holy Sacrifice of the Mass in the same manner and with the same value as if there were a thousand people around him" (1979a: 210).

In a sermon at an ordination he performed in spite of Vatican prohibitions, Lefebvre made his position clear:

> It is evident that the new rite . . . supposes another conception of the Catholic religion—another religion. It is no longer the priest who offers the Holy Sacrifice of the Mass, it is the assembly . . . And this is consistent with the mentality of modern man— absolutely consistent. For it is the democratic ideal which is the *fundamental* idea of modern man, that is to say, that the power lies with the assembly, that authority is in the people . . . and not in God. . . . The New Mass is not less than the expression that authority is at the base, and no longer in God. This Mass is no longer a hierarchical Mass; it is a democratic Mass . . . And this is what at present corrupts the entire Church. For by this idea of

power bestowed on the lower rank, in the Holy Mass, they have destroyed the priesthood! They are destroying the priesthood, for what is the priest, if the priest no longer has a personal power, that power which is given to him by his ordination, as these future priests are going to receive in a moment? They are going to receive a character . . . which will put them *above* the people of God! . . . They will no longer be men like other men. They . . . will be the intermediaries between God and God's people. (1979a: 208–10)

And in a sermon at the first Mass of those he ordained:

You are marked with the sacerdotal character [that] unites you to . . . the priesthood of our Lord Jesus Christ in a very special way, a participation which the faithful cannot have; and that is what permits you . . . to pronounce the words of consecration of Holy Mass, and in a way to make God obey your order, your words. At your words Jesus Christ will come personally, physically, substantially under the species of the bread and wine. (1979b: 219)

It was just this effective, working power of sacrifice that had so offended the Protestant reformers. But only a sacrifice that can cause what it signifies can order a social world. Archbishop Lefebvre is as aware of, and as dependent on, the constitutive power of sacrifice as are those who shape their social world in an ancestral cult. Says he, "The Church is essentially priestly because she offers the redemptive Sacrifice. . . . We cannot transform this Sacrifice into a simple commemorative meal, a simple repast at which a memory is recalled, this is not possible. To do such a thing would be to destroy the whole of our Religion" (quoted in M. Davies, 1979: 82–83).

The traditionalist movement is organized and led by priests, those with the most to lose from the liturgical reform (Dinges 1987: 149). Archbishop Lefebvre has been especially important to the movement because as its only bishop, he was its only source of new priests. For years the Vatican tolerated Lefebvre. It was only in 1988, when the eighty-two-year-old Archbishop consecrated four new bishops, thus making possible the eternal continuity of his schismatic sacrificial line of descent, that he and they were excommunicated.

From the point of view of traditionalists, Hans Küng is "the most notorious of the liberal theologians" who conspired to control Vatican II (M. Davies 1977a: 45). From a less partisan perspective, he is the most explicitly non-sacrificial of a number of professional theologians from advanced industrialized nations, such as Schillebeeckx, Rahner,

Congar, and others, whose effect on the council is widely recognized (McSweeney 1980: 135–95; Dinges 1987: 151–53; Wiltgen 1967). Prior to Vatican II, liturgical reform had been neither a grassroots movement of the laity nor a priority of the hierarchy. A non-partisan sociologist reports that the dramatic liturgical reforms were the accomplishment "of liturgical experts and scholars who provided both the theological rationale for the reforms and the administrative networking and practical know-how for carrying them out" (Dinges 1987: 152). For conservatives, this was travesty: "The new liturgy was simply not formed by saints, *homines religiosi* . . . but has been worked out by so-called experts" (von Hildebrand, 1973: 70).

For professional experts to be pivotal in decision making is a feature of advanced industrial society not consistent with traditional hierarchical order. Legitimation of authority among professional experts rests on entirely different criteria than does that of the priestly hierarchy. Those who are qualified to judge professional performance are other experts, peers, rather than superiors in a sacrificially maintained hierarchy. Judgment is horizontal, not vertical (Dinges 1987: 153). Authority is grounded on command of specialized knowledge in a modern scientific world view, not on supernatural transcendence. Alarmed traditionalists saw the de-sacralizing perspective of the experts eroding the supernatural basis of hierarchy: "Once the logic of making the active participation of the congregation the prime consideration of the liturgy is accepted there can be no restraint upon the self-appointed experts intent upon its total de-sacralization" (M. Davies 1977a: 238). It is true that Küng, a scholarly expert willing to turn to even such a secular discipline as "the sociology of religion" for support, finds that "there is neither a sociological nor even a theological basis for that sacralization of the Church's ministry . . . which sets its holder as a sacred person apart from the rest of men and raises him above ordinary Christians to be a mediator with God" (1972: 73, 77).

Using language not of the Church, but of the anticlerical revolutionaries who undermined the ancient principles of inequality, Küng calls for "democratization," the Church as community of "the original liberty, equality and fraternity of the gospel" (ibid.: 25). Since the traditional sacrificial "priest image has become untenable in both theory and practice," he offers a "'new' image of the Church leader, drawn from the New Testament and proposed for a new era" (ibid.: 108). Pointing out that the New Testament "avoids the word 'priest' in the sense of sacrificial priest," he does likewise, substituting terms like "leader," "presider," "pastor." Says Küng, "Jesus, himself a layman, had only once in all his parables introduced the figure of a priest (Luke 10:31), and there it is a warning example" (the callous priest in the parable of the Good Samaritan). Küng asks, "Did Trent even reflect on the original Christian message?" and concludes, "the definitions of Trent cannot constitute a decisive obstacle to a new understanding and a restructuring of the Church ministry" (1972: 58–59).

Küng rejects tradition both on scriptural grounds and in terms of modern secular democratic values. In addressing the crisis of identity among priests that followed Vatican II, Küng found a "state of emergency . . . taking on catastrophic proportions" (ibid.: 13). A similar assessment was made by traditionalists, but Küng's response was to give "an answer which will be open both to modern times and to the origins of Christianity," which "decisively clears the field of many a traditional view that can no longer be maintained" (ibid.: 14). He says explicitly, "The Eucharistic celebration is not itself a sacrifice" (ibid.: 68).

Without sacrifice there can be neither a hierarchical priesthood nor its institutionalized genealogy linking males in unilineal descent. For Küng, "the fundamental 'apostolic succession' is therefore that of the Church itself and of each individual Christian" (ibid.: 44. See also Küng 1968 passim). Finally, having de-sacralized and democratized the priesthood, abolished its descent line and its sacrifice, he calls for "the admission of women to all the Church's special ministries and to ordination" (1972: 81).[14]

For traditionalists, in contrast, the prime example of the "time bombs" hidden by experts in the *The Constitution on the Sacred Liturgy,* and accepted by unsuspecting bishops, is that lay participation in the Mass may include women (M. Davies 1977b: 227). The ultimate de-sacralizing of priestly status is this: "Only his consecrated hands had been allowed to touch the host—now it can be distributed by teen-aged girls" (M. Davies 1979: 329–30). The covers of two pamphlets by the traditionalist spokesman Michael Davies illustrate this contrast (see figs. 6 and 7).

The Tridentine Mass (1977a) emphasizes hierarchical structure among males in the elevation of the host, the priest's back to the congregation; *The New Mass* (1977c) displays the de-sacralizing consequences of lay participation by setting a young woman in a miniskirt as the active figure. The priest, now seated, faces the congregation; draperies behind him have replaced the altar, and microphones have replaced incense and the cross.

Traditionalists and Küng do not disagree about the content of the Roman Church's tradition of sacrifice. Their disagreement is about its value, its scriptural legitimation, and about the desirability and possibility of the kind of social order that sacrifice can maintain. Archbishop Lefebvre is committed to a vertical hierarchical social order, in which gender distinction is crucial; Küng, the professional expert, to a hori-

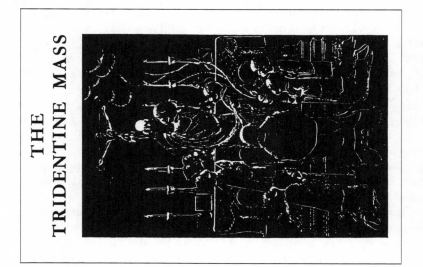

Fig. 6. Pamphlet cover (M. Davies 1977a).

Fig. 7. Pamphlet cover (M. Davies, 1977c).

zontal desacralized social order, in which gender distinction is almost irrelevant. Küng's antipathy to hierarchy, "holy domination" (1972: 40), is one source of his call for women's ordination. Ordaining women is as threatening to traditional hierarchical order as is rejection of sacrifice. In the sacrificial tradition the "supernatural" has always transcended a profane "natural" category of being, epitomized by sexuality, mortality, having-been-born-of-woman, and childbearing women themselves (Gossman 1968). In hierarchical order, "woman is by her very nature, subordinate to man. . . . The priest, on the other hand, as the man who offers sacrifices and mediates between God and men, is the exponent *par excellence* of the sacral scale of values" (Van Eyden 1972: 79).

The Church itself encompasses a great range of positions between the extremes represented by Küng and the traditionalists. Rome's official guardian of tradition, the Sacred Congregation for the Doctrine of the Faith, defends sacrifice and its social organization, but scholars and other groups continue to question or even to ignore them. The greater freedom for (and improved quality of) Roman Catholic historical and biblical research since Vatican II has not tended to strengthen the sacrificial tradition. Since Vatican II, some officially approved literature on the Eucharist shows a striking reduction of sacrificial themes. Much of this literature would not have been certified as free of doctrinal error in the 1950s; e.g., "in its basic structure . . . the Mass is a rite derived from a meal, not from a sacrifice. . . . The Lord left his Church the Eucharist, that is, the prayer of thanksgiving over bread and wine as elements of a meal. It was precisely this that he bade her do in memory of him. He did not tell her to carry out a sacrificial rite" (Emminghaus 1978: xx).[15]

Whatever new forms may revitalize the Church, a widespread return to cultic sacrifice does not seem likely to be one of them. In some popular recent Church developments, sacrifice has become peripheral or irrelevant. The Catholic charismatic movement is liturgically active but concerned with individual experience, not with hierarchical priesthood or apostolic succession. Liberation theology does address Church social structure, but not to support hierarchy. Base communities, organized around the Bible rather than the cult, are often without priests. Leonardo Boff, who favors ordaining women, ignores cultic sacrifice even while attacking its social organization: "Every baptized person . . . becomes an apostle . . . it is the entire community that is apostolic, and not only certain holders of sacred power. . . . Apostolic succession is not limited to hierarchical function, which divides the community" (1985: 122–23). Boff has been silenced by the Sacred Congregation for the Doctrine of the Faith, but base communities are growing while the priesthood shrinks.

The best source for measuring the continuing importance of the sacrificial cult for the Vatican is the debate over the validity of Anglican orders. In this enormous literature,[16] the role of sacrifice in maintaining the continuity of apostolic succession has been discussed from almost every perspective. The conflict began in the mid-sixteenth century, when all references to sacrifice were removed from the English ordinals. This was modified in succeeding centuries; and especially after 1833, with the Oxford Movement, renewed emphasis on the Catholic character of the Church of England developed (Franklin 1984). But in 1896, a papal bull shattered hopes of reconciliation:

> In the whole [Anglican] Ordinal not only is there no clear mention of the sacrifice . . . but . . . every trace . . . was deliberately removed and struck out. . . . In vain those who, from the time of Charles I, have attempted to hold some kind of sacrifice or of priesthood, have made additions to the ordinal. . . . Even if this addition could give the form its due signification, it was introduced too late, as a century had already elapsed . . . for as the Hierarchy had become extinct, there remained no power of ordaining. . . . we pronounce and declare that Ordinations carried out according to the Anglican rite have been, and are, absolutely null and utterly void. (*Anglican Orders* 1943: 11–12, 10,14; see also Hughes 1968b)

After Vatican II hope for reconciliation was reborn. The Anglican Roman Catholic International Commission (ARCIC) was appointed in 1968, and reached theological agreement on many topics, sometimes in the ambiguous language typical of efforts to reach consensus. In the final ARCIC report (1982), the Anglican Church accepted sacrifice, but this did not satisfy the Sacred Congregation for the Doctrine of the Faith. Supporting its argument with references to Trent, the Sacred Congregation found ARCIC's language ambiguous and inadequate on both sacrifice and the role of the priest, and condemned it for completely ignoring the "propitiatory value" of the Eucharist (SCDF 1982: I, 1). Concerning "Ministry and Ordination," sacrifice was still the obstacle: "Because the priestly nature of the ordained minister depends on the sacrificial character of the Eucharist, lack of clarity on the latter point would render uncertain any real agreement on the former" (ibid.: II, 1).

Finally, it is an insuperable obstacle for the Sacred Congregation that "some parts of the Anglican Communion" have ordained women (ibid.: II, 111). The consequent impasse can be described (with some freedom of expression) as looking something like this: The Anglicans say to Rome, we have accepted sacrifice, why don't you accept our orders? And Rome responds, you say you accept sacrifice, but you ordain women; therefore it cannot be sacrifice as we understand it.

Some of the voices in the conflict over Anglican orders have made the role of sacrifice in identifying and maintaining an "eternal," exclusively male, system of unilineal descent appear startlingly reminiscent of societies discussed earlier. Like patrilineage leaders, some churchmen have cited irregularities in descent generations ago as an insuperable barrier to sacrificing together today. For these, not religious meaning but continuity of descent is at issue. A conservative Jesuit historian writes,

> Roman Catholic apologists do not cease to point out that no matter how nearly Anglicans may advocate towards acceptance of the full Catholic doctrine of the priesthood and of the Eucharist, no matter how earnestly they may desire to attribute to their clergy the Catholic sacerdotal power, that cannot restore the loss if, as a consequence of the events of the mid-sixteenth century, the apostolic succession of order was extinguished in the Church of England. (Clark 1967: 15)

When apostolic succession and priesthood are identified by sacrificial power over the Eucharistic body, the criterion of membership is participation in a sacrificial cult just as it was in Athens, or among the Tallensi, the Nuer, and the Lugbara. In the conflict over Anglican orders, through all the confusing disagreements and the obscure technicalities, one theme remains clear: For the Vatican's official guardians of the doctrine of the faith, in the late twentieth century as at Trent, those who are outside the sacrificial cult are outside the true succession of Christianity.

NINE

Theories of Sacrifice

THEORIES OF SACRIFICE commonly exhibit notions of gender ranging from taken-for-granted male domination to explicit misogyny. In this they resemble the traditions they claim to illuminate. Theories offering universal explanations of sacrifice are especially susceptible to patriarchal presuppositions, which they universalize along with sacrifice. Some theorists have built visions of universal human nature on the gender dichotomies of specific sacrificial traditions, but it is more common for theorists to project notions from their own societies on to these traditions. Most of the early social-scientific theories of sacrifice were muddied by just such a projection: the European construction of totemism.

Late nineteenth-century European scholars, looking down from their unquestioned position at the pinnacle of civilization, identified its lowest stages by the presence of totemism, supposedly a single religious and social system found among "primitive races" all over the world. Since it provided a glimpse into human origins (when people were barely able to distinguish themselves from animals, thought some scholars), great efforts were made to lay bare its mysteries. As Freud said, "The more convinced we became that totemism had regularly formed a phase in every culture, the more urgent became the necessity of arriving at an understanding of it" (1950: 140). As the earliest phase in the unilineal progress of civilization, totemism held the key to the origin of another, more important, universal: sacrifice.

Those scholars, all from Protestant backgrounds, who saw European sacrificial religion as a "survival" from pre-rational times, characterized totemism by a savage irrationality as remote as possible from their own mentality. For example, Frazer's long search for the origin of totemism finally narrowed down to two cases of food taboos in Melanesia, one initiated by "influential old men," the other by pregnant women. Since the old men must have had some "reason" for their behavior, they could not be the true originators of so primitive a system.

So Frazer (soon to be an influential old man himself) turned to what he saw as completely irrational and wholly alien to identify "the tap-root of totemism, that is, the sick fancies of pregnant women" (1910, vol. II: 107).

Totemism, construed as a complete religious and social system, was manufactured by processing together raw material from different cultural sources into a single finished product, omitting only a "made in Britain" label. Its origin can be traced to an influential old man in Scotland (MacLennan 1865, 1869), and it spread so rapidly and gained such credibility that not only British specialists in "primitive religion" such as MacLennan, Robertson Smith, and Frazer, but also Durkheim in 1912 (*The Elementary Forms of the Religious Life*) and Freud in 1913 (*Totem and Taboo*) published major studies of it. These two works, and the traditions to which they have contributed, are still influencing theories of sacrifice.

I turn first to *Totem and Taboo* and theories influenced by it. For Freud, totemism had everywhere formed the original social order, and among savages still, "the system of *Totemism* takes the place of all religious and social institutions" (1950: 5). To study totemism is to investigate society at its point of origin, when culture and morality first appear. It is not surprising that Freud produced a kind of social contract theory, an account of how an original violent state of nature was overcome. Social contract theories usually take gender relations so for granted as to ignore them. *Totem and Taboo* has the great advantage of making them explicit.

According to the first great social contract theorist, Thomas Hobbes, in the original state of nature men are all violent but equal in strength, "and therefore if any two men desire the same thing, which nevertheless they cannot both enjoy, they become enemies" (1963: 142). Such is the cause of the war of all against all, which makes "the life of man solitary, poor, nasty, brutish and short" (ibid.: 143). This "ill condition, which man by mere nature is actually placed in," being intolerable, men got together to invent the state. (Ibid.: 145). All association and all morality begin with the state. Before its creation, there was neither right nor wrong, justice nor injustice, for "they are qualities that relate to men in society, not in solitude" (ibid.: 143). Probably men's original solitude was not so total that they had never enjoyed the company of their mothers, but Hobbes ignores this association, most likely because motherhood is strictly natural. As the Greeks knew, even animals have mothers. Men's relations with women, like relations between women and children, contribute nothing to socialization. Society is the rational creation of adult males, who alone contribute to it.

In Freud's hands, this story was fleshed out. In the state of nature, there was the primal horde (as imagined by Darwin), ruled over by the primal father, who drove away his sons and kept all the women for himself. "One day the expelled brothers joined forces, slew and ate the father, and thus put an end to the father horde" (1950: 183). The brothers each wished to be like the father; that's why they ate him, each acquiring a part of his strength. Only then did the war of all against all get going, for each of the brothers wanted all the women for himself, but since they were equal in strength, none could succeed. "Thus there was nothing left for the brothers . . . but to erect the incest prohibition . . . through which they all equally renounced the women whom they desired" (ibid.: 186). The ambivalent brothers did not just hate the father; they also longed for him. So they resurrected him as the totem animal and forbade his murder except in ritual repetition of the original murder. That is, *they invented sacrifice:* "the repetition and commemoration of this memorable criminal act with which so many things began, social organization, moral restrictions and religion" (ibid.: 183). Once again, society and morality are the creation of adult males. Women do exist this time, but only as passive objects of desire, not as subjects and certainly not as socializers. Relations with women are the opposite of social order; they are the natural source of strife.

This theory of sacrifice fell on hard times, but nearly sixty years later, in 1972, it was revived in René Girard's *Violence and the Sacred* (1977). Girard returns to taken-for-granted rather than explicit gender relations, but he still grounds all community and culture on male control of male violence. For Girard, "violence and the sacred are one and the same" (ibid.: 262). Violence (like libido in some of Freud's accounts) is a kind of liquid. "If left unappeased, violence will accumulate until it overflows its confines and floods the surrounding area. The role of sacrifice is to stem this rising tide . . . and redirect violence into 'proper' channels" (ibid.: 10).[1]

For Girard, men do not desire their female relatives or anything else in particular. Rather, desire is "mimetic": men desire whatever another man desires.[2] The trouble is, "the effects of mimetic rivalry . . . invariably end in reciprocal violence" (ibid.: 174). "Reciprocal violence" is the new name for the war of all against all, and once again, culture and community are the product of sacrificing enemy brothers. The father has vanished, but fighters in the war of all against all are still typified as "enemy brothers" because they are undifferentiated in desire and equal in strength. The war is not ended by rational contract or by incest taboos, but by a united attack on a scapegoat, the "surrogate victim."

Where only shortly before a thousand individual conflicts had raged unchecked between a thousand enemy brothers, there now appears a true community, united in its hatred for one alone of its numbers. All the rancors scattered at random among the divergent individuals, all the differing antagonisms, now converge on an isolated and unique figure, the *surrogate victim*. (1977: 79)

Freud was right, there *was* an original murder: "an absolute beginning, signifying the passage from nonhuman to human" (ibid.: 309). With this primordial event, "reciprocal violence" became "violent unanimity," the "generative violence" that alone creates community and culture. All sacrifice repeats this original murder, and functions like it, to centralize and redirect violence. Sacrificial rituals are "booster shots": a bit of violence under control prevents violence out of control (ibid.: 289–90). Without sacrifice, the hierarchical differences essential to social order disappear, and the war of all against all returns. Only modern societies with "judicial systems" can survive without sacrifice. "Primitive" societies that fail to sacrifice inevitably self-destruct: "Coherent thinking collapses and rational activities are abandoned. All associative forms are dissolved . . . all values, spiritual and material, perish" (ibid.: 51).

Girard's theory resembles many sacrificial mythologies and ideologies; for example, he illustrates his ideas with Euripides' *The Bacchae*, in which Pentheus's refusal to sacrifice leads to loss of distinction between males and females, humans and animals, and to the most terrible violence. In Christian sacrificial ideology (which he does not cite), the death of an innocent victim is the violent origin of a hierarchical society maintained by ritual repetition of the founding event. Girard's theory is itself a sacrificial ideology, legitimating hierarchical distinction as essential for a social order maintained only by sacrifice (and therefore only by males), a social order threatened everywhere by what he understands as its only alternative: chaos.[3]

Girard does not explain why, if sacrifice is the origin of all culture and society, hunter-gatherers do not sacrifice. For him, *all* rituals are the same (ibid.: 274–308) and all are sacrificial. Even all cultures are essentially the same (ibid.: 56). There is no point in paying much attention to what sacrificers themselves say, since they "do not and must not comprehend the true role of the sacrificial act" (ibid.: 7). (As Freud said, "It is useless to question savages" [op. cit.: 43].) Ignoring the trivial differences between cultures, Girard builds a theory explaining all sacrifice with fragments of ritual and culture taken from here and there—a common practice in Freud's day, but rare by 1972.[4] From Girard's perspective, this is perfectly legitimate since he already knows what is important about all cultures: "There can be nothing in the whole range of human culture that is not rooted in violent unanimity—nothing that does not find its source in the surrogate victim" (1977: 297). Everything that arises from the sociability of mothers and infants or from any other affectionate relationship is irrelevant.

Also in 1972, Walter Burkert produced a similar theory offering a genetic, rather than psychological, explanation for the violent origin of sacrifice and culture. In *Homo Necans*, he built his theory on "the fundamental role played in biology by intraspecific aggression" (1983: 1). ("Intraspecific aggression" is still another name for the war of all against all.) Since genes are affected only by long evolutionary processes, Burkert rejected Freud's single murder and put millennia of hunting kills in its place. But because the aggression of the hunt was originally intraspecific (directed toward humans only), the quarry "was experienced as human," even becoming "a father substitute," partially confirming "Freud's intuition that a patricide stands at the start of human development" (ibid.: 75). In the hunt, intraspecific aggression was redirected against other species, saving humans from self-destruction. By the time the supply of wild animals ran out, hunting behavior was genetically fixed and the behavior was retained, becoming sacrifice of domestic animals.[5]

Human evolution is the achievement of males only. "Man became man through the hunt, through the act of killing" (ibid.). There were no gatherers, and women stayed home "indoors," apparently in separate residences, for there was no community among women (ibid.: 18). "Community is defined by participation in the bloody work of men" (ibid.: 20).

Most important for evolution

> was the development of a social order leading to sharp sexual differentiation, which has even become part of our inherited biological constitution. Among human beings, hunting is man's work—in contrast to all animal predators—requiring both speed and strength; hence the male's long slender thigh. By contrast, since women must bear children with ever larger skulls, they develop round, soft forms. . . .
>
> The success of the "hunting ape" was due to his ability to work cooperatively, to unite with other men in a communal hunt. Thus, man ever since the development of hunting has belonged to two overlapping social structures, the family and the *Männerbund*. . . . At the core of this new type of male community . . . are the acts of killing and eating. (Ibid.: 17–18)

Girard made all sacrifice expiatory and ignored eating. Burkert makes all sacrifice alimentary to fit its hunting origin.[6] But basically their theoretical perspectives are the same.

Burkert is a great scholar of Greek religion, but in *Homo Necans,* he chose to interpret it as preservation of Paleolithic hunting practices about which nothing is known. The giant detour to northern Paleolithic hunters for the origin of Greek culture is the invention of Burkert's teacher, Karl Meuli. Meuli wrote at a time when German classicists, seeking an Aryan origin for Greek civilization, ignored influences from neighboring Semitic or Egyptian civilization that the Greeks identified as the source of much of their own civilization (Bernal 1987). The distinction between *Männerbund* and family is more suggestive of Nazi Germany than it is of Greece, where the sacred male community *was* the family.[7] (Girard's patriarchal formulation, "a father and son—that is, a family,"—is more Greek [op. cit.: 217].)

Critics of social contract theories point out that grounding explanation on a time about which nothing is known, and therefore on imagination, obliges the theorist to explain the origin of society by notions abstracted from contemporary society. As Durkheim said, social contract theories presuppose the society they claim to explain, or, as Hegel put it, "the guiding principle for the *a priori* is the *a posteriori*" (quoted in Benhabib 1986: 25). Projecting an image of human nature drawn from contemporary society onto imagined origins eternalizes this image, making it ahistorical and universal.

Both Girard and Burkert present sacrifice in terms of a universal human nature, including gender relations determined by biologically given male violence. But their arguments are not scientific theories, biological or otherwise; insofar as they universalize their ideas of gender and sacrifice, they are arguing ideologies. To do better, a feminist theory of sacrifice must recognize the historically contingent nature of the gender relations of different traditions, seeing them neither as universal nor as biologically determined, but as historical social products.

By changing our theoretical lens, we can see the war of all against all itself as a historical social product, neither a natural state nor an eternal threat. For example, Marx's critique of social contract claims theorists have lifted the war of all against all from contemporary bourgeois society, where men treat others as means to their own ends. He called this realm of economic striving and bourgeois private family life "civil society." This "sphere of egoism and of the *bellum omnium contra omnes*" (1978a: 35) is in opposition to the political state, which as illusory, unreal community, "in relation to civil society, is just as spiritual as is heaven in relation to earth" (ibid.: 34). In the opposition between state and civil society, "man leads, not only in thought, in consciousness, but in *reality*, in *life*, a double existence—celestial and terrestrial" (ibid). For Marx, this opposition is not salvation from biological drives to self-destruction, but alienation to be overcome in history.

I turn now to the Durkheimian tradition, which has been more important for theories of sacrifice, and is also closer to my own work. The first Durkheimian study of sacrifice, *Sacrifice: Its Nature and Function* (1964), was published in 1898 by two of Durkheim's disciples, Hubert and Mauss. In a number of ways this is a startlingly modern book, comparatively free of the ethnocentric and misogynist presuppositions of its contemporaries. Way ahead of their time, Hubert and Mauss challenged the unity and universality of totemism and abandoned the search for the origin of sacrifice. "Above all," they accurately observed, "it is difficult to find sacrifices that are properly totemic" (ibid.: 5). But the unity of sacrifice was not similarly challenged. Selecting a single complex Vedic sacrifice as the paradigm of all sacrifices, they concluded that sacrifices "are all the same in essence . . . They are the outer coverings of one single mechanism" (1964: 18).[8]

The role of gender in sacrificial ritual was not addressed, which gave an illusion of freedom from patriarchal presuppositions. Gender issues in the social contexts of sacrifices were not raised because the social contexts themselves were ignored throughout. If sacrifices are the same everywhere, there is no reason to locate them in their own varied contexts, and conversely, uprooted from their contexts, sacrificial rituals and their fragments become malleable and can be shown to be the same everywhere.

In its "single mechanism," sacrifice mediates, by means of a victim, between two opposed terms: the sacred and the profane. These polar terms are both united and separated by the sacrificial action, which involves two complementary processes: sacralization, a movement from profane to sacred, and its reciprocal, de-sacralization. In some ways, sacralizing and de-sacralizing resemble the reciprocal processes I have called communion and expiation,[9] but the sacrificial "mechanism" joins and separates not social groups, but a great dichotomy: the sacred and the profane. Like sacrifice, this opposition is the same everywhere. But what are the sacred and the profane? We are given a hint at the end of the book: "Sacred things are social things" (ibid.: 101). The profane receives not even such minimal illumination, nor does the nature of their opposition, the great gulf between them that can only be crossed by a victim in death. It was Durkheim who explicated this dichotomy, and in doing so revealed its gendered aspects.

In *The Elementary Forms of the Religious Life*, Durkheim defined all religion in terms of the opposition between sacred and profane:

All known religious beliefs . . . always suppose a bipartite division of the whole universe, known and knowable, into two
classes which embrace all that exists, but which radically exclude
each other. Sacred things are those which the interdictions protect and isolate; profane things those to which these interdictions
are applied and which must remain at a distance. . . . In all the
history of human thought there exists no other example of two
categories so profoundly differentiated or so radically opposed to
one another. (1965: 52–56)

Like Hubert and Mauss, he understood sacrifice in terms of this opposition, but unlike them, he turned to totemism and the search for origins. Since he identified sacrifice with a universal social quality, moral
renunciation, he was convinced that totemism must contain an elementary form of sacrifice.[10]

Durkheim was not an ex-Protestant like Frazer, but the son, grandson, and great-grandson of rabbis. He made totemism the most elementary religion not to denounce it as savage nonsense but to find there the
origin of conceptual thought itself. He claimed that Australian aboriginal men represented their society to themselves in ritual, making aspects of it available to consciousness in conceptual form for the first
time. In these "collective representations" originated ideas such as time,
space, class, and causality: the Kantian categories of understanding
(1965: 22). For Durkheim, the categories, on which "all thought" depends, are *products* of religion, but the sacred/profane dichotomy is a
precondition for religion, based on the eternal and universal dichotomy
between social and individual.

Two years after the publication of *The Elementary Forms,* complain-
ing that critics had "not perceived the principle" on which it rests, Durkheim set out to remedy their misperceptions by explicating the eternal
duality of human nature, a duality that is "only a particular case of that
division of things into the sacred and the profane that is the foundation
of all religions" (1979: 335). "In every age man has . . . conceived of
himself as being formed of two radically heterogeneous beings: the
body and the soul" (ibid.: 326). These two represent the opposition
between what is social in us (and consequently transcendent and sacred) and what is merely individual (and consequently amoral, unen-
during, and profane), especially our bodies. The opposition of social and
individual is a spirit/flesh dichotomy, in which moral rules are opposed
to sensual appetites and stable conceptual thought to shifting sense per-
ceptions.

Man's duality (it is not clear that it is woman's too) is a source of suffering as well as transcendence: He is torn in two and must endlessly renounce physical satisfaction for the sake of moral principle. With the inevitable progress of civilization, the tension of dualism must grow ever greater—but possibly not for women, who as less social than men are less given to moral rules and conceptual thought. With evolving civilization comes increasing division of labor. "The two great functions of psychic life are . . . dissociated . . . one of the sexes takes care of the affective functions and the other of intellectual functions" (1964: 60). As reason and emotion grow apart, women's very crania are shrinking (ibid.: 57–58).

Durkheim described Australian aboriginal people as leading a double life, very like the one Marx saw Europeans leading: For a part of the year, separated in individual families, they pursued purely private utilitarian economic interests; part of the year they met in great social gatherings to perform their rituals. All ordinary sexual activity took place during the profane individual-pursuit-of-economic-interests part of the year when the sexes were together. During the social, and sacred, part of the year men were separated from women and children. According to Durkheim, Australian women, who were profane in relation to men, were excluded from all rituals, even from knowledge about them.[11] That is, women had no access to *any* of the process by which conceptual thought is formed. Over and over he described their exclusion. The exclusion of women even provided an identifying sign to distinguish religious practices from those that were mere magic. If the capacity for conceptual thought is acquired only through participation in a process that excludes women, how does it come about that women can think? If you hold fast to Durkheim's analysis, there is no way to answer this question.[12]

Why are women so solidly on the "individual" side of what is in essence a social/individual split? Doesn't socialization begin in relation to women? For Durkheim, true social life, in France as well as in Australia, takes place among men only. His dedicated band of disciples was exclusively male. Only in such professional groups did he see a future for religious life in an increasingly secular world. At manhood, his son was admitted to that community, but his daughter, forbidden any access to higher education, was excluded. In France as well as in Australia, women and children are not fully socialized. Little is known of what they do together in the absence of males, but in any case it is not social. Probably it involves too much physical gratification and not enough moral renunciation.

Durkheim's search for origins led him into a universalizing projection much like the social contract theories he rejected. Although structures something like his sacred/profane dichotomy can be recognized in the Catholicism of his time, and even in the Judaism of his youth, that dichotomy is certainly not universal. It has not been found by most good ethnographers studying "primitive" religion. Evans-Pritchard, Nadel, Lienhardt, Goody, Turner, all fail to find it.[13] In particular, it is not to be found in aboriginal Australia. As a respected ethnographer of Australian religion has said of it, "To use the dichotomy is to disregard what is the case" (Stanner (1967: 230).

Like other "origin" theorists, Durkheim made eternal human nature from the historical divisions of his own society, finding in Australia the same dichotomy of sacred male community and profane individual pursuit of economic and sexual interests that Marx had located in nineteenth-century Europe. Like Marx, Durkheim saw "man" torn in two by the social/individual dichotomy. They both identified this as the ground of religion, differing in their evaluations of it.[14] Even though Durkheim rejected social contract theories, he recreated their social/individual dualism.[15]

In spite of this critique, my work is indebted to Durkheim in the recognition that people, sometimes men only, bring aspects of their society into being in ritual action. Disagreement with Durkheim has also contributed to my work. Many of Durkheim's accounts of sacred and profane are phrased (although not labeled) as contradictory dichotomy, "A/Not-A." The "logic of sacrifice" I describe in chapter 2 takes the form it does partly because I want to account for religious forms of contradictory dichotomy (such as the Israelite clean/unclean) as social products, not as universal structures established for eternity in the nature of reality.

Just while Durkheim was discovering sacrifice in totemic ritual, the whole system of totemism began to be questioned by American anthropologists, who, in the early twentieth century, were perhaps not so securely in place at the pinnacle of civilization, and who certainly found it more difficult than European scholars to snatch a custom, a phrase, or an aspect of social organization from the Ojibwa or the Omaha and blend it smoothly into place in Australia among the Arunta. By the mid-twentieth century, totemism, as a complete religious and social system, had lost credibility everywhere. Its final passing has been elegantly recorded by a student of Mauss's, Claude Lévi-Strauss, whose discussion of sacrifice is a by-product of his account of the rise and fall of the European "totemic illusion."[16]

Lévi-Strauss abandoned the search for origins and made a theory of sacrifice without reference to gender[17]—or even to religion—but nevertheless he did not escape entanglement in Durkheim's social/individual polarity. This appears in his theory as filtered through the work of the Swiss linguist Ferdinand de Saussure. Influenced by Durkheim, Saussure thought of language as social (a feature of the transcendent collective consciousness) in contrast to speech as individual (idiosyncratic and unpredictable). He built his theory of language by excluding speech from the subject matter of linguistics. Like Durkheim's social/individual dichotomy, Saussure's language/speech dichotomy is a spirit/flesh division. Language is spiritual, ordered and intelligible; speech is embodied, imperfect, and sometimes makes little sense.

Saussure's dichotomy underlies Lévi-Strauss's theory of sacrifice. Sacred and profane are gone; now sacrifice and totemism are polarized. Lévi-Strauss was right to oppose them,[18] but the *way* he did it made nonsense of sacrifice. He placed totemic classification on the social, intelligible side of the split, and sacrifice on the individual, unintelligible side, and so threw it away as worthless: "a private discourse wanting in good sense" (1966: 228). In order to make sacrifice "private," he had to throw out all its social contexts too. My own understanding of sacrifice has been enriched by what I fished out of Lévi-Strauss's trash barrel.

Lévi-Strauss opposed sacrifice and totemism not as religious systems, but as modes of classifying natural species. According to him, people who have been described as practicing "totemism" (an institution that does not exist as such) have really been making systems of classification. Totemic classification accurately correlates two systems of differences: differences between natural species, and differences between groups of people. Social groups are not *like* natural species, rather, they *differ* from other social groups in the same way that natural species differ from one another. By adopting the differences between animals, social groups do away with their own resemblances, for where there is no discontinuity there is neither order nor intelligibility. In totemic classification, "one beast can never be taken for another," nor can a member of the bear clan ever be confused with a member of the eagle clan (1966: 223).

Totemic classification is true, "there really are natural species and they do indeed form a discontinuous series" (ibid.: 222), but sacrifice "adopts a conception of the natural series which is false," for it represents it as continuous (ibid.: 228). In sacrifice (reminiscent of Hubert and Mauss), the series of natural species "plays the part of an intermediary between two polar terms, the sacrificer and the deity, between which there is initially no homology nor even any sort of relation," except as one is established through the victim "by means of a series of successive identifications" (ibid.: 225). Citing the Nuer substitution of cucumber for ox as victim, Lévi-Strauss claims, "In default of the prescribed object, any other can replace it. . . . Sacrifice therefore belongs to the realms of continuity" (ibid.: 224).

Sacrificial classification makes natural species "oriented" as well as continuous:

> A cucumber is sacrificed if there is no ox but the sacrifice of an ox for want of a cucumber would be an absurdity. In [totemic classification] . . . on the other hand, relations are always reversible. In a system of clan appellation in which both figured, the oxen would be genuinely equivalent to the cucumbers. (Ibid.)

For Lévi-Strauss, totemic classification accurately correlates two real systems of difference, natural species and social groups: it is a metaphoric system. In contrast, since neither natural species nor social groups are really continuous and oriented, sacrifice establishes relations not of resemblance, but only of contiguity: it is not metaphoric but only metonymic.

Lévi-Strauss relies on a structural model of language as a system of discontinuous oppositions within which continuity in any form means cognitive disorder. But sacrifice is not only false because it belongs to the realms of continuity, it belongs to continuity because he has already rejected it as false. Having put it on the individual, unintelligible side of the dichotomy, he cannot see that it too indexes social groups and distinctions between them. Generalizing wildly from one to all traditions, he cannot see that sacrifices create selective continuity, not obliteration of distinction throughout the natural and social worlds.[19] He thinks of sacrifice as operating in the same timeless conceptual "space" as totemic classification. He has even sketched a little geometry of sacrifice (1966: 225). But this is why the continuity and orientation of species are "false" to him. The medium of sacrifice is time, not simply conceptual space. Natural species are indeed discontinuous synchronically, but they are continuous diachronically. He finds continuity and orientation of species unintelligible because he has stripped them of their temporal dimension. (For more on sacrifice and time, see Appendix.)

Modern theories of biological evolution describe natural species as precisely continuous and oriented. Like theories of evolution, ancestor cults are "about" continuity and discontinuity of descent. Behind both sacrifice and theories of biological evolution is a common concern with time and continuity, generation and mortality, entirely lacking in totemic classification, which orders a timeless world. A dodo totem would not be affected by extinction because it is not the living, breeding species, but the idea of a dodo, as not a penguin, not a pelican, that is required.[20] Groups of people, however, are not timeless; a clan can die out, destroying the structural arrangement of the remaining clans. Lévi-Strauss describes "a permanent conflict" between totemic classification and history, an "obstinate fidelity" between totemic classification and history, an "obstinate fidelity" with which totemic systems of classification cling "to a past conceived as a timeless model, rather than as a stage in the historical process" (1966: 231–36). His discussion of the "fundamental antipathy between history and [totemic] systems of classification" continues in a most interesting way:

> This perhaps explains what one is tempted to call the "totemic void," for in the bounds of the great civilizations of Europe and Asia there is a remarkable absence of anything which might have reference to totemism, even in the form of remains. The reason is surely that the latter have elected to explain themselves by history and that this undertaking is incompatible with that of classifying things and beings (natural and social) by means of finite groups. (1966: 232)

Without observing that these "great civilizations of Europe and Asia" are all rooted in sacrificial religion, he continues:

> When . . . a society sides with history, classification into finite groups becomes impossible because the derivative series, instead of reproducing the original series, merges with it to form a single series in which each term is derivative in relation to the one preceding it and original in relation to the one coming after it. . . . a continuous evolution is postulated within a single series that accepts an unlimited number of terms. (Ibid.: 233)

This "continuous evolution" resembles the continuity and orientation he has rejected as false in sacrifice, but he cannot make his own theory serve him because he has thrown sacrifice away as false and denied it metaphorical significance. It does not occur to him that ancestral cults celebrate oriented continuity. The priestly source of Genesis was surely a historian of sorts, and P's genealogies, so perfect and so one-dimensional, are indeed an ordering of the whole of the past into a continuous linear series, in which "each term is derivative in relation to the one preceding it and original in relation to the one coming after it."

Lévi-Strauss's model is based on an exclusion as fundamental, as distorting, and as purifying as is P's exclusion of mothers from genealogies: Saussure's exclusion of speech from language. Saussure's language, like Lévi-Strauss's totemic classification, is a timeless structure of discontinuous oppositions and correlations. It excludes speech as embodied action, as oriented, linear series of events *in time*. As linguistic structure is disembodied (for Durkheim, the body was *the* individuating factor) so too Lévi-Strauss's classificatory systems are disembodied. Totemic classification chooses natural species "not because they are 'good to eat' but because they are 'good to think'" (1963: 89). In contrast, sacrifice is fundamentally an alimentary ritual, even in being sometimes specifically anti-alimentary. Classificatory systems "are not, or are not primarily, means of communication. They are means of thinking" (1966: 67). In contrast, sacrifice is a means of communication, and of severing communication. It is an active *doing*, not a finished system. Like speech, it is necessarily an affair of the flesh.[21]

As P purified descent by casting out mothers, Saussure purified language by casting out speech. But he did not render speaking unintelligible by depriving it entirely of linguistic structure. For Saussure, acts of speech are imperfect because they are individualized, but they are not wholly private and therefore not entirely wanting in sense. Lévi-Strauss's notion of sacrifice has no such restraint:

> It is not enough, then, to say that [totemic classification] is a system of reference and [sacrifice] a system of operations . . . that one is true and the other is false. Rather, to put it precisely, classificatory systems belong to the level of language: they are codes which . . . aim always to make sense. The system of sacrifice, on the other hand, represents a private discourse wanting in good sense for all that it may be frequently pronounced. (1966: 228)

Lévi-Strauss freed sacrifice from its supposed roots in "totemism," but in so doing he put it on the irrational, individual, profane side of the great dichotomy and made it unintelligible. He might almost have made it an invention of women, like Frazer's totemism.

A branch of this French structuralist line of descent has influenced my account of Greek sacrifice. Vernant, Detienne, and colleagues, following Lévi-Strauss and structural linguistics, insist that the elements of Greek myth must be understood, not as individual symbols of this or that isolated category, but in opposition to other such elements within particular systems of classification. An important difference from Lévi-Strauss is their emphatic rejection of any universal category of sacrifice. Descendants of Hubert and Mauss, they see Greek sacrifice mediating between men and gods by means of a victim that both joins and separates them (Vernant 1989: 34–35). But the sacred/profane split is rejected as ethnocentric projection (Durand 1979: 89) and the oppositional structure has become threefold, the middle term mediating between the poles: natural/social/divine; animals/humans/gods; raw/cooked/burnt. Sacrifices are restored to their social contexts, gender becomes an important category of analysis, and Greek misogyny is interpreted as a feature of its own historical social contexts, not of eternal human nature.

The final Durkheimian theory to be considered here is Valeri's *Kingship and Sacrifice* (1985). This is both a detailed account of Hawaiian sacrifice and a formulation of principles for interpreting ritual in general. Valeri's theory is grounded in Durkheim and Mauss but breaks out of eternal dichotomy by understanding ritual as dialectical process. Durkheim is modified by Hegel and Feuerbach.

For Hegel, says Valeri, "religion is 'objective spirit,' that is, the objectified system of ideas of a community. This view is essentially the same that is found not only in Hegel's pupils—such as Feuerbach and Marx—but also in . . . Durkheim" (1985: x). For Hegel, in the course of history the collective subject (spirit and mind) appears in its own products (gods, institutions, and other cultural artifacts) as objectified and consequently as estranged from itself. Now divided, subjectivity relates to itself as object and doesn't recognize itself there; human creations appear as immutable givens. When recognition does come, the dialectical circle is completed.[22] Hegel's subject/object divisions can take spirit/flesh form, but unlike Durkheim's spirit/flesh dichotomy (which equals his social/individual distinction), Hegel's divisions are not eternal. They are moments in an ongoing process in which estrangement comes into being and is also overcome.

Valeri puts an essentially Durkheimian account of ritual in Hegelian terms. In the public work of sacrifice, Hawaiians produce the concept of the collective subject (in Durkheimian language, Hawaiians represent society in conceptual form), but (now back to Hegelian language) this concept is produced in objectified, estranged form—for example, as the god Ku.[23]

> The dialectical circle in which the subject unconsciously reflects himself in the objects, then apperceives himself in them, is not completed. The subject becomes aware of his properties in the object, but not of their subjective nature. In other words, he only half recognizes himself in them: he conceives them as an external, human active being that underlies the natural objects—as a god. (1985: 345–46)

For Durkheim too, the concept of the collective subject is produced in ritual, but he does not see this as alienation. For him, the collective subject (society as *"conscience collective"*) is actually transcendent. To represent it as sacred or divine is adequate conceptualization rather than alienation. Sacred and profane represent the real opposition between two fundamental aspects of human existence: social and individual. This dichotomy is eternal and universal, not historically contingent, not an estrangement to be dialectically surpassed. (Try using Durkheim's eternal dichotomy to interpret Liholiho's eating with women. Or the Christian Apostles' eating with the profane uncircumcised. As Paul said,

"Neither circumcision counts for anything, nor uncircumcision, but a new creation" [Gal. 6:15].)

Hegel's pupil Feuerbach is also important for Valeri's theory. Both Feuerbach and Durkheim see religion as the product of a collective subject. For Durkheim, this is "society"; for Feuerbach it is "species being." Like Durkheim's "society," "species being" transcends an opposed, devalued, individual aspect of human life. For Feuerbach, our failings are aspects of our individuality. Collectively we overcome them all, even death: as individuals we die; as species being we are immortal.

Just as for Durkheim the content of religious representation is the social, so for Feuerbach it is species being, but there is an important difference between them. For Durkheim, religious representation is the way society originally becomes conscious of itself. Without such representation society cannot begin to know itself or anything else in conceptual form. Religious representation enriches society. For Feuerbach, in contrast, precisely what is given in religious representation is lost to humans, alienated from them. Whatever is put into God impoverishes a humanity that cannot recognize its own essence in objectified form (1957: passim).

In Valeri's synthesis of Durkheim and Feuerbach, ritual representation both reveals and conceals. "The ordering virtue of ritual is not due simply to enlightening, but also to blinding" (ibid.: xii). Ritual makes conceptual thought available to consciousness—but only in disguised form. Sacrificers "only half recognize" themselves in their victims and divinities.

For Valeri, to understand Hawaiian sacrifice we need to recognize the ways in which knower and known are entangled. We must stop presupposing a world divided into an objective, non-symbolic nature and a detached, pure subjectivity. If all natural species are divinized in Hawaii it is because they have an objectified subjective content. This comes about because the activities in which people encounter nature, the ways they come to know it, are perceived in part as aspects of nature itself. Hawaiians see their own "species properties" most vividly in agricultural species because these are "congealed" labor and because, as potential food, they also contain "human life in potential form" (ibid.: 80–81). All victims contain the subject in objective form; this must be given to the gods where it belongs (for they too are objectified subjectivity) before the remainder can be used as profane food. Species especially evocative of human activities, such as pigs, can never be fully desacralized; they are too charged with subjective content and must remain in a ritual context.[24]

Valeri pays careful attention to the social contexts of sacrifices, he recognizes gender as fundamental for his analysis, and he describes the gender hierarchy as a historically contingent feature of Hawaiian sacrifice, not as universal human nature. Nevertheless, he appears to fall into a particularly Durkheimian dilemma. Ritual is "creation of awareness through 'model experience'"; it is "programmed learning through activities that involve the apperception of codes, principles, concepts, and their reproduction in practice" (ibid.: 345, 344). Some basic cultural concepts are learned in no other way. For example, the great cycle of sacrifices to Ku, in which a tree becomes a god, "furnishes all participants in the ritual with the only experience they can have of society manifesting itself as unity and multiplicity, that is, of the unity of the species realized as a coordinated complex of social actors" (ibid.: 345). If this is so, what about the "awareness" of those who are never participants in sacrifice, who are denied all opportunities for such "programmed learning"? Do *they* learn of the unity of the species? If so, how?

Valeri never addresses these questions, which are very like the one that Durkheim's definition of religion created for his sociology of knowledge: If access to conceptual thought is gained only through a process that excludes women, how does it come about that women can think? Durkheim resolves this by making women mentally deficient and also by equating "society" with the sacred male community: women really are individualized outsiders, unsocialized barbarians. Valeri accepts only the latter solution—whether as a student of Durkheimian theory or of Hawaiian sacrificial ideology is unclear. In Hawaiian sacrificial ideology, as in Durkheimian theory, the collective subject, the big concept maker, is male; the opposed female pole is hardly equipped to be a subject at all.

That women are individualized also follows from Valeri's interpretation of hierarchy. Hierarchy is unity in diversity, and Hawaiian society is "a coherent whole" only as hierarchy. Ascending hierarchical ranks include in themselves more of the collectivity as they subsume inferior ranks—"the human male . . . stands for the entire human species because he is its superior form" (ibid.: 270). Superior ranks are consequently more social as well as more pure. The divine king, "a visible personification of the human species," embodies the whole of society, and sure enough, there is nothing collective about a common woman: she embodies no one but herself (ibid.: 158). The pure/impure opposition on which the hierarchy is built is another version of the old social/individual split.[25]

Most of the above theories, whether they are variants of social contract theory or Durkheimian theory, posit a collective subject. To do this, they have to separate consciousness from mortal individuals and make it unitary and transcendent, as, for example, Durkheim's "collective consciousness." Even Freud grounded *Totem and Taboo* on a biologically inheritable (and therefore immortal) "mass psyche" (1950: 203). Burkert is less explicit, but by putting culture in shared DNA, he puts himself in an analogous theoretical position. Girard, who recognizes two societies, has two collective subjects: "the primitive mind" and "the modern mind."

When theory posits a collective subject, some people's subjectivity will be more collective than others', and when theory construes society as one and whole, some people are always going to be more "social" than those whose voices, if heard, would damage the unity of the model. (Remember Hawaiian women's roles in the fall of the sacrificial tradition.) When theory presents society as a single coherent whole, the ideas of those in power appear as those of the big concept maker (the collective consciousness, mind, species being, or whatever his name is) and therefore of all who are true members of society. In that case, those true members will very likely all turn out to be men.

A theory that denies reality to "society" as one and whole, and to its spirit, the collective subject, will interpret sacrifice somewhat differently. Marx did not always keep clear of the collective subject, but in his notion of ideology, he described how systems of ideas serving the interests of only some persons or classes can masquerade as universal truths; the view from one particular social situation is presented as everyone's perspective (1978b: 172–75). This is achieved in the same way a collective subject is made, by detaching consciousness from concrete individuals and making it universal.

Any social practice will take on different meanings as it is looked at through different theoretical lenses. Take the sacrificial construction of the Hawaiian state as an example and look at it through some of these theories. It is not so easy to make this appear as genetically determined ritualization of the practices of Paleolithic Siberian hunters, but it *can* be interpreted as a crucial lifesaving method for controlling the repeated outbreaks of the war of all against all (reciprocal violence) that follow every king's death. Such a theory is a sacrificial ideology and will legitimate male domination as it legitimates royal sacrifice. This theory, of course, requires that we ignore the fact that the repeated outbreaks of anarchy in Hawaii were not aspects of universal human nature but features of the sacrificial tradition and disappeared with it. From still another theoretical perspective, Hawaiian royal sacrifice appears to exemplify a universal religious process mediating and differentiating between pure and impure, sacred and profane, social and individual, male and female. This perspective too will legitimate and universalize sacrificial gender domination. From still one more theoretical perspective, the one that I prefer, Hawaiian royal sacrifice can be seen as a historically contingent practice for production of a political ideology in which the perspective of male nobles is elaborated as transcendent divine truth, legitimating one particular historical form of male domination by making it appear universal and eternal.

TEN

Conclusion

A S FEMINIST SCHOLARSHIP, this is a contribution to the struggle toward a perspective that is at least partially free of patriarchal presuppositions. Like every perspective, the one developed here cannot bring all dimensions of any tradition into central focus, but it does illuminate aspects of sacrifice that have been regularly left in darkness. As is common in feminist scholarship, what it lights up has not been hidden but only ignored, has not been invisible but only irrelevant. That is, sacrificial traditions have rarely been questioned about the ways they are grounded in the social relations of reproduction or about the ways they work to achieve male domination. Most theories have ignored the ways in which sacrifice remedies having-been-born-of-woman, establishing bonds of intergenerational continuity between males that transcend their absolute dependence on childbearing women.

I have not produced a universal theory reducing all sacrificial traditions to a single strand of meaning or purpose. Instead, a set of questions has been developed about relations between sacrificial practices, social organization, and gender from which any well-described tradition may be examined. I have been asking questions such as these: What role does sacrificing (in any particular tradition) play in indexing social groups and their boundaries? What kinds of social structures are so identified? Who is included? Who excluded? What is the relation of women, especially childbearing women, to sacrificial practices? How is intergenerational continuity between males maintained? Are there oppositions between sexual reproduction and social reproduction? What forms do they take? And so on. Societies in which sacrifice is in tension with recognized or latent descent through women (such as Ashanti, Hawaii, or ancient Israel) are perhaps the most interesting to look at from this perspective. Sacrificial solutions to descent through women (such as the Ashanti use of latent patrilineal descent or the Hawaiian coopting of childbearing in sacrifice) may be more illuminating than smooth affinities between sacrifice and patriliny.

What I have taken as problematic, and therefore the conclusions I have reached, follow from my original interest in religious legitimation of male domination and oppositions between blood sacrificial religions and childbearing women. But this is not an account of the origin (the taproot as Fraser would say) of patriarchy. Like sacrifices, those theories that make sacrifice coterminous with patriarchal civilization (e.g., Girard 1977, 1987; Burkert 1983, 1987) work to legitimate a world in which male domination is eternalized. These theories do reflect real aspects of sacrificing societies, but they see them as aspects of eternal human nature rather than as historically contingent products of one or another particular social world. Blood sacrificial traditions, and the kinds of social organization they are at home in, arise only with agrarian and pastoral societies and disappear with them. Only some of the many forms of patriarchy have been constituted in sacrifice.

When Martin Luther said to the Church of Rome, "In truth, your re-sacrificing is a most impious re-crucifying," sacrificially maintained domination was sorely wounded, but patriarchy itself took new forms. There is more than one way to exclude women from control of the production of religious meaning. In Europe, family structures were already changing when Luther rejected the priestly sacrifice of the Mass. Lineages and extended kin groups were giving way to separate conjugal families of husband, wife, and children, and feudal property was giving way to private bourgeois family property. (Atkinson 1991: chap.6; Herlihy 1985: chap.4; Davis 1977: 100). Each separate bourgeois family could still be ruled by its own patriarch, but these families embodied different kinds of gender domination, and they too must be recognized as historically contingent, not as evidence of eternal human nature. Conjugal families without ties to lineage or lineage property are not built on enduring intergenerational continuity, nor do they depend on sacrifice for their legitimation.

Because gender relations link historical social relations to a biological base, they appear natural, inevitable. (Even Marx, who refused to see nature in a cherry tree,[1] saw gender as natural.) This apparently natural quality makes gender unequaled as a cornerstone of domination. Growing up in families, people learn, along with gender, systems of domination that can be elaborated on a tribal and state level. Building political systems of domination on gender relations makes political domination too appear inevitable and unchangeable.

One of the most striking and widespread aspects of sacrifice is its prominence in the development of the state in ancient and pre-industrial societies. This is true of traditions as different and unrelated as those of the Aztecs and Incas, of ancient Israel, of the nineteenth-century West African city states, Hawaii, Athens, Rome, and a large number of others. Combes-Schilling (1989), in an excellent work on the Islamic-based Moroccan monarchy, convincingly argues the central role of Islamic sacrifice in the historical formation and maintenance of that state. Sacrifice is an extraordinarily efficient method for control of the production of religious meaning, especially effective in centralizing and making exclusive the means of communication with the transcendent powers that legitimate the social order.

There is more than efficiency involved in the dependence of ancient states on sacrifice. This dependence reflects the underlying gender and family base of their systems of political domination. Those states depending on sacrifice were what Max Weber called "patrimonial" states, in which the state is an extension of the ruler's household and political power is inherited within families and lineages. Enduring tradition, not a rational legal constitution, legitimates the apparently immutable system of domination. A particularly clear example of the gender base of domination is the Hawaiian state cult in which the domination of male superior over male inferior explicitly replicates male-female domination. Benin and Dahomey are also classic examples. In Ashanti, where ordinary family structures involved far less male domination, the state turned to patrilineal family organization to embody its sacrificially legitimated power.

Any foundation for apparent similarities in meaning systems between unrelated traditions must be sought in common conditions of life, such as the way agrarian and pastoral systems of production may lead to a concern for birth- and death-transcending male intergenerational continuity. Set in such contexts, sacrificially maintained meaning systems regularly value social and religious reproduction over sexual reproduction, the *pater* over the *genitor* as well as paternity over maternity. In unrelated traditions, the body of the victim undergoes an analogous transformation. Death disorganizes the victim (a product of sexual reproduction) only to permit re-organization on another level, that of "eternal" social structures (e.g., see Durand 1979: 155). That is, in the destruction of its living organic whole, the victim's body becomes the effective sign of the social order that is indexed by the distribution— and non-distribution—of its flesh.

It is a mistake to see this in terms of a spirit/flesh distinction. In alimentary sacrifice the victim's body does not de-materialize; it is still flesh, even if its organization has become that of the social group. Social structures are never purely spiritual either. ("The people are put together as a bull is put together," say the Dinka [Lienhardt 1961: 23].) Just as the victim does not become a disembodied idea, neither was it purely physiological before the act of sacrifice. Social and symbolic organization regularly characterize any potential victim before it is sacrificed. Simply as property, domestic animals are not purely physiological beings. The "property" aspect of anything (that it is mine, not yours) is not physical, but is a mode of relationship between people.

These social aspects of potential victims are variously represented. For example, at a Lugbara sacrifice, the living eat the victim's flesh and the ancestors eat its soul. Only domestic animals have souls, so it is worse than meaningless to offer wild animals in sacrifice (Middleton 1960). In the Vedic tradition, animal victims must belong to a ranked series: man, horse, ox, sheep, goat. Wild animals belong to an opposed, unranked category (Das 1983).[2] Different as these two sacrificial systems are, domestic animals share social and religious qualities (souls, hierarchical order) with humans, and both traditions strongly forbid any non-sacrificial slaughter of domestic animals. In these traditions, as in many others, a victim that already has social qualities is violently further socialized in sacrificial ritual.

Blood sacrificial religions are disappearing as modern industrial production, the world market, democracy, and science expand. Blood sacrifice does not even make sense in contemporary industrial society, where separate individuals, joined in temporary, voluntary association, are thought of as the basic units of society; where social institutions are not conceived as integrated by descent, real or metaphorical. But even if sacrifice may not be a major future means of disempowering women, it is still important to understand sacrificially maintained domination. All of the historical and contemporary methods by which male domination is achieved need to be demystified. Feminist scholarship is correctly committed to recovering women's silenced voices, but it must also look critically at all the varied methods for silencing them.

APPENDIX:

SACRIFICIAL CALENDARS

R ELATIONS BETWEEN SACRIFICE AND TEMPORAL CONTINUITY are particularly evident when sacrifice is recognized as maintaining not merely the continuity and discontinuity of social groups, but the continuity and discontinuity of social time itself. The world's great calendrical systems were developed in relation to sacrifices. Ancient calendrical systems are chronological orderings of sacrificial festivals; examples are Greek, Israelite, Egyptian, Roman, Hawaiian, Ashanti, Chinese, Vedic, Aztec, and Mayan calendars. In ancient Greece, for example, "the order of the calendar is largely identical with the sequence of festivals. For this reason the calendars exhibit an extreme particularism; there are virtually as many calendars as there are cities and tribes" (Burkert 1985: 225). The sacrificial calendar was the largest public inscription in Athens. Demosthenes asks why the festivals are always on time when the military expeditions "invariably arrive too late," and answers, "at the festivals everything is ordered by statute; every man among you knows long beforehand who of his tribe is [to do exactly what] . . . nothing is undetermined, but in what pertains to war and its equipment, everything is ill-arranged, ill-managed, ill-defined" (IV 35–36; in 1989: 88–91).

Many ancient sacrificial calendars were based on twelve lunar months. (Intercalary months or days were inserted to adjust the lunar year of 354 days to the solar year.) In the Israelite, Greek, and Roman traditions, the ordering of agnatic descent groups was articulated with the ritual ordering of time (Noth 1960: 88). In Genesis, not only Jacob had twelve sons, so did Nahor, Ishmael, and Esau. In Athens, before the reform of Kleisthenes, the four tribes each contained three phratries, and these in turn were divided into thirty *gene*. (A lunar month contains twenty-nine and one-half days.)

Israelite priests also recognized a solar calendar, divided into fifty-two weeks (Vermes 1975: 43). The Dead Sea Scrolls tells of "the fifty-two heads of family in the congregation," and the "twenty-six leaders of the priestly divisions." Both lunar and solar social organization figure in the Dead Sea Scrolls: "And the twelve Chief Priests shall minister at the daily sacrifice before God, whereas the twenty-six leaders of the priestly divisions shall minister in their divisions" (ibid.: 125).

The Aztec and Mayan calendars were organized in a 260-day purely ritual, non-astronomical year of 13 non-lunar months of twenty days, running concurrently with a 365-day solar year. The two systems completed one joint cycle every fifty-two solar years. Perhaps Aztec anxiety about solar continuity was a feature of the very lack of correlation between astronomical and ritual years. Frazer described Aztec human sacrifice as based on astronomical error, but Aztec sacrifice was less an astronomical affair than were many Old World sacrifices. Social time, not purely astronomical time, was at issue in sacrifices "to make the sun rise." Aztec priests were not, as Frazer thought, manipulating a purely physical universe but were maintaining the continuity of the social world by homicidal means. A better analogy to Frazer's Europe is not to astronomers, but to the World War I generals who sent hundreds of thousands of young men to certain death in an attempt to preserve a particular social order. (This observation is in memory of Robert Hertz and André Durkheim, victims. For an account of Hertz's "sacrificial" death, see Evans-Pritchard's introduction to Hertz 1960.)

INTRODUCTION

1. In many African traditions, a man must wait until his own father is dead and he has become the patriarch of an extended family before he can offer sacrifice himself. In the Vedic tradition, only after his marriage could a man begin to offer sacrifice (daily offerings in the domestic fire); only after he had begotten a son could he offer the solemn sacrifices requiring three fires (Biardeau 1976: 34).

2. Among the West African Ashanti, even to draw water for sacrifice a woman must be past menopause (Rattray 1923: 96). In ancient Athens, Demeter's priestesses were reported to have been virgins, while "the priestess of Athena Polis is not a virgin but a mature woman who has put conjugal life behind her" (Burkert 1985: 98).

Detienne, moreover, in his essay "The Violence of Well Born Ladies" (1989), painstakingly re-examined all the evidence apparently showing that in Athens as well as in other ancient Greek city-states certain categories of women, especially among the "well born," had prominent sacrificial roles, even to wielding the knife in blood sacrifices. He concluded that all these reports and references were rooted in male fantasy fears of the power of women, especially that of mature childbearing women, women as mothers, and by a kind of negative relief simply emphasized the absolute control of sacrifice by men. Some references to women as priests he traced back to ritual in which male priests dressed up as women, rather like the male priests in Benin, noted below, who on certain sacrifical occasions masqueraded as pregnant women. He finally concluded,

> Iphigenia is right: in Greek societies it is not the woman who can hold the knife. There is not a single example of a *mageiros,* butcher-sacrificer-cook, who is not male. Moreover, the word *mageiros* has no feminine forms. . . .
> In other words, the Greek system does not allow any thought of women as butchers and sacrificers. (Ibid.: 143)

Such illustrations could go on and on. I know of only one traditional society in which married, childbearing women are reported to be the major sacrificers, the Lovedu of southern Africa. But the sacrificing role of these women, though neither virginal nor post-menopausal, is still specifically non-childbearing. A Lovedu woman never sacrifices for the lineage to which her children belong but only for that of her father and brothers. This is because she is recognized as the one who enabled the line of descent from father to son to continue—but notice it is not by bearing children that she performs this service. Her children are born for her husband's lineage, for which she never sacrifices. She is responsible for the continuity of her brother's lineage because it is her marriage cattle, the bride-wealth given by her husband's lineage, that enables her brother to marry and beget offspring (Krige and Krige 1943 and 1954).

The only important truly atypical exception I know to the rule excluding childbearing women from the regular practice of sacrificing is contemporary Haiti, where traditional family structure has been doubly dislocated. The first disruption of West African descent systems was a consequence of transporting slaves to the New World. In rural Haiti family structure was partially reconstituted around inheritance of land, but during slave times, when land did not perform that organizing function, women probably assumed atypical positions in family structure in spite of any enduring patriarchal ideology. More recently, in moves to the city, where only women are likely to find employment and inherited land loses its organizing power, family structure is further reorganized. Families with a heritage of patriarchal ideology find themselves organized around women as exclusive economic producers. Today, urban Haitian voodoo priestesses regularly sacrifice small animals, although they will call in a male priest to sacrifice large ones. Women are not ordinarily sacrificers in the traditional West African religions from which Haitian voodoo takes its roots, nor do they ordinarily sacrifice in rural Haiti (Karen McCarthy Brown, personal communication; see also Brown 1991).

3. See chapter 8 for more discussion and references.

4. For example, the Australian *intichiuma* ritual, Southeast Asian headhunting, Iroquois ritual torture of prisoners of war.

5. A purely empirical, statistical cross-cultural study is not an option because determining what is "sacrifice" and what is not is itself an interpretive procedure.

CHAPTER 1

1. The Revised Standard Version of the Bible (Holy Bible 1952) is used throughout the book, unless otherwise specified, but I have sometimes altered the translation slightly to make it more literal. Here I have altered "forgiveness" to the older "remission."

2. My account draws on Talcott Parsons's discussion of the positivists and their dilemma in chapters 1–3 of *The Structure of Social Action*, vol. 1.

3. For interesting neo-Tylorian accounts see Horton 1971 and Goody 1961.

In my opinion, by far the most consistent of intellectual positivist interpretations of religion is Mary Baker Eddy's *Science and Health with Key to the Scriptures*. Christian Science certainly draws on nineteenth-century positivism. Eddy and Tylor were contemporaries for seventy-eight years; their major works were published within four years (*Science and Health* in 1875 and *Primitive Culture* in 1871).

4. Among several failings of this kind of approach is one Durkheim pointed out: "As for the theory of Frazer, it presupposes a thorough-going idiocy on the part of the primitive which known facts do not allow us to attribute to him" (1965: d203).

5. Harner 1977; Harris 1977. This illustration gives perhaps too pejorative an account of anti-intellectual positivism. What is particularly offensive about the Harner-Harris interpretation is the combination of the extreme poverty of what it is able to take into account from Aztec life and the exaltedness of its claim to truth. See Sahlins 1978 for further criticism. In contrast, Rappaport's *Pigs for the Ancestors* (1967) draws on a wealth of ethnographic data and claims only to show what can be seen from an anti-intellectualist perspective.

6. Although there are exceptions (Douglas 1966, Beidelman 1974), many modern readers dismiss this remarkable book wholesale. Lévi-Strauss (1963), for example, assumes that since Smith was so thoroughly wrong about totemism he was equally wrong about everything else. Since Smith's better-known followers, Durkheim and Freud, in their major works on religion acknowledge their debt to what appear now as his errors, Beidelman's book is especially valuable in demonstrating Durkheim's great debt to Smith.

7. The instrumental/expressive split re-phrases sacrifice precisely in terms of the world in which it is no longer intelligible. It makes a Protestant-like interpretation of ritual as only effective as its meaning is understood. But sacrifice is more like Counter-Reformation rituals, whose purpose was not merely to signify, but to sanctify, and which were effective *ex opere operato* (from the acts done) quite separately from whether they were correctly understood or not.

8. Talcott Parsons, who can be thought of as a father of the instrumental/expressive split, conceived of symbols in this way:

> The essence of a symbol is first that its importance, value or meaning is not inherent in the intrinsic properties of the symbol itself, but in the thing symbolized, which is by definition something else; secondly, that in so far as it is a symbol it has no intrinsic causal connection with its meaning, the thing it symbolizes, but looked at in such terms the relation between them is arbitrary, conventional. (1968: 416)

9. See Tambiah 1981 for a valuable discussion of performative and indexical aspects of ritual.

10. For example, Edmund Leach: "I hold that the rite is prior to the explanatory belief. This will be recognized as essentially the view of Robertson Smith." (1968: 524)

11. Interpreting even our own action is always a separate state of consciousness from doing our own action. As Alfred Schutz has shown in meticulous detail (1967: chap. 2), insofar as we are caught up in our own ongoing action, our attention is within the continuous flow of experience of the ongoing action. It is not upon the act, as something discrete, in such a way that we can grasp it reflectively. We attend to the continuous doing of it, not to interpreting it, except

as, even instantaneously, we move in thought out of the undifferentiated flow of experiencing the ongoing action and reflect upon it as if it were a complete act. We can, of course, as observers, reflect upon another's ongoing action, but then we are not doing it.

12. Some of the diversity of members' interpretation is reported as follows:

> Of the twenty cult members, seven said the main purpose of the ritual was to find and establish proper relations with the Christian God who lies beyond death and of whom the Fang had no traditional knowledge. Eight said that the main purpose of the cult was to reestablish contact with the abandoned ancestors and regain their tutelary blessing. The remaining three [sic] informants declared the purpose of the cult ritual to be various: guaranteeing the well-being and tranquility of . . . the village, demonstrating to the European the validity of African religion, and curing individual illnesses of the worshippers. (Fernandez 1965: 906)

CHAPTER 2

1. In a fragment from Aristophanes, a hero speaking from beyond the grave threatens thieves with "enlarged spleen, coughs, dropsy, colds, itches, gout, insanity, rashes, mumps, chills, fever . . ." Aristophanes, *Fragments* 58. Quoted in Burkert 1985: 208, from Merkelbach 1967: 97–99.

2. See especially Thompson 1963; also Kaufmann 1972.

3. Harrison's chronology is surprising since she admits the earliest source, Homer, "ignored or suppressed" the very expiatory notions which she understood as early on no other grounds than their supposed irrational character (1922: vii). Robertson Smith's chronology was supported by textual evidence.

4. The authors' commitment to that illusion of French sociology, the social reality of the universal opposition between sacred and profane, led them to find the "unity" of sacrifice in its work of "establishing a means of communicating between the sacred and profane worlds" (1964: 97). Their own opposed positive and negative sacrificial modes are "sacralizing" and "desacralizing."

5. See "atone" in the unabridged *Oxford English Dictionary* for the history of this word, which originally meant "to set or make at one."

6. Cf. Jay 1981.

7. Louis Dumont claims that members of that most conservative of all social organizations, the Indian caste system, conceptualize these distinctions as the social elaboration of "a single true principle, namely the opposition of the pure and the impure" (1970: 43).

8. My version of the myth draws on Jean-Pierre Vernant's interpretations of Hesiod's *Theogony* and *Works and Days*. See "The Myth of Prometheus in Hesiod," in Vernant 1980, pp. 168–85; and Vernant 1981 and 1983. See also Detienne 1977, 1979; Detienne and Vernant 1989; and Vidal-Naquet 1981.

9. The same structure encodes botanical species: cereals occupy the center position, between plants that are cold and wet, like lettuce, and spices that are

hot and dry. See especially Detienne 1977. For marriage and sacrifice, see Vernant 1980: 138–40.

10. Vidal-Naquet 1981, p. 85. See also Vernant 1981, pp. 75–77, and Vernant 1980, pp. 110–29. For discussion of the two aspects of Greek religion see especially Nock 1944. Also Burkert 1985, especially pp. 199–203; Farnell 1921; Ferguson 1944; Guthrie 1955, especially pp. 221–22; Moulinier 1952; Harrison 1922.

11. *Enagismos* could be holocaust or *sphagia,* in which parts of a victim might be burnt but most were disposed of in some other way such as throwing into the sea. *Sphagia* was used for all human victims except the *pharmakoi,* human scapegoats for the purification of a city. Victims of alimentary sacrifice were always domestic animals.

12. An example is sacrifice to Pelops at Olympia. As was common at other sacred sites, the "grave" of Pelops, a hero, was near, but separate from, an altar to an Olympian, in this case Zeus. (The Erechtheon on the Acropolis was a hero shrine, near the temple of Athena.) A good description of sacrifice to Pelops and Zeus at Olympia is in Burkert 1983, pp. 93–103. Unfortunately in this book a wealth of erudition is made to serve a remarkably impoverished theory. Trying to construe Greek sacrifice as a preservation of Paleolithic hunting practices, Burkert conflates alimentary and non-alimentary sacrifices. Of sacrifice to the hero Pelops he says, "This chthonic, dark, nocturnal sacrifice is for eating, but the 'eaters' must subsequently shun the daytime sky god, Zeus" (1983: 101). See also Vernant's comment on Burkert's conflating alimentary and funeral sacrifice: 1981: 75–77.

13. Vernant rejects it entirely: "It is not the case that there are two kinds of gods, one devoted to the sacred that is pure, the other to the sacred that is impure . . . Depending on the time, the circumstances and the place the very same gods either preside over defilement or else delight in purity alone" (1980: 117).

14. This abbreviated description is based on LeVine's account of funeral sacrifices in the nineteen-fifties. He also describes how they had changed twenty years later, but notes that even then they combined communion and expiation.

15. These accounts often conflict with one another. See Daly 1978 and de Vaux 1964 or, for a short account, Rogerson 1980.

16. One of very few variations was that if a peace offering were a "freewill" offering, the meat could be eaten on the second day. The meat of ordinary peace offerings must be eaten on the day of sacrifice.

17. Except in temple service, accounts of burnt offerings performed alone are rare and always in unusual circumstances; for example, the ram sacrificed instead of Isaac (Gen. 22); the sacrifice of Jephthah's daughter (Judg. 11:31); or Elijah's sacrifice on Carmel (1 Kings 18:38).

18. The *Septuagint* translates *"zebah,"* one of the words translated in English as "peace offering," as *"thysia."* They are indeed similar and possibly even historically related. The vocabulary of chthonic sacrifice, however, was not used, with the exception of *"holocautoma"* to translate *"olah,"* burnt offering. In the

Catholic tradition, the English word "holocaust" is regularly used instead of "burnt offering." There is nothing wrong with this except when it is claimed, as do Yerkes (1952) and de Vaux (1964: 48–49), that Greek holocaust and Israelite burnt offerings are equivalent. There was no Greek sacrifice like the burnt offering. The closest parallel would have been the burnt portion of the *thysia*, if it were greatly intensified, which it most definitely was not. The Greek holocaust, a purifying expiatory sacrifice which nevertheless could make performers ritually unclean, was usually burnt whole (not in pieces like the burnt offering) in a place quite separate from the altars of the heavenly gods. It was much more like the red heifer sacrifice, or even those portions of sin offerings burnt outside the camp. Israelite burnt offerings, even of human victims, like Jephthah's daughter, or the near sacrifice of Isaac, were not intensely apotropaic. The burnt offering in which the Moabite king sacrificed his own son to get rid of the about-to-conquer Israelite army (2 Kings 3:27) was indeed powerfully apotropaic. But it was not done on an altar, but instead as far outside the city as was possible under the circumstances, and it was not an Israelite sacrifice.

CHAPTER 3

1. "Sacrifice and marriage appear to occupy the same position at the center of the system, this being exactly compared to that of cereals which, placed between the wet rawness of grasses on the one hand (the food of animals) and the incorruptible dryness of the aromatic plants (the food of the gods) on the other, represent the midway position, the human norm" (Vernant 1980: 150).

2. Kuper (1982) very usefully and critically reviews the issue of "descent theory" in anthropology, stressing its inadequacies as a model. Comaroff (1987) extends this critique to issues of "gender" and "kinship," stressing the work of construction that has gone into these terms in Western society and especially in anthropology. I am indebted to John Comaroff for these references.

A good deal of deconstructionist work has been done recently by anthropologists critically examining these and related anthropological concepts. I suggest that "sacrifice," exhibiting a unified logic in its action that transcends cultural boundaries, provides a context for reexamining the *sociological* utility of such concepts as "gender," "lineage," and "descent" critically but less dismissively.

3. This may seem remarkable since Smith was concerned ultimately with Israelite sacrifice and the covenant relation between the Israelites and Yahweh is often phrased as marriage. He was correct in his choice however. The Israelites did not use marriage as a model of sacrificial relations with Yahweh. That would have put the sacrificers in the position of married women.

4. There was probably a real ground in Semitic patrilineal endogamy for Smith's ignoring of affines and related difficulties. Nevertheless he had to forget, for example, all the tensions between Jacob and his father-in-law, Laban.

5. Why did Freud, who relied on Smith so heavily and so indiscriminately for *Totem and Taboo*, not suspect something here?

6. Fortes (1953: 26) is here discussing "collective responsibility in blood

vengeance." Smith based his notion of kinship as a "physical unity of life" primarily on his understanding of collective blood vengeance.

7. I am using the term "unilineal descent group" as a gloss covering a variety of different unilineal descent structures: clan, sib, lineage (maximal and minimal), etc.

8. This account draws on Meyer Fortes, "The Structure of Unilineal Descent Groups" (1953: 24).

9. Modern capitalist corporations have certain resemblances to corporate lineages, in ownership of property, enduring continuity, etc. (As Sir Henry Maine said, "Corporations never die.") But when there is no longer even a metaphor of descent in conceptions of legal or moral corporate unity, sacrificial ritual is wholly irrelevant.

CHAPTER 4

1. In *African Political Systems*, Fortes and Evans-Pritchard (1958) used this phrase as the technical term for the internal nesting of lineages within larger lineages. They claimed that the political organization of stateless societies, like the Tallensi, Lugbara, and Nuer, rests on such segmentary structure. In such a model, affairs such as lineage-related disputes involving parties across lineage lines typically engage only those lineage segments in the total structure that define and contain the action between units related as equals.

2. Nor do all African sacrificing patrilineal societies have segmentary lineage organization; for example, Dahomey, where lineages are hierarchically ranked, with the royal lineage on top incorporating inclusively the ultimate authority of the entire lineage system.

3. His student, Emile Durkheim, accused him of having "mistaken the cause for the effect" (1933: 179), but in Durkheim's last book he concluded that in giving symbolic representation to features of social organization, ritual creates and re-creates them.

4. From this perspective, "their social structure . . . moulds their ritual ideas and values" (1945: 97, 31). Fortes's claim is not based on a simple "expressive" understanding of ritual, but on his understanding of a difference in perspective between "native thought" and his own generalized view of Tallensi social structure. See 1945: 115ff.

5. The *anchisteis* was a bilateral kindred. As a kindred, it was not a corporate group but a tracing of cognatic ties from any given individual, "as far as the degree of 'children of cousins'" (J. K. Davies 1977: 108).

6. The historically changing roles of Greek agnatic descent groups are by no means always clear. But though scholars may disagree on many issues, they agree that sacrificially validated agnation was the fundamental organizing principle in ancient Greek society. For an appreciation of some of the subtleties and uncertainties of Greek kinship, see the following, as well as those references cited in the text: Andrewes 1961; Connor 1971; Ferguson 1944; Humphreys 1977, 1978.

7. There are differences of opinion about the nature and importance of the

family cult of the dead. According to Burkert and others, individual families differentiated themselves from one another especially in their cults of the dead, celebrated at the graves with non-alimentary sacrifices, as well as with sacrificial feasts at home. But Humphreys point out that non-kin also participated in funerals and commemoration feasts, and that archaeology does not show "an unbroken tradition of patrilineal tomb groupings stretching back into the mists of time" (1983: 79, 117).

8. The dead of the Roman family were "somewhat lost . . . in the immense mass of the 'divine' Manes" (Dumézil 1970: 617). And the *di manes*, deified ancestors and/or gods of the lower world, are themselves hard to disentangle from the Lars, Penates, and other divinities of family worship.

9. As with the Tallensi, lineage segmentation occurs at points of maternal origin. Middleton says (1960: 66) that women may sacrifice at these external ancestrix shrines, but provides no further information except that such sacrifices are not part of the politics of cultic agnation. Presumably these women are lineage daughters past childbearing.

Internal ghost shrines may be set for a mother's agnatic relatives, especially for her brother. "These matrilateral shrines are all 'placed' by a mother's brother or one of his lineage and they provide the offering" (1960: 59). There is no ritual congregation for these matrilateral shrines.

10. Surely it was a consequence of Evans-Pritchard's own personal theological interest that *Nuer Religion* was the first ethnography to take "primitive" religion seriously on strictly religious grounds.

CHAPTER 5

1. This is the ethnographic present tense. The time is the 1930s.

2. Richards mentions, but does not describe, sacrifices at the founding of a chief's village, at the burial of a chief. A few previous Paramount Chiefs had celebrated a national sacrifice at shrines of dead chiefs. The detailed descriptions of ritual in *Chisungu* includes "miming, singing, dancing and handling of sacred emblems" (1956: 17) and many other ritual forms, but no sacrifice. In describing the annual cycle of agricultural rituals (1939: 362–80), Richards mentions no blood sacrifice, although offerings of food and beer are important. The only sacrifice she mentions in an agricultural context is one offered very rarely by the priest of the Paramount Chief for rain: "One such sacrifice was apparently performed in 1930" (1939: 380).

Richards describes informal village distribution of parts of slaughtered cattle without mention of sacrifice. When cattle are sacrificed at court, the distribution follows detailed prescriptions which she does not describe because they "cannot be understood without knowledge of the functions of the different dignitaries of the court" (1939: 141). Since a chief's sons and his paternal relatives all receive positions at court, and some chieftainships are transmitted patrilineally (1940: 89, 93) it would be interesting to know much more about the social context of Bemba sacrifice. The information available indicates that while Bemba sacrifice may legitimate the chief's authority, it does not maintain matrilineal descent in any family sense.

3. The ethnographic and historical sources on Ashanti include Rattray's detailed studies on religion, begun shortly after the conquest, as well as more recent ethnographic studies by Fortes and others, including Busia, who was himself an Ashanti. There is also excellent historical work by Ivor Wilks and others.

4. Instead, the conflict was mitigated by laws forbidding reference to another's descent: in precolonial days it was a capital offense to mention anyone's descent, possibly calling attention to slave forebears, and even in Fortes's day it was a legally actionable offense (1950: 225).

5. This is Wilks's term. Ashanti "bureaucracy," although unaligned with matrilineal structures, was not independent of central authority as Max Weber understood bureaucracy.

6. The king's position was also strengthened by laws giving him power of life and death over all subjects. As in Benin and Dahomey, all ritual killings of humans took place under his authority alone. Still, in Ashanti, tension always remained between the national kingship and the chiefs holding offices sanctioned by the matrilineal ancestor cult. In contrast, the kings of Benin and Dahomey represented the apex of all patrilineal ancestor cults, centralizing, not conflicting with, cults of other lineages and sibs.

7. Uneven use of verb tenses in the following account is a consequence of drawing on both ethnographic and historical sources. (Historians do not use the timeless ethnographic present.) I have tried to resolve this by writing in the past tense about events, such as human sacrifice, that predate any ethnographic account, but using the present for describing events witnessed by any ethnographer, whatever the date. Nevertheless, it is important to remember that Fortes wrote more than a generation after Rattray.

8. Other aspects of this Ashanti annual ceremony (the *Odwira*), such as a period of general license and freedom from social constraints, were markedly unlike the unrelieved rigidity of Dahomean ritual (Herskovits and Herskovits 1933: 35).

9. The gods are willing to associate with women in increasing degrees as they descend in generation. The river god Tano, father and grandfather of lesser gods, is "especially indifferent or even hostile to women . . . No woman is allowed to touch his shrine, and he has no female priests of his own." "Pure, pure Tano," his priests chant, "he devours rams" (ibid.: 183, 102).

10. The ashes of the Israelite red heifer sacrifice (Num. 19) had similar qualities of being both polluting and powerfully apotropaic.

11. Fortes associates the *sunsum,* one of the patrilineal souls, more than the *ntoro* with naming, but that is equally patrilineal, and the terms are often synonymous.

12. Sometimes these are used synonymously and sometimes distinctions are made between them. Anthropologists as well as informants differ in their uses of these terms, and even Rattray admitted to being confused. Rattray, Fortes, Busia, and Herskovits all understand them somewhat differently. In Rattray's last account he makes no real distinction between *sunsum* and *notro* (consistent

with Busia, but not with Fortes or Herskovits) but distinguishes between *ntoro* and *'kra:* "The ntoro is very often loosely called by the name *'kra,* and is confused with it, or even considered the same by the uninformed; but this is not, I think, correct" (1927: 318). Herskovits (1937) substitutes *'kra* entirely for *ntoro* and uses *ntoro* to refer to the matrilineages, but Fortes (1950: 266, n. 4) says this is because his informants were the descendants of slaves and did not have a real *ntoro* and so claimed one in the matrilineage.

13. Were the preferred partners in the two forms of cross-cousin marriage to be named from a woman's point of view, the kinship connections would be reversed.

14. In Rattray's day the preference for cross-cousin marriage was so strong that he concluded that Ashanti had once been organized in two intermarrying moieties so that all marriages would have been, in classificatory terms, both matrilateral and patrilateral cross-cousin marriages (1927: 328). Fortes discounts this (1969: 160).

15. Although he does not specify here which form of cross-cousin marriage is intended, surely it is preferably patrilateral.

16. Fortes's inability to get a clear account of stool ancestral spirits may be a consequence of the relative lack of stress on *ntoro* and patrilateral cross-cousin marriage, except among chiefs, in his time. By then, "the strongest argument for cross cousin marriage in general is on grounds of property and wealth . . . importance is still attached, also, to the transmission of names, though not so much as when Rattray wrote" (1950: 282). Matrilateral cross-cousin marriage protects interests in property and wealth, although it cannot preserve names.

17. In *The Ritual Process,* Victor Turner presents Ashanti and Tallensi as mirror images in descent and religion. According to Turner, Tallensi sacrifice represents formal, organized patrilineal "structure," while rituals connected with the relatively powerless and "spiritual" kinship through women represent benign but powerless "communitas." Ashanti reverses this: the matrilineages, controlling all power and material wealth, express "structure" in their sacrifices and are opposed to a structurally weak but "almost totally auspicious" (1969: 125), benign, and spiritual patrilineal principle whose rituals express "communitas." According to Turner, as a consequence of matrilineal organization, the Ashanti unite "femininity . . . killing . . . menstrual pollution and the sacrifice of men and beasts" (1969: 124).

One source of this distortion is Turner's ahistorical approach. He draws indiscriminately on Fortes (mid-twentieth century) for kinship, and Rattray (early twentieth century looking back to the nineteenth) for religion, so that he sets "the sacrifice of men" in the same context as mid-twentieth-century ancestral cult sacrifice. He makes no distinction between expiatory and communion sacrifice and because there is menstrual blood in the *kunkuma* fetish, he conflates menstrual blood and sacrifice. It is also misleading to compare the Ashanti to the Tallensi, subsistence farmers with no central government and no past involvement in international slaving. Comparison with Benin and Dahomey is more appropriate.

CHAPTER 6

1. I want to acknowledge my debt to Douglas Oliver's 1966 seminar on Hawaii, for which I read all the accounts of Hawaii written before the missionaries' arrival in 1820 and many of the remembrances of ancient Hawaii written after that time.

2. For the sake of simplicity I have omitted two other major gods, Kane and Kaneloa, and a host of inferior gods.

3. This example of "communitas" vs. "structure" would have pleased Victor Turner.

4. Liholiho's heirs struggled against her niece, Kinau, with little more success than Liholiho had had against Kaahumanu. The regency was abolished in 1833, but two years later King Kamehameha III (the younger brother who succeeded after Liholiho's death from measles in 1824) was obliged to give most of his power back to Kinau (Kuykendall 1938: 136).

CHAPTER 7

1. This chapter, somewhat revised, was previously published in *Vetus Testamentum*. Cf. Jay 1988.

2. See *Essays on the Patriarchal Narratives*, A. R. Millard and D. J. Wiseman, eds., 1980, for discussion of the historicity of the narratives.

3. Wellhausen 1885: 151–61. See Cross 1973: 195–215 for an excellent, more recent discussion and bibliography.

4. See especially R. J. Thompson 1963, and Yehezkel Kaufmann 1972.

5. In this verse I have changed the RSV's "he became the father of a son" to "he begot a son."

6. An interest in purity and continuity of patrilineal descent is a widespread feature of hereditary sacrificing priesthoods. For example, "The Egyptian families of the first Millennium B.C. for whom genealogies were compiled were mainly, one might almost say exclusively, priestly" (Redford, 1970: 5). Or Lienhardt on the (pre-literate) Dinkas hereditary priesthood, "In fact also the spearmaster clans can on the whole produce clearer and longer genealogies than the rest" (1961: 168).

7. As the name implies, J had a special relation with Yahweh; only J used the name before the Mosaic revelation. Yahweh differed from all surrounding pagan deities especially in the absence of patrilineal descent. Unlike all other regional gods, Yahweh was neither begotten nor begetting. Also unlike regional gods, Yahweh never received sacrifices. See Kaufmann 1972, especially chapter 3, for a discussion of Yahweh's differences from regional gods. Kaufmann believes Yahwism was originally entirely non-sacrificial, only later incorporating Canaanite sacrifice. See also *The Book of J* (1990), where Harold Bloom speculates that "J" was a woman.

8. Malinowski found that the Trobrianders, a society stressing "matrilineal" descent, stubbornly refused to recognize any male role in procreation; they were

politely incredulous of his "modern scientific" explanation: "When . . . I directly advanced the embryological [*sic*] view of the matter, I found the natives absolutely ignorant of the process suggested. To the simile of a seed being planted in the soil and the plant growing out of the seed, they remained quite irresponsive" (ibid.: 223)—a classic example of a patriarchal formulation, reduced as typical to the "natural," confronting a matrilineal ideology. Malinowski appeared to notice no contradiction between this formulation and his *accurate* understanding of embryology, expressed two pages earlier: "impregnation, that is the idea of the father having a share in building up the body of the child" (ibid.: 221). As he said himself on the preceding page, though referring to the Trobrianders, "But any drawing of conclusions, or arguing by logical contradiction, is absolutely futile in the realm of belief, whether savage or civilized. Two beliefs, quite contradictory to each other on logical grounds, may coexist, while a perfectly obvious inference from a very firm tenet may be simply ignored" (ibid.: 220)—a perfect argument also, with a demonstration (though unintended), for how patriarchal assumptions in Western society can be maintained unexamined, taken for granted, in the face of modern scientific knowledge.

9. Goode 1970: 93–95; Murphy and Kasdan 1959 and 1967; Patai 1965. See also Wander 1981.

10. The problem of "the matrilineal principle" in Judaism is analogous; see Cohen 1985.

11. See M. J. Selman, "Comparative Customs and the Patriarchal Age," in Millard and Wiseman, eds., 1980, pp. 93–138, for a good discussion and bibliography.

12. The names Abram and Abraham are probably just dialectical variants of the same name. They both can be translated as "the (divine) father is exalted."

13. The rest of chapter 16, from the hand of J, is full of conflict.

14. I am assuming here that J's Abraham, like E's, was not lying, i.e., that his marriage to Sarah was patrilineally endogamous.

15. As von Rad comments, "The Elohist insists that Abraham resisted [Sarah's] demand and yielded to it only upon God's express directive" (1961: 227).

16. The Revised Standard Version has "offspring." I have changed it to "seed" (as in the King James version) to indicate that it is the same Hebrew word spoken to Hagar.

17. See Martin Noth's discussion of the importance of twelve tribes for Israelite and other cultic organization (1960: 88). See also Appendix.

18. For more detailed discussion of Abraham's near sacrifice of Isaac as an indication of paternity and patriarchy, see Delaney 1977 and Bakan 1971.

19. Gen. 15:7–12 (J) is not an Israelite sacrifice; there was no altar and the flesh was neither eaten nor burned. Speiser 1964: 112–13; Van Seters 1975: 258; Westermann 1985: 225.

20. See, for example, Das 1983: 456; Middleton 1960: 88, 97–99; J. Z. Smith 1987.

21. These are terms used by anthropologists that mean, respectively, "at the home of the wife" and "at the home of the uncle." They are common living arrangements in matrilineally organized societies.

22. An objection might be based on 31:1 (J); but sons' resentment of sisters' sons' inheritance is a common feature of matrilineal, not of patrilineal, societies.

23. Attribution to sources is based on Noth 1972, von Rad 1961, and Speiser 1964. Westermann (1985: 490) says Gen. 31 is entirely J. See note 30 below.

24. See Selman, in Millard and Wiseman 1980, for discussion and bibliography. Also Huehnegard 1985: "Biblical Note on some New Akkadian Texts from Emar."

25. Gen 31:53 is attributed entirely to E by von Rad and Speiser. Noth attributes Laban's invocation, 53a, to J. If Noth is correct, it does not make much difference, since J too was recording a patrilineal resolution.

26. Albright translates this as "kinsman" (1957: 248). My work would support Albright, but see Hillers 1972 and Westermann 1985: 497.

27. Alt (1967: 22–23) says the phrase "the god of their father" was added later to remedy invocation of two different gods, but in ancestral cults, for a sacrifice of alliance like Jacob's, an apical ancestor is necessary at the time of sacrifice. (The plural "their fathers" in the English translation misrepresents Alt's "Vaters" [1953: 16–17].)

28. Joseph's Egyptian name (Gen. 41:45) may indicate continuity of patrilineal descent through offspring not adopted by Jacob—but in an Egyptian lineage.

29. For example: "Les mamelles et les seins mentionnés au verset 25b ont pris la place de deux divinités feminines cananéennes" (Coppens 1956: 103).

30. Many attributions to E in chapters 25–36 made by Noth, von Rad, and Speiser are rejected by Westermann: "J's plan is clearly discernible . . . One must be able to demonstrate a corresponding plan for E. This has not succeeded so far even in outline . . . E is entirely missing in the two chapters (27 and 33) in which J's blue print is moored" (1985: 572). According to my interpretation, E's "plan" is an antidote to J's chapter 27.

CHAPTER 8

1. A. von Harnack almost does. According to him, during the eight centuries from Augustine to Thomas, ecclesiology remained unchanged, but liturgy and theology of sacrifice were transformed, as was Church social organization (1961, vol. 6: 127ff.).

2. These changes are extensive. E. g. See Rahner 1979 for a discussion of Vatican II as initiating the transition from European Church to World Church— in his view, a change comparable only to that from Jewish to Gentile Christianity.

3. Analogously, according to Louis Dumont, traditional Indian caste hierarchy is built on the social elaboration of "a single true principle, namely the opposition of the pure and the impure" (1970: 43).

4. Exceptions were allowed for those dioceses and orders able to demonstrate that their liturgy was over two hundred years old.

5. Trent adopted three separate decrees on the Eucharist. From Trent until Vatican II, the Church systematically protected its sacrificial practice and hierarchical organization, but at a price of liturgical rigidity and an increasingly defensive posture toward the modernizing world (McSweeney 1980).

6. Schillebeeckx's little book on the Eucharist (1968) takes the incompatibility between transubstantiation and modern physics as a central problem. Science, now the almost inescapable standard for valid knowledge, not Thomism, was the winner.

7. Consistent with the supernatural basis of hierarchy, the commonest interpretation of the phrase "without father or mother," recurring throughout Christian history (except in modern Protestantism), is that "without father" refers to Christ's humanity, in which he died, and "without mother" to his divinity and immortality (Demarest 1976: 11–12, 28–29, 30–31, 88).

8. There are two brief references (13: 7, 17) to church "leaders," but these are not priests but preachers.

9. These accelerating changes in eucharistic theology and practice provoked the anti-sacrificial wrath of the nineteenth-century Lutheran scholar A. von Harnack. Said he, "In the whole history of religions there is probably no second example of such a transformation, extension, demoralization and narrowing of a simple and sacred act" (vol. 4: 228). But in the whole history of religions there is surely no second example of such a centralization of sacred and political power in one enduring hierarchical social organization.

10. Within their own contexts, these changes appear less radical. Cyprian's statement that "the passion of the Lord is, indeed, the sacrifice we offer" (1964: 213–14) was made in the context of insisting that a mixture of water and wine be used in the Eucharist, in opposition to a contemporary use of water alone. His insistence on only one line of episcopal succession was in response to the Novatian schism.

11. Celibacy ended an interesting fourth-century development: the inheritance of a bishopric from father to son through several generations in one family (Mohler 1970: 99).

12. The Church is, of course, working to define more clearly its postconciliar identity. See Rahner 1979 for a good example.

13. Davies does not identify the emphasis as his.

14. Strangely, Küng never observes that ordination is itself non-scriptural.

15. For a contrast, see Amiot's *History of the Mass*, first published only seven years before Vatican II. According to Amiot, "The Mass is the very sacrifice of Jesus Christ himself, an extension of the sacrifice on Calvary" (1959: 7). He finds sacrifice already present in the accounts of the Last Supper in the Gospels of Matthew and Mark: "The supper already seems to have been relegated to a position of secondary importance and was soon to disappear altogether" (ibid.: 12).

16. A bibliography of over 465 works is "clearly incomplete" (Hughes 1968a: 145).

CHAPTER 9

1. According to Girard, "In the language of pure sacredness," violence "flows everywhere and impregnates on contact" (1977: 258).

2. As with Freud's primal father, mimetic desire is based on imitation of an admired model.

3. Girard's theory is less successful in reference to the non-mythical world. He has been able to find only one non-mythical case of that universal danger, self-destruction by reciprocal violence: a Brazilian tribe whose internal feuding was out of control. That the Kaingang had been driven from their own territory, that their population had shrunk to one-third of its number from disease, and that they were being systematically killed by hunters hired by local settlers, are all incidental. "The process of self destruction . . . is basically internal," and could be prevented by sacrifice (ibid.: 53). Jules Henry, whose ethnography (1964) is Girard's source, mentioned these disasters but still interpreted the Kaingang tragedy as endogenous cultural neurosis, an interpretation analogous to Girard's. Today, few but Girard accept Henry's theory at face value.

4. For example, Girard discusses the Chuckchi at length (1977: 16–17, 25–28) on the basis of a comment in Lowie's *Primitive Society* (1961) without ever thinking it might be worth his while to read the only ethnography about them.

5. As Burkert says, his theory reduces "ideas" to the imprinting effect of cultural transfer. Konrad Lorenz's *On Aggression* is the source for much of this.

6. See Vernant's scornful comments on this (1981: 75–77).

7. Burkert himself appears to be guilty only of naive devotion to his teacher. For example, he might have been more suspicious of Meuli's extra-archaeological access to Paleolithic ritual: "The continuity between the hunt and sacrificial ritual appears most forcefully in the ritual details that leave no tangible archaeological trace; these have been set out in detail by Meuli" (1983: 16).

8. Hubert and Mauss's distinction sacrificer/sacrifier (priest/benefiter) has become a convention in sacrificial literature. The Vedic sacrifice cannot be described without using such a distinction. Since I have not used this distinction, I sometimes refer to "the offerer," or use the cumbersome phrase "the man for whose benefit the sacrifice was performed." But it does not follow that their distinction is either necessary or appropriate for all other traditions. Their analysis is based exclusively on priestly sacrifice. They ignore Israelite sacrifices outside the priestly tradition, such as the Genesis sacrifices I analyze and for which their distinction is meaningless.

9. In general, alimentary sacrifices sacralize while non-alimentary sacrifices de-sacralize. A single sacrifice may involve both processes. In an Israelite peace offering, for example, the blood rite and the burning of parts of the victim sufficiently de-sacralize the remainder that it becomes safe for human consumption. It sacralizes those who eat it, but only to a tolerable degree.

10. The one he found, or rather, invented, in the *intichiuma ritual*, is now universally rejected as sacrifice.

11. Actually, Australian women do take part peripherally in some men's rituals, and they also have their own rituals from which men are excluded. See Kaberry 1939 (*Aboriginal Women, Sacred and Profane*). The male ethnographers who were Durkheim's source did not describe women's rituals, and Durkheim himself gave little significance to women's marginal role in men's rituals.

12. See Jay 1981 for further discussion.

13. For discussion, see Goody 1961, Lukes 1972, Stanner 1967.

14. See also Martin Buber's discussion of the sacred/profane dichotomy as alienation in *I and Thou*.

15. Sometimes he sounds just like France's own social contract theorist, Jean-Jacques Rousseau: "This passage from the state of nature to the civil state produces quite a remarkable change in man, for it substitutes justice for instinct in his behavior and gives his actions a moral quality they previously lacked. Only then, when the voice of duty replaces physical impulse and right replaces appetite, does man, who hitherto had taken only himself into account, find himself forced to . . . consult his reason before listening to his inclinations" (Rousseau 1987: 150–51).

16. See Lévi-Strauss 1963. Some Americans also rejected any evolutionary relationship between totemism and sacrifice; for example, Paul Radin's scornful rejection of Durkheim: "If the *intichiuma* rites of the Australians represents an initial form of sacrifice, then it can be said with equal show of reason that chaos is an initial form of order or that zero is an initial form of the integer" (1937: 183–84).

17. His position as a patriarchal theorist is secure, however. See Gayle Rubin 1975, "The Traffic in Women."

18. Perhaps because he saw them as mutually exclusive, he ignored evidence supporting his opposition from societies practicing both. For example, the Dinka distinguish sharply between them. Like the Nuer, they offer sacrifice *to*, but never *of* their totemic clan-divinities. Animals identified as emblems of clan-divinities must never be injured by their clansmen (Lienhardt 1961: 114). Dinka who have cattle of a particular color pattern as clan-divinities will not keep such animals in their herds, from which victims are chosen (ibid.: 107–8). Contact with "the blood of the emblem of one's clan-divinities is one of the greatest misfortunes that can happen" (ibid.: 128); it causes the same disease as does incest, another profound confusion of categories. In Ashanti, Rattray described the annual ritual pollution of the entire kingdom, a period of complete license in which the world was turned upside down, inferiors abusing superiors with impunity. This was inaugurated by the sacrifice of a bull, a "totem" of the patrilineal descent group to which most kings belonged. Order was restored, and the kingdom purified, by the subsequent sacrifice of a non-totemic victim, a sheep (1927: 136; 1923: 47).

19. For example, the Vedic tradition opposed two categories of animals, *pasu* and *mrga*. The former consists of man, horse, ox, sheep, and goat, each a

suitable victim for certain sacrifices, and is indeed an oriented category. The latter, in its widest sense, consists of wild animals in general, or, in a restricted sense, of antelope, animals whose sacrificial role is sharply opposed to that of victim (Das 1983: 456). For an entirely different classification, see Valeri's account of the complex, but not continuous, categories of natural species in Hawaiian sacrifice (1985).

20. Here again, Lévi-Strauss could have turned to the Dinka for support: "I asked men of the Padiangbar clan who had never seen a giraffe how Giraffe could help them, when it was no longer found in their part of Dinkaland, and what indeed would happen if all giraffes were exterminated. . . . They replied that it would make no difference at all . . . that even if all giraffes were dead there would still be the *atiem mir,* the "ghost" or "shade" of giraffe which would support them as strongly as ever." (Lienhardt 1961: 107).

21. Sometimes dangerously so. After sacrifices in their honor, Dahomean ancestors were told in song "to take away the songs that had been sung in their honor, but not the voices of the singers; to take the drum rhythms, but not the hands of the drummers" (Herskovits 1938, vol. 1: 227).

22. For an illustration, see the discussion in chapter 1 (p. 14–15) of MacIntyre's portrayal of the Nuer concept of god, *kwoth,* as non-logical. MacIntyre conceives of *kwoth* as object, but the logical difficulties vanish when *kwoth* is recognized as subject.

23. I believe Valeri uses the term "alienation" only once, in reference to Lono, whose worshipers take back their offerings: "In this god man is less alienated from himself than he is in the others. This is why sacrifices offered to Lono are less serious." (1985:224.)

24. Valeri's theory can illuminate the importance of domestic animals in many sacrificial traditions. Those who learn about nature in books and desacralize meat through the market may not need to sacrifice. But for others, to eat a domestic animal without sacrifice may be uncomfortably close to cannibalism.

25. Given this view of hierarchy, Valeri might have done well to avoid the use of gendered words for the species ("man") and of ungendered words ("one," "everyone") for males.

CHAPTER 10

1. He insisted that cherry trees were found in Germany only as a consequence of history and commerce (1978: 170).

2. Here also can be found one of the rare cases of sacrifice of wild animals: late in the tradition a kind of reverse sacrifice developed, offered not to divinities but to female demons, and requiring a wild victim.

Abbott, Walter M., S.J., ed. 1966. *The Documents of Vatican II.* Introduction by Lawrence Cardinal Shehan. Translations directed by Joseph Gallagher. New York: Herder and Herder.

Aeschylus. 1926. *Eumenides.* Translated by Hugh Lloyd-Jones. Loeb Classical Library. Cambridge, Mass.: Harvard University Press.

Albright, William Foxwell. 1957. *From the Stone Age to Christianity: Monotheism and the Historical Process.* Baltimore: Johns Hopkins Press.

Alt, Albrecht. 1953. *Kleine Schriften zur Geschichte des Volkes Israel,* vol. 1. Munich.

———. 1967. *Essays on Old Testament History and Religion.* Translated by R. A. Wilson. Garden City, N.Y.: Doubleday and Co.

Amiot, François, 1959. *History of the Mass.* Translated by Lancelot C. Sheppard. New York: Hawthorn Books.

Andrewes, A. 1961. "Philochoros on Phratries." *Journal of Hellenic Studies* 81: 1–15.

Anglican Orders. 1943. *Anglican Orders (English). The Bull of His Holiness Leo XIII, September 13, 1896, and the Answer of the Archbishops of England, March 29, 1897.* Published for the Church Historical Society. London: Society for Promoting Christian Knowledge.

Anthony, James. 1957. "The System Makers: Piaget and Freud." *British Journal of Medical Psychology* 30: 255–69.

Atkinson, Clarissa W. 1991. *The Oldest Vocation: Christian Motherhood in the Medieval West.* Ithaca, N.Y.: Cornell University Press.

Austin, J. L. 1962. *How to Do Things with Words.* Cambridge, Mass.: Harvard University Press.

Baden-Powell, Robert. 1896. *The Downfall of Prempeh: A Diary of Life with the Native Levy in Ashanti 1895–96.* London: Methuen and Co.

Bakan, David. 1971. *Disease, Pain and Sacrifice: Toward a Psychology of Suffering.* Boston: Beacon Press.

Beidelman, Thomas O. 1974. *W. Robertson Smith and the Sociological Study of Religion.* Chicago: University of Chicago Press.

Benhabib, Seyla. 1986. *Critique, Norm and Utopia: A Study of the Foundations of Critical Theory.* New York: Columbia University Press.

Bernal, Martin. 1987. *Black Athens: the Afroasiatic Roots of Classical Civilization.* New Brunswick, N.J.: Rutgers University Press.

Biardeau, Madeleine, and Charles Malamoud. 1976. *Le Sacrifice dans l'Inde ancienne.* Paris: Presses Universitaires de France.

Bible. See Holy Bible.

Boff, Leonardo. 1985. *Charism and Power, Liberation Theology and the Institutional Church.* Translated by John W. Diercksmeier. New York: Crossroad.

The Book of J. 1990. Translated from the Hebrew by David Rosenberg; interpreted by Harold Bloom. New York: Grove Weidenfeld.

Bourdillon, M. F. C., and Meyer Fortes. 1980. *Sacrifice.* London, New York: Academic Press.

Bradbury, Robert Elwyn. 1957. *The Benin Kingdom and the Edo-speaking Peoples of South-Western Nigeria.* London: International African Institute; Oxford University Press.

————. 1967. "The Kingdom of Benin." In *West African Kingdoms in the Nineteenth Century.* Edited by Daryll Forde and P. M. Kaberry. London: International African Institute; Oxford University Press.

————. 1973. *Benin Studies.* Edited by Peter Morton-Williams. London: International African Institute; Oxford University Press.

Brown, Karen McCarthy. 1991. *Mama Lola: A Vodou Priestess in Brooklyn.* Berkeley: University of California Press.

Brown, Raymond E., S.J. 1970. *Priest and Bishop: Biblical Reflections.* Paramus, N.J.: Paulist Press.

Buber, Martin. 1970. *I and Thou.* New York: Charles Scribner's Sons.

Burkert, Walter. 1983. *Homo Necans: The Anthropology of Ancient Greek Sacrificial Ritual and Myth.* Translated by Peter Bing. Berkeley, Los Angeles, London: University of California Press.

————. 1985. *Greek Religion.* Translated by John Raffan. Cambridge, Mass.: Harvard University Press.

————. 1987. "The Problem of Ritual Killing." In *Violent Origins. Walter Burkert, René Girard and J. Z. Smith on Ritual Killing and Cultural Formation.* Edited by Robert G. Hamerton-Kelly. Stanford, Calif.: Stanford University Press.

Burks, Arthur W. 1949. "Icon, Index, and Symbol." *Philosophy and Phenomenological Research* 9: 673–89.

Burton, Sir Richard Francis. 1893. *A Mission to Gelele, King of Dahome.* London: Tylston and Edwards.

Busia, K.A. 1954. "The Ashanti of the Gold Coast." In *African Worlds: Studies in the Cosmological Ideas and Social Values of African Peoples.* Edited by Daryll Forde. London: International African Institute; Oxford University Press.

————. 1968. *The Position of the Chief in the Modern Political System of Ashanti. A*

Study of the Influence of Contemporary Social Changes on Ashanti Political Institutions. London: Frank Cross.

Campenhausen, Hans, Freiherr von. 1969. *Ecclesiastical Authority and Spiritual Power in the Church of the First Three Centuries.* Translated by J. A. Baker. Standard, Calif.: Stanford University Press.

Cantarella, Eva. 1987. *Pandora's Daughter: The Role and Status of Women in Greek and Roman Antiquity.* Translated by Maureen B. Fant. Baltimore and London: Johns Hopkins University Press.

Carr, Anne Elizabeth. 1976. "The Church in Process: Engendering the Future." In *Women and Catholic Priesthood: An Expanded Vision. Proceedings of the Detroit Ordination Conference.* Edited by Anne Marie Gardiner. New York, Paramus, N.J., Toronto: Paulist Press.

Cazelles, H. 1978. Review of J. Van Seters, *Abraham in History and Tradition. Vetus Testamentum* 28: 241–55.

Chrysostom, John. 1844. *The Treatise of John Chrysostom on the Priesthood.* Translated by E. G. Marsh. London: Seeley, Burnside, and Seeley, Fleet Street.

Clark, Francis, S.J. 1967. *Eucharistic Sacrifice and the Reformation.* Oxford: Basil Blackwell.

Cohen, S. J. D. 1985. "The Matrilineal Principle in Historical Perspective." *Judaism* 34: 5–13.

Comaroff, John L. 1987. "Sui Genderis: Feminism, Kinship Theory, and Structural 'Domains.'" In *Gender and Kinship: Essays toward a Unified Analysis.* Edited by Jane Fishburne Collier and Sylvia Junko Yanagisako. Stanford, Calif.: Stanford University Press.

Combes-Schilling, M. E. 1989. *Sacred Performances: Islam, Sexuality, and Sacrifice.* New York: Columbia University Press.

Connor, W. R. 1971. *The New Politicians of Fifth-Century Athens.* Princeton, N.J.: Princeton University Press.

Coppens, J. 1956. "La Bénédiction de Jacob. Son cadre historique a la lumière paralleles ougaritiques." *Supplements to Vetus Testamentum* 4: 97–115. Leiden: E. J. Brill.

Cross, Frank Moore. 1973. *Canaanite Myth and Hebrew Epic: Essays in the History of the Religion of Israel.* Cambridge: Harvard University Press.

Cyprian. 1964. *Saint Cyprian: Letters.* Translated by Sister Rose Bernard Donna, C.S.J. Washington, D.C.: The Catholic University of America Press.

Daly, Robert J. 1978. *Christian Sacrifice. The Judaeo-Christian Background before Origen.* Washington, D.C.: The Catholic University of America Press.

Das, Veena. 1983. "The Language of Sacrifice." *Man* 18: 445–62.

Davenport, William. 1969. "The Hawaiian 'Cultural Revolution': Some Economic and Political Considerations." *American Anthropologist,* n.s. 71: 1–20.

Davies, John K. 1977. "Athenian Citizenship: The Descent Group and the Alternatives." *The Classical Journal* 73: 105–21.

———. 1984. *Wealth and the Power of Wealth in Classical Athens.* Salem, N.H.: The Ayer Company.

Davies, Michael. 1977a. *The Tridentine Mass.* Devon: Augustine Publishing Company.

———. 1977b. *Pope John's Council; Part Two of Liturgical Revolution.* Devon: Augustine Publishing Company.

———. 1977c. *The New Mass.* Devon: Augustine Publishing Company.

———. 1979. *Apologia pro Marcel Lefebvre.* Dickinson, Tex.: The Angelus Press.

Davis, Natalie Zemon. 1977. "Ghosts, Kin and Progeny: Some Features of Life in Early Modern France." *Daedalus* 106: 87–114.

Delaney, Carol. 1977. "The Seed and the Soil: the Legacy of Abraham." In *Beyond Androcentrism: New Essays on Women and Religion.* Edited by Rita M. Gross. Missoula, Mont.: Scholars Press for the American Academy of Religion.

Demarest, Bruce. 1976. *A History of Interpretation of Hebrews 7:1–10 from the Reformation to the Present.* Tübingen: J. C. B. Mohr.

Demosthenes. 1964. *Demosthenes,* vol. 5. Translated by A. T. Murray. Loeb Classical Library. Cambridge, Mass.: Harvard University Press.

———. 1988. Ibid., vol. 6. Translated by A. T. Murray.

———. 1989. Ibid., vol. 1. Translated by J. H. Vince.

Denzinger, Henricus, ed. 1976. *Enchiridion Symbolorum.* 26th edition. Barcelona: Herder.

Detienne, Marcel. 1977. *The Gardens of Adonis: Spices in Greek Mythology.* Translated by Janet Lloyd. Atlantic Highlands, N.J.: Humanities Press.

———. 1979. *Dionysos Slain.* Translated by Mireille Muellner and Leonard Muellner. Baltimore and London: The Johns Hopkins University Press.

———. 1989. "The Violence of Well Born Ladies: Women in the Thesmophoria." In *The Cuisine of Sacrifice among the Greeks.* Edited by M. Detienne and J.-P. Vernant. Translated by Paula Wissing. Chicago: University of Chicago Press.

Detienne, Marcel, and Jean-Pierre Vernant, eds. 1989. *The Cuisine of Sacrifice among the Greeks.* Translated by Paula Wissing. Chicago: University of Chicago Press.

Dewey, John. 1938. *Logic: The Theory of Inquiry.* New York: Holt.

Didache. 1912. In *The Apostolic Fathers,* vol. 1. Edited and translated by Kirsopp Lake. Cambridge, Mass.: Harvard University Press.

Dinges, William D. 1987. "Ritual Conflict as Social Conflict: Liturgical Reform in the Roman Catholic Church." *Sociological Analysis* 48: 138–57.

Douglas, Mary. 1954. "The Lele of the Kasai." In *African Worlds: Studies in Cosmological Ideas and Social Values of African People.* Edited by Daryll Forde. London: Oxford University Press.

———. 1955. "Social and Religious Symbolism of the Lele of the Kasai." *Zaire* 9: 385–402.

———. 1957. "Animals in Lele Religious Symbolism." *Africa* 27: 46–58.

———. 1963. *The Lele of the Kasai*. London: Oxford University Press.

———. 1966. *Purity and Danger: An Analysis of Concepts of Pollution and Taboo*. London: Routledge and Kegan Paul.

———. 1973. *Natural Symbols: Explorations in Cosmology*. New York: Vintage Books.

———. 1975. *Implicit Meaning: Essays in Anthropology*. London and Boston: Routledge and Kegan Paul.

Dumézil, Georges. 1970. *Archaic Roman Religion*. Translated by Philip Krapp. Chicago and London: University of Chicago Press.

Dumont, Louis. 1970. *Homo Hierarchicus: An Essay on the Caste System*. Translated by Mark Sainsbury. Chicago: University of Chicago Press.

Durand, Jean-Louis. 1989. "Greek Animals: Toward a Topology of Edible Bodies." In *The Cuisine of Sacrifice among the Greeks*, edited by M. Detienne and J.-P. Vernant. Translated by Paula Wissing. Chicago: University of Chicago Press.

Durkheim, Emile. 1964. *The Division of Labor in Society*. Translated by George Simpson. New York: Macmillan.

———. 1965. *The Elementary Forms of Religious Life*. Translated by Joseph Ward Swain. New York: The Free Press.

———. 1979. *Durkheim: Essays on Morals and Education*. Edited by W. S. F. Pickering. London: Routledge and Kegan Paul.

Eddy, Mrs. Mary Baker. 1918. *Science and Health with Key to the Scriptures*. Boston: A. V. Stewart.

Emminghaus, Johannes H. 1978. *The Eucharist: Essence, Form, Celebration*. Translated by Matthew J. O'Connell. Collegeville, Minn.: The Liturgical Press.

Evans-Pritchard, E. E. 1940. *The Nuer: A Description of the Modes of Livelihood and Political Institutions of a Nilotic People*. Oxford: Clarendon Press.

———. 1945. "Some Aspects of Marriage and Family among the Nuer." The Rhodes-Livingstone Papers, No. 11. Livingstone, S. Rhodesia (Zimbabwe): The Rhodes-Livingstone Institute.

———. 1951. *Kinship and Marriage among the Nuer*. Oxford: Clarendon Press.

———. 1956. *Nuer Religion*. New York and Oxford: Oxford University Press.

———. 1962. *Essays in Social Anthropology*. London: Faber and Faber.

———. 1964. Introduction to *Sacrifice*, by Hubert and Mauss, 1964. London: Cohen and West.

———. 1965. *Theories of Primitive Religion*. Oxford: Clarendon Press.

Farnell, Lewis Richard. 1921. *Greek Hero Cults and Ideas of Immortality*. Oxford: Clarendon Press.

Fenton, William N. 1936. *An Outline of Seneca Ceremonies at Coldspring Longhouse*. Yale University Publications in Anthropology, no. 9. New Haven: Yale University Press.

Ferguson, William Scott. 1944. "The Attic Orgeones." *Harvard Theological Review* 37: 61–140.

Fernandez, James W. 1965. "Symbolic Consensus in a Fang Reformative Cult." *American Anthropologist,* n.s. 67: 902–29.

Feuerbach, Ludwig. 1957. *The Essence of Christianity.* Translated by George Eliot. New York: Harper and Row.

Forde, Daryll. 1962. "Death and Succession, an Analysis of Yako Mortuary Ceremonies." In *Essays on the Ritual of Social Relations.* Edited by Max Gluckman. Manchester: Manchester University Press.

———. 1964. *Yakö Studies.* London, New York: International African Institute; Oxford University Press.

Fortes, Meyer. 1945. *The Dynamics of Clanship among the Tallensi: Being the First Part of an Analysis of the Social Structure of a Trans-Volta Tribe.* London: International African Institute; Oxford University Press.

———. 1949. *The Web of Kinship among the Tallensi: The Second Part of an Analysis of the Social Structure of a Trans-Volta Tribe.* London: International African Institute; Oxford University Press.

———. 1950. "Kinship and Marriage among the Ashanti." In *African Systems of Kinship and Marriage.* Edited by A. R. Radcliffe-Brown and Daryll Forde. London: International African Institute; Oxford University Press.

———. 1953. "The Structure of Unilineal Descent Groups." *American Anthropologist,* n.s. 55: 17–41.

———. 1963. "Time and Social Structure: An Ashanti Case Study." In *Social Structure: Studies Presented to A. R. Radcliffe-Brown.* Edited by M. Fortes. New York: Russell and Russell.

———. 1965. "Some Reflections on Ancestor Worship in Africa." In *African Systems of Thought.* Edited by M. Fortes and G. Dieterlen. London: International African Institute; Oxford University Press.

———. 1969. *Kinship and the Social Order: The Legacy of Lewis Henry Morgan.* Chicago: Aldine Publishing Co.

Fortes, Meyer, and E. E. Evans-Pritchard, eds. 1940. *African Political Systems.* London: International African Institute: Oxford University Press.

Franklin, R. W. 1984. "An Outline of Arguments on *Apostolicae Curae* from 1896 to 1984." Anglican/Roman Catholic Consultation, unpublished Consultation paper. New York, Dec. 11, 1984.

Frazer, Sir James George. 1910. *Totemism and Exogamy, A Treatise on Certain Early Forms of Superstition and Society.* 4 vols. London: Macmillan.

———. 1951. *The Golden Bough, A Study in Magic and Religion.* Abridged edition. New York: Macmillan.

Freud, Sigmund. 1950. *Totem and Taboo: Some Points of Agreement between the Mental Lives of Savages and Neurotics.* Authorized translation by James Strachey. London: Routledge and Kegan Paul.

Fustel de Coulanges, Numa Denis. 1956. *The Ancient City: A Study on the Religion,*

Laws, and Institutions of Greece and Rome. Garden City, N.Y.: Doubleday and Co.

Garfinkel, Harold. 1967. *Studies in Ethnomethodology.* Englewood Cliffs, N.J.: Prentice-Hall.

Girard, René. 1977. *Violence and the Sacred.* Translated by Patrick Gregory. Baltimore and London: Johns Hopkins University Press.

———. 1987. "Generative Scapegoating." In *Violent Origins: Walter Burkert, René Girard and J. Z. Smith on Ritual Killing and Cultural Formation.* Edited by Robert G. Hamerton-Kelly. Stanford, Calif.: Stanford University Press.

Godelier, Maurice. 1973. *Horizon, trajets marxistes en anthropologie.* Paris: François Maspero.

Goode, W. J. 1970. *World Revolution and Family Patterns.* New York: The Free Press.

Goody, John Rankin. 1957. "Anomie in Ashanti?" *Africa* 27: 356–63.

———. 1961. "Religion and Ritual, the Definitional Problem." *British Journal of Sociology* 12:142–64.

Gordon, R. L., ed. 1981. *Myth, Religion and Society: Structuralist Essays by M. Detienne, L. Gernet, J.-P. Vernant and P. Vidal-Naquet.* Cambridge, London, New York: Cambridge University Press. Paris: Editions de la Maison des Sciences de l'Homme.

Gossman, Elizabeth. 1958. "Women as Priests?" In *Apostolic Succession: Rethinking a Barrier to Unity. Concilium,* vol. 34. Edited by Hans Küng. New York/ Glen Rock, N.J.: Paulist Press.

Greenberg, Moshe. 1962. "Rachel's Theft of the Teraphim." *Journal of Biblical Literature* 81: 239–48.

Greengus, Samuel. 1975. "Sisterhood Adoption at Nuzi and the 'Wife-Sister' in Genesis." *Hebrew Union College Annual* 46: 5–32.

Guthrie, W. K. 1955. *The Greeks and Their Gods.* Boston: Beacon Press.

Handy, E. S. C., and Mary Kawena Pukui. 1972. *The Polynesian Family System in Ka-'u, Hawai'i.* Rutland, Vt.: C. E. Tuttle Co.

Harnack, Adolph von. 1961. *History of Dogma,* vols. 1–7. Translated from the third German edition by Neil Buchanan. New York: Dover Publications.

Harner, Michael. 1977. "The Enigma of Aztec Sacrifice." *Natural History* 236: 46–51.

Harris, Marvin. 1977. *Cannibals and Kings: The Origins of Cultures.* New York: Random House.

Harrison, Jane Ellen. 1922. *Prolegomena to the Study of Greek Religion.* 3d ed. Cambridge: Cambridge University Press.

Henry, Jules. 1964. *Jungle People: A Kaingang Tribe of the Highlands of Brazil.* New York: Vintage Press.

Herlihy, David. 1985. *Medieval Households.* Cambridge: Harvard University Press.

Herskovits, Frances S., and Melville Jean Herskovits. 1933. *An Outline of Daho-*

mean Religious Belief. Menasha, Wis.: American Anthropological Association.

Herskovits, Melville Jean. 1937a. "The Ashanti Ntoro: A Re-examination." *Journal of the Royal Anthropological Institute of Great Britain and Ireland* 67: 287–96.

———. 1937b. *Life in a Haitian Valley.* New York: Alfred A. Knopf.

———. 1938. *Dahomey, an Ancient West African Kingdom.* 2 vols. New York: J. J. Augustin.

Hertz, Robert. 1960. *Death and the Right Hand.* Translated by Rodney and Claudia Needham, with an introduction by E. E. Evans-Pritchard. Glencoe, Ill.: Free Press.

Hesiod. 1973. *Theogony, Works and Days.* Translated by Dorothy Wender. Hammondsworth, Middlesex, England; Baltimore: Penguin.

Heusch, Luc de. 1985. *Sacrifice in Africa: A Structuralist Approach.* Translated by Linda O'Brien and Alice Morton. Bloomington: Indiana University Press.

Hildebrand, Dietrich von. 1973. *The Devastated Vineyard.* Chicago: Franciscan Herald Press.

Hillers, D. R. 1972. "Pahad Yishaq." *Journal of Biblical Literature* 91: 90–92.

Hirsch, Samson Raphael. 1959. *The Pentateuch, Translated and Explained, vol. 1, Genesis.* Translated and published by Isaac Levy, London.

Hobbes, Thomas. 1963. *Leviathan.* Cleveland, Ohio: World Publishing Co.

Holy Bible. 1952. Revised Standard Version. New York: Thomas Nelson and Sons.

Horton, Robin. 1971. "African Traditional Thought and Western Science." In *Rationality.* Edited by Bryan R. Wilson. New York: Harper and Row.

Hubert, Henri, and Marcel Mauss. 1964. *Sacrifice: Its Nature and Function.* Translated by W. D. Halls. London: Cohen and West.

Huehnegard, John. 1985. "Biblical Notes on Some New Akkadian Texts from Emar (Syria)." *Catholic Biblical Quarterly* 47: 428–34.

Hughes, John Jay. 1968a. "Recent Studies of the Validity of Anglican Orders." In *The Sacraments in General, a New Perspective. Concilium,* vol. 31. Edited by Edward Schillebeeckx, O.P., and Boniface Willems, O.P. New York/Glen Rock, N.J.: Paulist Press.

———. 1968b. *Absolutely Null and Utterly Void: The Papal Condemnation of Anglican Orders, 1896.* Washington, D.C.: Corpus Books.

Humphreys, S. C. 1974. "The Nothoi of Kynosarges." *Journal of Hellenic Studies* 94: 88–95.

———. 1977. "Public and Private Interests in Classical Athens." *The Classical Journal* 73: 97–104.

———. 1978. *Anthropology and the Greeks.* London, Boston: Routledge and Kegan Paul.

———. 1983. *The Family, Women and Death. Comparative Studies.* London, Boston, Melbourne, and Henley: Routledge and Kegan Paul.

Jay, Nancy. 1981. "Gender and Dichotomy." *Feminist Studies* 7: 38–56.

————. 1985. "Sacrifice as Remedy for Having Been Born of Woman." In *Immaculate and Powerful.* Edited by C. W. Atkinson et al. Boston: Beacon Press.

————. 1988. "Sacrifice, Descent and the Patriarchs." *Vetus Testamentum* 38: 52–70.

Jerome. 1884. "Commentariorum in Epistolam ad Ephesios," Bk III. In *Patrologiae Latinae,* vol. 26. Edited by J.-P. Migne. Paris: Apud Garnier Fratres, Editores et J.-P. Migne successores.

Kaberry, Phyllis. 1939. *Aboriginal Women, Sacred and Profane.* London: Routledge and Sons.

Kalakaua, His Hawaiian Majesty King David. 1888. *The Legends and Myths of Hawaii: The Fables and Folklore of a Strange People.* New York: Charles L. Webster and Co.

Kapelrud, A. S. 1955. "King and Fertility." In *Interpretationes ad Vetus Testamentum Pertinentes.* (Festschrift Mowinckel.) Oslo: Fabritius and Sonner.

Kaufman, Yehezkel. 1972. *The Religion of Israel from Its Beginnings to the Babylonian Exile.* Translated by Moshe Greenberg. New York: Schocken Books.

Krige, E. Jensen, and J. D. Krige. 1943. *The Realm of a Rain-Queen: A Study of the Pattern of Lovedu Society.* London: International African Institute; Oxford University Press.

Krige, J. D., and Krige, E. J. 1954. "The Lovedu of the Transvaal." In *African Worlds: Studies in the Cosmological Ideas and Social Values of African Peoples.* Edited by Daryll Forde. London: Oxford University Press.

Kroeber, A. L. 1948. *Anthropology.* New York: Harcourt, Brace.

Küng, Hans, ed. 1968. *Apostolic Succession: Rethinking a Barrier to Unity. Concilium,* vol. 34. New York/Glen Rock, N.J.: Paulist Press.

————. 1972. *Why Priests? A Proposal for a New Church Ministry.* Translated by Robert C. Collins, S.J. Garden City, N.Y.: Doubleday and Co.

Kuper, Adam. 1982. "Lineage Theory: A Critical Retrospect." In *Annual Review of Anthropology 1982.* Palo Alto Calif.: Annual Reviews, Inc.

Kuykendall, Ralph S. 1938. *The Hawaiian Kingdom 1778–1854; Foundation and Transformation.* Honolulu: The University of Hawaii Press.

Leach, Edmund Ronald. 1965. *Political Systems of Highland Burma.* Boston: Beacon Press.

————. 1968. "Ritual." In *The International Encyclopedia of the Social Sciences,* vol. 13. Edited by David L. Sills. New York: Macmillan Co. and The Free Press.

Leeuw, Gerardus van der. 1967. *Religion in Essence and Manifestation: A Study in Phenomenology.* Translated by J. E. Turner, with appendices to the Torchbook edition incorporating the additions of the second German edition by Hans H. Penner. Gloucester, Mass.: Peter Smith.

Lefebvre, Marcel. 1979a. "The Ordination Sermon." In Michael Davies, *Apologia pro Marcel Lefebvre.* Dickinson, Tex.: Angelus Press.

————. 1979b. "Sermon. Mars in Geneva." In Michael Davies, *Apologia pro Marcel Lefebvre*. Dickinson, Tex.: Angelus Press.

Lévi-Strauss, Claude. 1963. *Totemism*. Translated by Rodney Needham. Boston: Beacon Press.

————. 1966. *The Savage Mind*. Translated by George Weidenfeld and Nicolson Ltd. Chicago: University of Chicago Press.

————. 1967. *Structural Anthropology*. Translated by Claire Jacobson and Brooke Grundfest Schoepf. Garden City, N.Y.: Anchor Books, Doubleday and Co.

————. 1968. *The Elementary Structures of Kinship*. Revised edition. Translated by James Harle Bell and John Richard von Sturmer, and edited by Rodney Needham. Boston: Beacon Press.

Levin, Stephanie Seto. 1968. "The Overthrow of the *Kapu* System in Hawaii." *Journal of the Polynesian Society* 77: 402–30.

LeVine, Robert A. 1982. "Gusii Funerals: Meanings of Life and Death in an African Community." *Ethos* 10: 26–65.

Lienhardt, Godfrey R. 1956. "Religion." In *Man, Culture and Society*. Edited by Harry L. Shapiro. New York: Oxford University Press.

————. 1961. *Divinity and Experience, the Religion of the Dinka*. Oxford: Clarendon Press.

Lloyd, G. E. R. 1966. *Polarity and Analogy. Two Types of Argumentation in Early Greek Thought*. Cambridge: Cambridge University Press.

Lowie, Robert H. 1956. *The Crow Indians*. New York: Rinehart and Co.

————. 1961. *Primitive Society*. New York: Harper.

Lukes, Stephen. 1972. *Emile Durkheim, His Life and Works: A Historical and Critical Study*. New York: Harper and Row.

MacIntyre, Alasdair. 1971. "Is Understanding Religion Compatible with Believing?" In *Rationality*. Edited by Bryan R. Wilson. New York: Harper and Row.

MacLennan, John Ferguson. 1865. *Primitive Marriage: An Inquiry into the Origin of the Form of Capture in Marriage Ceremonies*. Edinburgh: Adam and Charles Black.

————. 1869. "The Early History of Man." *North British Review* 50: 516–49.

Malinowski, Bronislaw. 1948. "Baloma: The Spirits of the Dead in the Trobriand Islands." In *Magic, Science and Religion and Other Essays*. Garden City, N.Y.: Doubleday and Co.

Marx, Karl. 1978a. "On the Jewish Question." In *The Marx-Engels Reader*. 2d ed. Edited by Robert C. Tucker. New York, London: W. W. Norton and Co.

————. 1978b. "The German Ideology." In *The Marx-Engels Reader*. 2d ed. Edited by Robert C. Tucker. New York, London: W. W. Norton and Co.

Mauss, Marcel. 1967. *The Gift: Forms and Functions of Exchange in Archaic Societies*. Translated by Ian Cunnison, with an introduction by E. E. Evans-Pritchard. New York: W. W. Norton and Co.

McSweeney, Bill. 1980. *Roman Catholicism: The Search for Relevance.* Oxford: Basil Blackwell.

Merkelbach, R. 1967. "Die Heroen als Geber des Guten und Bosen." *Zeitschrift für Papyrologie und Epigraphik* 1: 97–99.

Middleton, John. 1960. *Lugbara Religion: Ritual and Authority among an East African People.* London, New York, Toronto: Oxford University Press.

———. 1965. *The Lugbara of Uganda.* New York and London: Holt, Rinehart and Winston.

Millard, A. R., and D. J. Wiseman, eds. 1980. *Essays on the Patriarchal Narratives.* Leicester, Eng.: Inter-Varsity Press.

Mohler, James A., S.J. 1970. *The Origin and Evolution of the Priesthood: A Return to the Sources.* Staten Island, N.Y.: Alba House, Division of the Society of St. Paul.

Moulinier, Louis. 1952. *Le Pur et l'impure dans la pensée des grecs d'Homère à Aristote.* Paris: Librarie C. Klincksieck.

Murphy, Robert Francis, and Leonard Kasdan. 1959. "The Structure of Parallel Cousin Marriages." *American Anthropologist,* n.s. 61: 17–29.

———. 1967. "Agnation and Endogamy: Some Further Considerations." *Southwestern Journal of Anthropology* 23: 1–14.

Newbury, Colin W. 1961. *The Western Slave Coast and Its Rulers: European Trade and Administration among the Yoruba and Adja-speaking Peoples of Southwestern Nigeria, Southern Dahomey and Togo.* Oxford: Clarendon Press.

Nilsson, Martin P. 1925. *A History of Greek Religion.* Translated by F. J. Fielden. Oxford: The Clarendon Press.

Nimkoff, M. F., and Russell Middleton. 1960. "Types of Family and Types of Economy." *American Journal of Sociology* 66: 215–25.

Nock, Arthur Darby. 1944. "The Cult of Heroes." *Harvard Theological Review* 37: 141–74.

Noth, Martin. 1960. *The History of Israel.* 2d ed. New York: Harper and Brothers.

———. 1972. *A History of Pentateuchal Traditions.* Translated by Bernhard W. Anderson. Englewood Cliffs, N.J.: Prentice-Hall.

Ovid. 1958. *The Metamorphoses.* Translated by Horace Gregory. New York: Viking Press.

Paige, Karen Ericksen, and Jeffrey M. Paige. 1981. *The Politics of Reproductive Ritual.* Berkeley, Los Angeles, London: University of California Press.

Palmer, Leonard. 1972. *Descriptive and Comparative Linguistics.* London.

Parker, Robert. 1983. *Miasma: Pollution and Purification in Early Greek Religion.* Oxford: The Clarendon Press.

Parsons, Talcott. 1954. "The Theoretical Development of the Sociology of Religion." In *Essays in Sociological Theory.* Revised ed. New York: The Free Press.

———. 1968. *The Structure of Social Action: A Study in Social Theory with Special*

Reference to a Group of Recent European Writers. 2 vols. New York: The Free Press.

Patai, Raphael. 1965. "The Structure of Endogamous Unilineal Descent Groups." *Southwestern Journal of Anthropology* 21: 325–50.

Pausanias. 1979. *Guide to Greece.* Translated and with an introduction by Peter Levi. New York: Penguin Books.

Peirce, Charles. 1958–60. *Collected Papers.* 6 vols. Edited by C. Hartshorne and P. Weiss. Cambridge, Mass.: Belknap Press of Harvard University.

Pfeiffer, Robert Henry. 1947. *Introduction to the Old Testament.* New York, London: Harper and Brothers.

Plato. 1952. *Plato's Phaedo.* Translated by R. Hackforth. New York: The Liberal Arts Press.

Polanyi, Karl, and Abraham Rotstein. 1966. *Dahomey and the Slave Trade: An Analysis of an Archaic Economy.* Seattle: University of Washington Press.

Powers, Joseph M., S.J. 1967. *Eucharistic Theology.* New York: Herder and Herder.

Rad, Gerhard von. 1961. *Genesis: A Commentary.* Translated by John H. Marks. Philadelphia: Westminster Press.

Radin, Paul. 1937. *Primitive Religion: Its Nature and Origin.* New York: Viking Press.

Rahner, Karl, S.J. 1979. "Towards a Fundamental Theological Interpretation of Vatican II." *Theological Studies* 40: 716–27.

Rappaport, Roy Abraham. 1967. *Pigs for the Ancestors: Ritual in the Ecology of a New Guinea People.* New Haven: Yale University Press.

Rattray, Robert Sutherland. 1923. *Ashanti.* Oxford: Clarendon Press.

———. 1927. *Religion and Art in Ashanti.* London: Oxford University Press.

———. 1929. *Ashanti Law and Constitution.* Oxford: Clarendon Press.

Redford, Donald B. 1970. "A Study of the Biblical Story of Joseph." *Supplements to Vetus Testamentum* 20. Leiden: E. J. Brill.

Richards, Audrey Isobel. 1939. *Land, Labour and Diet in Northern Rhodesia: An Economic Study of the Bemba Tribe.* London: International African Institute; Oxford University Press.

———. 1940. "The Political System of the Bemba Tribe—North-eastern Rhodesia." In *African Political Systems.* Edited by M. Fortes and E. E. Evans-Pritchard. London: International African Institute; Oxford University Press.

———. 1956. *Chisungu, a Girls' Initiation Ceremony among the Bemba of Northern Rhodesia.* London: Faber and Faber.

Richardson, Alan. 1958. *An Introduction to the Theology of the New Testament.* London: S.C.M. Press.

Rogerson, J. W. 1980. "Sacrifice in the Old Testament: Problems of Method and Approach." In *Sacrifice.* Edited by M. F. C. Bourdillon and Meyer Fortes. London: Academic Press.

Roth, H. Ling. 1903. *Great Benin. Its Customs, Art and Horrors*. London: Routledge and Kegan Paul.

Rousseau, Jean-Jacques. 1987. *The Basic Political Writings*. Translated by Donald A. Cress. Indianapolis: Hackett Publishing Co.

Rubin, Gayle. 1975. "The Traffic in Women: Notes on the 'Political Economy' of Sex." In *Toward an Anthropology of Women*. New York: Monthly Review Press.

Sacred Congregation for the Doctrine of the Faith. 1982. *Observation on the Final Report of the Anglican Roman Catholic International Commission*. London: Catholic Truth Society, Catholic Information Services.

Sahagun, Bernadino de. 1951. *The Florentine Codex and General History of the Things of New Spain. Book 2. The Ceremonies*. Translated from the Aztec into English by Arthur J. O. Anderson and Charles E. Dibble. Santa Fe, N.Mex.: The School of American Research and the University of Utah.

Sahlins, Marshall. 1978. "Culture as Protein and Profit." *New York Review of Books* 30 (Nov. 23, 1978): 45–53.

———. 1981. *Historical Metaphors and Mythical Realities: Structure in the Early History of the Sandwich Islands Kingdom*. Ann Arbor: The University of Michigan Press.

———. 1985. *Islands of History*. Chicago and London: The University of Chicago Press.

Schillebeeckx, E. 1968. *The Eucharist*. Translated by N. D. Smith. New York: Sheed and Ward.

Schutz, Alfred. 1967. *The Phenomenology of the Social World*. Translated by George Walsh and Frederick Lehnert. Evanston, Ill.: Northwestern University Press.

Selman, M. J. 1980. "Comparative Customs and the Patriarchal Age." In *Essays on The Patriarchal Narratives*. Edited by R. Millard and D. J. Wiseman. Leicester, Eng.: Inter-Varsity Press.

Smith, Jonathan Z. 1987. "The Domestication of Sacrifice." In *Violent Origins. Walter Burkert, René Girard and J. Z. Smith on Ritual Killing and Cultural Formation*. Edited by Robert G. Hamerton-Kelly. Stanford, Calif.: Stanford University Press.

Smith, W. Robertson. 1972. *The Religion of the Semites: The Fundamental Institutions*. New York: Schocken Books.

Soggin, J. Alberto. 1976. *Introduction to the Old Testament, from Its Origins to the Closing of the Alexandrian Canon*. Translated by John Bowden. Philadelphia: Westminster Press.

Speiser, Ephraim A. 1963. "The Wife-Sister Motif in the Patriarchal Narratives." In *Biblical and Other Studies*. Edited by Alexander Altmann. Cambridge, Mass.: Harvard University Press.

———. 1964. *Genesis: The Anchor Bible*. Garden City, N.Y.: Doubleday and Co.

Stanner, William. 1967. "Reflections on Durkheim and Aboriginal Religion."

In *Social Organization; Essays Presented to Raymond Firth*. Edited by Maurice Freedman. London: Frank Cass and Co.

Szemler, G. J. 1972. *The Priests of the Roman Republic. A Study of Interaction between Priesthoods and Magistracies*. Bruxelles: Latomus, Revue d'Etudes Latines.

Tambiah, Stanley. 1981. "A Performative Approach to Ritual." *Proceedings of the British Academy* 65: 113–69. London: Oxford University Press.

Thomas Aquinas. 1923. *Summa Theologica*. Translated by the Fathers of the English Dominican Providence. London: Burns, Oates and Washbourne.

Thomas, Keith. 1958. "Women and the Civil War Sects." *Past and Present* 3: 42–62.

———. 1971. *Religion and the Decline of Magic*. New York: Charles Scribner's Sons.

Thompson, R. J. 1963. *Penitence and Sacrifice in Early Israel outside the Levitical Law: An Examination of the Fellowship Theory of Early Israelite Sacrifice*. Leiden: E. J. Brill.

Tooker, Elizabeth. 1964. *An Ethnography of the Huron Indians, 1615–1649. Bulletin of American Ethnology no. 190*. Washington, D.C.

———. 1965. "The Iroquois White Dog Sacrifice in the Latter Part of the Eighteenth Century." *Ethnohistory* 12: 129–40.

Turner, Victor Witter. 1968. *The Drums of Affliction: A Study of Religious Processes among the Ndembu of Zambia*. Oxford: Clarendon Press.

———. 1969. *The Ritual Process: Structure and Anti-Structure*. Chicago: Aldine Publishing Co.

———. 1975. *Religion and Divination in Ndembu Ritual*. Ithaca and London: Cornell University Press.

———. 1977. "Sacrifice as Quintessential Process: Prophylaxis or Abandonment?" *History of Religions* 16: 189–215.

Tylor, Sir Edward Burnett. 1924. *Primitive Culture: Researches in the Development of Mythology, Philosophy, Religion, Language, Arts and Custom*. New York: Brentano's.

Valeri, Valerio. 1985. *Kingship and Sacrifice: Ritual and Society in Ancient Hawaii*. Translated by Paula Wissing. Chicago/London: University of Chicago Press.

Van Eyden, René. 1972. "The Place of Women in Liturgical Functions." In *Liturgy: Self Expression of the Church. Concilium*, vol. 72. Edited by Herman Schmidt, S.J. New York: Herder and Herder.

Van Seters, John. 1975. *Abraham in History and Tradition*. New Haven and London: Yale University Press.

Vatican Council II. 1975. "The Constitution on the Sacred Liturgy (Sacrosanctum Concilium)." In *Vatican Council II: The Conciliar and Post-Conciliar Documents*. Edited by Austin Flannery. Northport, N.Y.: Costello Publishing Company.

Vaux, Roland de. 1964. *Studies in Old Testament Sacrifice.* Cardiff: University of Wales Press.

Vawter, Bruce. 1955. "The Canaanite Background of Genesis 49." *Catholic Biblical Quarterly* 17: 1–18.

Vermes, Geza. 1975. *The Dead Sea Scrolls in English.* 2d ed. Harmondsworth, Middlesex, Eng.; New York: Penguin Books.

Vernant, Jean-Pierre. 1980. *Myth and Society in Ancient Greece.* Translated by Janet Lloyd. Sussex: Harvester Press; N.J.: Humanities Press.

———. 1981. "Sacrificial and Alimentary Codes in Hesiod's Myth of Prometheus." In *Myth, Religion and Society: Structuralist Essays by M. Detienne, L. Gernet, J.-P. Vernant and P. Vidal-Naquet.* Edited by R. L. Gordon. Cambridge, New York: Cambridge University Press.

———. 1983. *Myth and Thought among the Greeks.* London, Boston, Melbourne and Henley: Routledge and Kegan Paul.

Vidal-Naquet, P. 1981. "Slavery and the Rule of Women in Tradition, Myth and Utopia." In *Myth, Religion and Society: Structuralist Essays by M. Detienne, L. Gernet, J.-P. Vernant and P. Vidal-Naquet.* Edited by R. L. Gordon. Cambridge, New York: Cambridge University Press.

Vilanova, Evangelista, et al. 1969. *The Crisis of Liturgical Reform. Concilium,* vol. 42. New York/Glen Rock, N.J.: Paulist Press.

Walker, W. O. Jr. 1975. "First Corinthians 11:2–16 and Paul's Views Regarding Women." *Journal of Biblical Literature* 94: 94–110.

Wander, N. 1981. "Structure, Contradiction, and 'Resolution' in Mythology: Father's Brother's Daughter Marriage and the Treatment of Women in Genesis 11–50." *Journal of the Ancient Near Eastern Society* 13: 75–99.

Webb, M. C. 1965. "The Abolition of the Taboo System in Hawaii." *Journal of the Polynesian Society* 74: 21–39.

Wellhausen, Julius. 1885. *Prolegomena to the History of Israel.* Translated by J. Sutherland Black and Allen Menzies. Edinburgh: A. and C. Black.

Westermann, Claus. 1985. *Genesis: A Commentary,* vol. 2. Translated by John J. Sullivan. Minneapolis, Minn.: Augsburg Publishing House.

Wilks, Ivor. 1967. "Ashanti Government." In *West African Kingdoms in the Nineteenth Century.* Edited by Daryll Forde and P. M. Kaberry. London: International African Institute; Oxford University Press.

———. 1975. *Asante in the Nineteenth Century: The Structure and Evolution of a Political Order.* London, New York: Cambridge University Press.

Willoughby, W. C. 1928. *The Soul of the Bantu: A Sympathetic Study of the Magico-Religious Practices and Beliefs of the Bantu Tribes of Africa.* Garden City, N.Y.: Doubleday and Co.

Wilson, Robert R. 1977. *Genealogy and History in the Biblical World.* New Haven and London: Yale University Press.

Wiltgen, Ralph. 1967. *The Rhine Flows into the Tiber.* New York: Hawthorn.

Winch, Peter. 1971. "The Idea of a Social Science." In *Rationality*. Edited by Bryan R. Wilson. New York: Harper and Row.

Wittgenstein, Ludwig. 1968. *Philosophical Investigations. The English Text of the Third Edition*. Translated by G. E. M. Anscombe. New York: Macmillan Co.

Yerkes, Royden Keith. 1952. *Sacrifice in Greek and Roman Religions and Early Judaism*. New York: Scribner.

98–99; tensions over descent in, 97–101

Paul, 142–43

Pausanias, 22–23

Peabody Museum of Archaeology and Ethnology, 12

Peirce, Charles, 6

Pelops, 157n.12

Piaget, Jean, 8, 12

Pitt, Billy, 90–92

Pius V, 114

Pius IX, 114

Plato, 11

Pollution, xxiii, 20, 29

Principle of Contradiction, 19

Principle of Identity, 19

Principle of the Excluded Middle, 19

Prometheus, 21; and agriculture, 30; and marriage, 30

Property rights, 35

Protestant reformers, 113–15, 121

Puritans, 13

Rachel, 98–99, 105–11

Rad, Gerhard von, 164n.15, 165nn.25 and 30

Radin, Paul, 168n.16

Rahner, Karl, S. J., 121

Rappaport, Roy, 155n.5

Rattray, Robert Sutherland, 67, 69–70, 72–75, 161nn.3 and 7, 161–62n.12, 162nn.14, 16, and 17, 168n.18

Rebekah, 98–99, 103–5, 108, 110–11

Richards, Audrey, 63, 160n.2

Rites of passage, 27

Ritual, 1, 135, 144; and alienation, 142; and killing, 17; and language, 3; "politics of interpretation," 10–11; positivist interpretation of, 2, 8, 155n.5; and representation, 143; Robertson Smith on, 3; and speech acts, 5–6; symbolic interpretation of, 3

Robertson Smith, W., 3, 7, 9, 18, 129, 155nn.6 and 10, 156n.3,

158nn.3, 4, and 6; and alimentary participation, 56; on patriliny and sacrifice, 32–34

Roman Church: Apostolic Succession, 112; and celibacy, 117; and laity, 117; priestly hierarchy, 32, 113–14, 118, 122–23; status of deaconesses, 117; succession of the clergy, 37; and validity of Anglican orders, 126–27; women, 117, 123–27

Roman Empire, 116

Romans, 36, 148; agnation, 42; ancestor cult, 46, 49; cognation, 41, 53; *dies lustricus*, 45; *di manes*, 160n.8; family cults, 46; Lars, 160n.8; *paterfamilias*, 45; Penates, 160n.8; sacrifice compared with Ndembu, 64–65; sacrificial calendars, 151; women, 48

Rousseau, Jean-Jacques, 168n.15

Sacred Congregation for the Doctrine of the Faith, 126; on the Eucharist, 125

Sacrifice: alimentary, 6–7, 17, 28, 149; and alimentary nature, 141; and ancient state, 148–49; clan, 32; expiatory and communion, 17–29; fertility, 9; funeral, 23–24; and historical change, 24–25, 89–91; and logical oppositions, 19–21, 27–29; piacular, 17, 27; as symbolic action, 19; unity of expiation and communion in, 17–19, 28

Sahlins, Marshall, 83, 88–90, 92

Sarah, 98–99, 101–2, 105, 164n.14

Saussure, Ferdinand de, 137–38, 140–41

Schillebeeckx, E., 121, 166n.6

Schutz, Alfred, 155n.11

Semitic societies, 133; and endogamy, 98–99; and sacrificial ritual, 3

Seneca, 63